DEVELOPMENT OF RESEARCHES IN ANTHROPOLOGY IN INDIA

RANCHI ANTHROPOLOGY SERIES-2

Ranchi Anthropology Series

No.1 : Process, Performance and Pilgrimage: A Study in Comparative Symbology/ *Victor Turner*

No. 2 : Development of Researches in Anthropology in Inida: Bihar A Case Study/ *L.P. Vidyarthi* and *V.S. Upadhyay*

No. 3 : Nature-Man-Spirit Complex in Tribal India/ *R.S. Mann* and *Vijoy S. Sahay*

About the Editors

Lalita Prasad Vidyarthi, Ph.D. (Chicago) had the distinction of being President of both the International Union of Anthropological and Ethnological Sciences (1973-78) and the Xth International Congress of Anthropological and Ethnological Sciences (1978). Widely travelled, he is well known in academic circles through his several publications and the papers he has presented at international gatherings. He has also directed a number of projects in anthropological research in this country.

Currently he is Professor and Head of the Department of Anthropology, University of Ranchi and Director of the UGC Centre of Special Assistance in Anthropology. He is also Vice-President of the International Social Science Council and editor of the Unesco sponsored *International Journal of Asian Studies.*

Vijay S. Upadhyay, Ph.D., is Reader, Department of Anthropology, Ranchi University and has collaborated closely with Prof. Vidyarthi in more than one of his publications. He has done considerable field work among tribals in Bihar. His other area of interest is in the Sacred Cities of India.

RANCHI ANTHROPOLOGY SERIES-2

Gen. Editor : L.P. VIDYARTHI

Development of Researches in Anthropology in India

Bihar : A Case Study

Edited by

L.P. VIDYARTHI
V.S. UPADHYAY

CONCEPT PUBLISHING COMPANY PVT. LTD.
NEW DELHI-110059

ISBN: 978-81-7022-158-6

Edition 2025

Published and Printed by

Concept Since 1974

Concept Publishing Company Pvt. Ltd.
A/15-16, Commercial Block, Mohan Garden,
New Delhi-110059 (India)
T : 91-11-41101460
E : publishing@conceptpub.com, *W*: www.conceptpub.com

FOREWORD

THE Department of Anthropology of Ranchi University has celebrated its Silver Jubilee in 1978. Again, it has received the recognition of being the only U.G.C. Centre of Special Assistance in Anthropology in the country almost in the same year. During the tenure of my Presidentship of the International Union of Anthropological and Ethnological Sciences (1973-78) as well as of the Xth ICAES (1978), the Department was also called upon to perform several academic and professional roles involving it at the international level.

With this background, we ventured to launch a new series of publications entitled "Ranchi Anthropology Series" in the year 1980. This series is designed to provide short but scholarly treatments of key problem-areas in anthropology. Under this series, in addition to learned lectures delivered at Ranchi by scholars of national and international repute, we will also publish the theoretically-oriented research work of local scholars as well as proceedings of the national and international level seminars and symposia.

This series was initiated with the publication of one of our internationally distinguished anthropologists, Professor Victor Turner, who has been rightly termed as "a master interpreter of symbol and ritual in social life". Author of several books on symbol, myth and ritual, Professor Turner in this series of lectures, summarises the results of his research in this new field, which he terms as "Comparative Symbology".

The present volume, the second in the series, includes the papers presented at a national symposium on the development and trends in anthropology in India with special reference to Bihar. Such a case study of anthropological researches of Bihar enables us to understand, in depth, the traditions and trends in Indian anthropology of a particular region as well as its interactions and contributions to the rest of the country within a particular discipline.

I take this opportunity to thank the contributors to this volume particularly Dr Bhupinder Singh, Dr A.K. Danda and Professor Sachchidananda, who came to attend the symposium from outside Ranchi and made valuable contributions to our deliberations as well as to this volume. I am also thankful to all my collaborators particularly Dr V.S. Upadhyay who helped me in organising the symposium as well as editing this volume.

My thanks are due to Shri Naurang Rai and Smt. S. Ramaswamy of the Concept Publishing Company for taking keen interest in publishing this volume.

27 May 1981 L.P. VIDYARTHI

CONTENTS

PART II

INSTITUTIONAL EFFORTS TOWARDS RESEARCH

PART III

MAJOR THEMES OF STUDIES

LIST OF MAPS AND FIGURES

LIST OF CONTRIBUTORS

Sarat Borbora

Senior Lecturer in Anthropology, D.H.S.K. College Dibrugarh, Bihar.

M.R. Chakravarthi

Life Sciences Division, Post Graduate Centre, Jawaharlal Nehru University Imphal, Manipur.

Ajit K. Danda

Deputy Director, Anthropological Survey of India, Eastern Region, 27 Jawaharlal Nehru Road, Calcutta, West Bengal.

William Ekka

Anthropological Survey of India, Eastern Region, 27 Jawaharlal Nehru Road, Calcutta, West Bengal.

Guru Charan Ghosh

Anthropological Survey of India, Eastern Region, 27 Jawaharlal Nehru Road, Calcutta, West Bengal.

P.N. Gour

Retd. Librarian and Social Scientist, Indian Institute of Advanced Studies, Simla. (Patliputra Colony, Patna).

S. Prakash Gupta

Director, Bihar Tribal Welfare Research Institute, Ranchi, Bihar.

Amitava Das Gupta

Teacher Fellow (U.G.C.), Ranchi University Ranchi, Bihar.

A.K. Haldar

Lecturer, Department of Anthropology, Ranchi University Ranchi, Bihar.

Makhan Jha
Lecturer, Post Graduate of Anthropology, Ranchi University, Ranchi, Bihar.

B.M. Mukherjee
Department of Anthropology, Calcutta University, Calcutta, West Bengal.

Rajiv Ranjan Prasad
Research Fellow, Department of Anthropology, University of Delhi, Delhi.

Sachchidananda
Professor of Anthropology, A.N Sinha Institute of Social Studies, Patna, Bihar.

Abnindra Narayan Sandhwar
Lecturer, Post Graduate of Anthropology, Ranchi University, Ranchi, Bihar.

Vijoy S. Sahay
Research Associate, Department of Anthropology, Ranchi University, Ranchi, Bihar

Jyotirmoyee Sarma
6/1, New Road, Alipur, Calcutta-700 027.

Bhupinder Singh
Joint Secretary, Ministry of Home Affairs, Government of India, New Delhi.

Ajit Kumar Singh
Research Associate, Department of Anthropology Ranchi University, Ranchi, Bihar.

A.C. Sinha
Department of Sociology and Anthropology, North Eastern Hill University, Shillong, Meghalaya.

N.K. Sinha
Research Associate, Viswa-Bharati, Santiniketan, West Bengal.

Arbind K. Sinha
Space Applications Centre, Ahmedabad-380053, Gujarat.

Ratish Srivastava
Reader in Anthropology, Ravishankar University, Raipur, Madhya Pradesh.

Sita Toppo
Lecturer, Department of Anthropology, Ranchi College, Ranchi, Bihar.

V.S. Upadhyay
Department of Anthropology, Ranchi University, Ranchi, Bihar.

INTRODUCTION

THE result of any social scientific effort may have three kinds of usefulness : the findings and interpretations emerging from it may be of interest and value to other social scientists who will be asking such questions as, "How does this piece of work give us further insight into individual or collective human behaviour ?" "What new methods, hypotheses and generalizations are presented in this study ?" Thus utilization of a research model by fellow scientists has as its goal the production of a greater body of scientifically valid knowledge.

Secondly, the findings and interpretations may also be of value to professional workers of social leaders, those who have responsibility for public service and social action. Their goals are the improvement of policy-making, planning and acting in some area of social activity. They all look towards researches in the area/subject.

Thirdly, the findings and interpretations may also be of value to the community which is living in and adapting to the complex and changing 20th century society.

Thus when a person or an organization turns to the scientific stockpile for help on a research problem, he or it is faced with a number of important questions about the applicability of research done in a different setting. To what extent and in what ways is this situation comparable to those in which the research was done ? Does a theoretical principle hold for this situation also ? Unfortunately many persons have not considered these questions while looking for help from scientific sources. Hence the western research models had been followed in studies in India. There are certain manifest differences between situations or populations on which the researches were conducted in the West and in India. One cannot, therefore, uncritically accept all the findings and insights as relevant to the Indian situation and proceed on that assumption.

The development of researches in anthropology had been on the lines of Western research models. Hardly any themes had been in use a couple of decades ago that could be termed indigenous. Lately, however, there have been clear signs pointing towards what one can call the development of Indian research models. Researches in Bihar are not exceptional. As the review in various papers in this volume would show, the research has just entered what can be called a critical period in Bihar in that inter-disciplinary works have gained ground. Again, one of the important but neglected research areas is research on the process of applying research findings. Systematic research is needed urgently to provide an integrated body of knowledge on how best to apply knowledge.

A review of the current courses of study of systematic training in anthropology suggests that there is need to broaden the curriculum beyond the current teaching of research methodology to include more systematic training. The potential contribution of anthropology to the solution of social problems is tremendous but is largely unrealized. It is, therefore, important for anthropologists not to undersell anthropological research nor should they lack the confidence to use scientific methods as tools for solving complex social problems.

II

The principal objective of this volume is to cover anthropological research in the state of Bihar taking into consideration its quantum, quality, facility and the theory formulation and overall development of the science.

As a first step it was decided to carry out a survey of the researches done so far in the different fields of anthropology. The entire area of study was accordingly divided. An eminent anthropologist was requested to carry out a survey of the research work done so far to identify major trends that have developed in the past as well as the principal gaps that have yet to be filled. The overall findings are being compiled and should help identify the major areas in which researches are to be carried out on a priority basis. This will also serve as guidelines for future anthropologists.

It is hardly necessary at this stage to anticipate what it will offer to the coming generations. However, it appears that the major achievement of the post-independence period has been the growth of institutions like the Department of Anthropology, Ranchi University, which are engaged in imparting training facilities. A fair quantum of research has also been produced though the quality of research is still to achieve a high degree in the theoretical field and its designed utilization for human welfare is still far from satisfactory. It appears that for future development, the strengthening of institutions is of prime importance. It may be mentioned here that the establishment of the Centre for Special Assistance at the Department of Anthropology, Ranchi University, by the University Grants Commission and the creation of the Eastern Region by the Anthropological Survey of India are steps in this direction. This is bound to widen the basis of the institutions engaged in research, training and guidance and identification of young potential talent for research and its development. Each expansion of the research programmes by the University and other institutions is bound to reduce the imbalances in the development of researches in different branches and improve the quality of research.

The establishment of the Centre for Special Assistance in the Department of Anthropology, Ranchi University, under a scheme, will strengthen the Department by adding research personnel in the ranks of Senior Fellows, Research Associates, Senior and Junior Research Fellowships. The objects of the scheme are to enable social scientists in general and anthropologists in particular to spend their time on whole-time or part-time basis, in writing books or working for the same research project. It will also provide opportunities for further self-development to younger anthropologists.

It also becomes a responsibility of the institution to develop the necessary infra-structure to facilitate research and secure an improvement in its quality. Hence the development of library, and other documentation facilities which are the backbone of research. Collecting information can be made more useful only by disseminating it. It is normally done through publishing books and journals. Several anthropologists in Bihar have published a large number of books and journals like *Man in India* (Ranchi), *Journal of Economic and Social Change* (Patna) and *Journal of Social Research* to cater to the needs of researchers in Bihar.

III

This volume provides an overall picture of the researches and teaching in anthropology in Bihar. As would be clear from the papers, the teaching of anthropology as an independent subject is done only in Ranchi University. Right from the first year to the Master's stage students pass through different stages of learning and training in research. It is also to the credit of Ranchi University that the subject is under both the faculties of Arts and of Science. A specific background at the graduation stage enables a student to opt for an Arts or Science degree. Apart from this university, the subject finds a place as a paper in the syllabus for the Master's discipline in sociology in different universities of Bihar.

The research standards from graduation to project level have covered a large canvas as will be evident from the papers included in the volume.

In all more than two dozen papers were presented at a seminar on the status of teaching and research in anthropology in Bihar conducted by the Department of Anthropology, Ranchi University, under the auspices of the University Grants Commission in the last week of June, 1979. The selected papers have been grouped under four categories :

(i) General Overview
(ii) Institutional Efforts
(iii) Major Themes
(iv) Training and Influence

The first part gives an overall coverage of researches done till today. Bhupinder Singh has very rightly pointed out that it is the administration which can use anthropological data for the benefit of human beings. To bridge the gap between academic and developmental efforts, the administration has always played a crucial role. The paper of M.R. Chakravarthi emphasizes the need for bio-cultural studies today. Till now cultural and physical anthropology have been working as independent disciplines though both have to contribute to and control much of each other's role in human life. A.C. Sinha has categorized the researches in Bihar on four levels based on the treatment of the subject. V.S. Upadhyay in his paper has covered a large area of discussion on social anthropological researches. The problems and prospects have enumerated the present conditions of research areas still to be covered and the problems facing future researchers. William Ekka has proposed some new areas of research in tribal Bihar, while R. Srivastava has covered a period of 26 years to categorize the publications on a methodological basis. Looking through time, Ajit Danda in his paper presents a picture of the extraordinary glory of Bihar which, he says, has faded but which, he believes, can be restored by its elite and committed citizens.

The second part is allotted to institutional efforts to develop anthropological researches. Three experts have enumerated the works of three main institutions engaged in researches on anthropological themes— the A.N. Sinha Institute of Social Studies, Patna, the Tribal Welfare Research Institute, Ranchi, and the Anthropological Survey of India, Calcutta. Apart from these the Department of Anthropology, Ranchi University, may be reckoned as the premier institution of research in this field. There are many other institutions which, through their own efforts, touch on anthropological themes, but as their aim and training have a different orientation they have not been included here. Sachchidananda, in his paper, has listed works by the A.N. Sinha Institute of Social Studies. He has included only those which he thought to be anthropological, but many, which he called sociological, have not found a place. Having been Director of the Institute, he was of the inner orientation of the subjects of research, hence a controlled relation has been presented. Similarly S.P. Gupta of the Bihar Tribal Welfare Research Institute has covered the entire period right from the inception of the institute in 1954. V.S. Upadhyay's paper limits itself to providing a list of research proposals undertaken by the Anthropological Survey of India, Calcutta, between 1952 and 1975, which he has appended to his paper. He has rightly pointed out that the establishment of the Eastern India Station by the ASI will certainly improve the share of Bihar in the near future.

The third part of the book comprises the major themes of studies undertaken in Bihar. In the first paper of this section G.C. Ghosh discusses the researches in physical anthropology. He has brought it out clearly that a great deal remains to be done in the case of Bihar. Similarly the paper of N.K. Sinha brings out the much wanted researches and teac hing of linguistics. As it is a complete discipline in itself, linguistics has much to cover in Bihar. In his study of urban and industrial centres in Bihar A.K. Haldar has dwelt upon the modernization process in tribal Bihar. In a somewhat similar study Makhan Jha concludes that researches on the industrial complexes of Central India in general, and Chota Nagpur in particular, have made significant contributions towards the development of industrial anthropology, a comparative newcomer to the field of anthropology. Pioneering work has been done by Vidyarthi on Ranchi while others have dealt with centres like Tatanagar, Dhanbad, Patna, etc. Lately, applied anthropology has covered a larger part of studies on tribal development. A.K. Singh, in his study, has analysed the developmental studies by anthropologists. Again area studies are gaining importance in the field of tribal Bihar. S. Borbora has taken up the study of Asur as a case to develop and strengthen this approach. Another major theme is the study of tribal religion. Because of earlier studies on tribes, their religion has attracted the attention of administrators, missionaries and anthropologists alike. A. Das Gupta has tried to incorporate all such studies on tribal religion made in Bihar. In his paper A.N. Sandhwar has discussed one of the major themes—Nature-Man-Spirit-Complex which Vidyarthi brought out in his study of the Maler. A number of subsequent studies have been taken up to qualify the theory.

The fourth part of the book comprises papers which cover two primary aspects of research—training in and the influence of research. In the first paper itself, M.R. Chakravarthi discusses training for teaching physical anthropology. Being a man of deep insight, he has proposed several new ideas to be incorporated while framing a course for teaching physical anthropology. J. Sarma, in her paper, has taken up quite an unusual theme for study, that in parts of the country European culture has become the status symbol and describes how this has spread with the help of Christianity. R.R. Prasad has also put forth the new idea of communicating anthropological knowledge, not only to the specialists, but also to the masses. For this de-islanding he has suggested taking the help of journalism, and the introduction of a new course of study. S. Toppo has given details of the various standards of teaching anthropology in Bihar. B.M. Mukherjee has dealt at length with the anthropological training imparted by the various educational institutions in Bihar. A.K. Sinha has thrown a challenge to professional anthropologists and asked whether the subject has remained relevant today. Only a few points of anthropological studies bear any relation to practical problems while a larger part has remained confined to ideal research. Thus the question of relevance is bound to haunt one's mind. In the last paper of the section V.S. Sahay has tried to cover the over-all theoretical contributions of Ranchi, specially of the Department of Anthropology, Ranchi University, and has conceived the idea of calling it the Ranchi School. The themes of Sacred Complex and Nature-Man-Spirit Complex have proved successful in the study of the Hindu religion and simpler societies and are being followed to study such facts of life throughout India. Hence it justifies the recognition of this centre on theoretical grounds.

L. P. VIDYARTHI

PART I

AN OVERVIEW

ONE

Bhupinder Singh

ANTHROPOLOGICAL RESEARCH AND ADMINISTRATION

About two or three decades ago, it would have been unthinkable for an administrator to attend a seminar of academic nature and, perhaps, for academicians to invite an administrator. The two worlds were completely apart and its denizens lived in water-tight compartments, unaware of what was going on beyond the walls created by themselves. Needless to say, the insularity generated complexes which hardened the partition walls. The result was that theory and practice remained poles apart. The practitioner of anthropology, i.e., the administrator, scoffed at the hare-brained postulates of the academician, while the professor within the precincts of the university thought poorly of the people in the work-a-day field. The thought and experience of one denied to the other, both remained impoverished and inadequate. Both sets of men remained incomplete in their individual make-up, but the loss was more of the nation which called for a blending of their knowledge to be applied to the people for their benefit and enrichment. Happily, the past situation seems to be on the way out. Today, there is in evidence a commingling of fraternities to mutual advantage. I have no doubt now that a field practitioner like me can derive immense benefit by a dip into the treasure-ocean of knowledge in the university. Conversely, an exposition of field conditions by a penetrating field worker is liable to contribute significantly to conclusions which can become the foundation for hypotheses. The law of gravitation derived its substance from the observation of a falling apple by Newton.

The complementarity of the two can be illustrated with a little detail. We are aware of the tremendous role which applied science and technology have been playing in our life. They are born of pure sciences like mathematics, physics, chemistry. While the pursuit of pure scientific research continues to be an engaging and widening task, their Cinderella, i.e., applied science and technology, has wrought a veritable revolution in our life. Chemical engineering and petro-chemicals are examples, but examples are legion. Similarly, while a professor expatiates, in a college or at a university, on the logically developed science of anthropology, the applied aspect is practised in the field by the administrator. It has often been found that where the administrator is not versed in the theory of the science, he often gropes in the dark while grappling with the tasks confronting him. Were he familiar with the reservoir of systematized human knowledge proferred by the universities, he would go about his job in a much more enlightened way.

Let us take the case of primitive groups among tribals. In Bihar, you have the Pahariya, the Birhor and the like. You are aware that the nation is seriously engaged in bringing them to some level of advancement so that they could make use of the developed technology for their economic betterment. If the agent of change were conversant with their history, their sociology, their culture, their habitat, he would go about the task in an informed way. For example, some of the primitive groups practise shifting cultivation and their religious ceremonies and social festivities have got inextricably linked with the various stages of this cultivation starting with the felling of trees, burning of leaves and vegetation, dribbling of holes, etc. Now, if an administrator went about preventing shifting cultivation without an understanding of its significance in the life of the tribal community, his efforts would not only be doomed to failure from the beginning but would also result in alienating the group. On the other hand, if he informed himself properly of the culture of that group, he would not only succeed but gain the confidence of the group. Recently, we had the occasion to discuss some primitive tribal groups of the

Andamans and Nicobar Islands. You are well aware of the incalculable harm done before Independence by the British Government by their policy of hostility and repression of these groups, particularly the Great Andamanese. As a result, the Great Andamanese now number only 24. This and other groups like the Onge and the Sentinelese would, by now, have been extinct but for the enlightened and liberal policy followed after Independence. The examples can be multiplied. Similarly, if the academicians undertook field studies not only would they benefit but also the country as a whole. This would help them to formulate their theories and postulates with greater understanding and precision.

I have been directly engaged in the field of tribal development for the past 15 years or so. In common with many other people in this field, I have acutely felt the need of associating the tribal people themselves in the formulation of policies as well as implementation of development programmes. It is evident that, in a country like ours, association can take the shape of mass participation only in exceptional cases and on rare occasions. It has to be mostly association of representatives of the masses. This means that the tribal communities should be able to throw up competent leadership and these leaders should be enabled to participate in decision-making processes and supervision of implementation of schemes of development. Many patterns and devices whereby the association could be secured have been thought of. It could be through nomination of their headmen or representatives in the traditional village councils, called by various names in various communities, e.g. Gomango among the Saora of Orissa, Manjhi among the Santhals of Bihar, Majhi among the Gond of Bastar. The Miji of the north-east have village affairs administered by regularly selected village officials and groups of Miji villages are administered by formally constituted "Shubang" councils consisting of the village headmen. Apart from these traditional political systems dating back to historical times, statutory Panchayati Raj bodies like the Gram Panchayat for a group of villages, Panchayat Samiti at the Block level and Zila Parishads at the district level have, since the advent of Independence, been introduced. Incidentally, the Asoka Mehta Committee has suggested a change-over from the three-tier to a two-tier system comprising a Mandal Panchayat and a Zila Parishad. The policy of the Government has been that representatives of tribals in both the traditional and the statutory bodies should be involved in the formulation and implementation aspects.

One difficulty that has cropped up in complying with this policy is that, notwithstanding the organization of the Panchayati Raj bodies, the actual representation of tribals on these bodies has been rather poor and, hence, their association with tribal development rather inadequate. As an administrator dealing with tribal development, perhaps I would have continued, vainly, my search for an apt solution for long. However, the fortunate circumstance of my undertaking research in tribal leadership in Orissa obliged me to make a probe into various facets of leadership on the academic plane initially, to lead ultimately to application of the ideas obtained to the field. The principles of classification of leadership related to (a) nature of the social system in terms of egalitarianism, ranking and stratification, (b) socio-political situation, (c) level of socio-cultural integration and (d) mode of succession. Weber's classification (1922) of leadership into (i) charismatic authority, (ii) traditional authority, (iii) legal or administrative technical competence, Lippit and White's (1943) classification into (i) autocratic, (ii) democratic and (iii) laissez-faire, Otterbein's (1977) attributes of formality and power for constructing typology for (i) kings (formal with absolute power), (ii) dictators (informal with absolute power), (iii) chief (formal with limited power) and headmen (informal with limited power) were enlightening. In this context, the work of B.N. Sahay among the Maler and the Santhal of Santhal Parganas of Bihar leading to classification of leaders into (a) traditional, (b) emergent and (c) traditional-emergent came in as relevant. For the purpose of my research, the classification into traditional, elected and functional leaders proved to be useful. I found that out of 159 Sarpanchs in the said area, only 40 were Saora (the tribe of the area) and out of 11 chairmen of the Panchayat Samiti not one was a Saora. This led me to propose, much before the Asoka Mehta Committee recommended likewise, that there should be reservation for the Scheduled Tribes in the elected places in Panchayati Raj bodies. I hope, by now, the point I have been trying to make is clear, that only by optimal conjunction of the theory and practice of a subject can the best results be achieved.

An individual is an amalgam of many attributes and he has several roles to play in society. Similarly, the nation is like a multi-faceted personality, consisting of many communities, races, religions, etc., whose economic, social and political aspects call for attention. It will be conceded that a solution which is based on an integrated view of the various aspects is liable to be the most satisfactory. The integrated view can be obtained by juxtaposing and effectively coordinating diverse interpretations of the situation by men belonging to different fields like economists, political scientists, sociologists, psychologists, administrators, etc. The composition of the Planning Commission at the national level is a reflection of this need. And we must extend this principle to the lower levels also. The nation must be assured that the thinking of savants of disciplines involved on a particular plane has been fused in the crucible of highest thought and action and that the best by-product has been obtained. I do not think that a bigger justification exists for a durable bridge between the two gulfs of erudition and practice.

I would now hark to the need and scope of the contribution that is called for from the academic side in our own field of endeavour, i.e., tribal development. We are aware that since the Fifth Plan period, the country has launched a serious programme of tribal development. For the purpose, in each State, areas of predominant tribal population have been identified and 180 Integrated Tribal Development Projects (ITDP) have been constituted. The idea is that in each of these ITDPs there should be an administrative apparatus capable of undertaking well-conceived integrated tribal development programmes with the help of the totality of financial resources available for the ITDP area. The underlying idea of totality requires to be emphasized. It means that there should be no effort outside the project reports prepared for the ITDP and the plan so prepared should rest on all the financial resources available. I may add that the Government of India has gone out of its way to support the programme with the help of funds they have specially earmarked for it.

Some features of this programme called the "Sub-Plan for Tribal Areas" of the concerned States, deserve notice. Firstly, the sub-Plan programme aims at extending protection to the Scheduled Tribes in various ways. Regulations have been framed and legislation enacted for preventing illegal alienation of lands from tribals and restoration of illegally transferred land to tribals. Money-lending is sought to be regulated or prohibited; in lieu thereof, the effort is to enable the tribal to borrow money at differential rate of interest (4%) from cooperative institutions. Bonded labour has been abolished and freed bonded labourers are to be rehabilitated under the schemes framed for the purpose. Broadly speaking, the excise policy to be adopted by the States would abolish all shops which sell liquor in the tribal areas while the tribals would be allowed to brew their own liquor for domestic or social purposes. The worst form of exploitation occurs when the farm and forest produce of the tribals is subjected to short weighment and under-payment. To check this, arrangements for marketing of the tribals' produce through cooperative institutions are to be made. We are, therefore, laying stress on the creation of an adequate and meaningful credit-cum-marketing structure in the form of cooperative institutions. We hope that these protective measures will make a significant dent in the unhealthy socio-economic condition of the tribal communities. Secondly, apart from these protective measures, positive steps for development are to be taken concomitantly. It is well known that the predominant occupation of a tribal is agriculture, horticulture and animal husbandry. However, the level of technology which they practise produces low return while their natural resource endowment (soil, water) is rather poor. Application of an intermediate technology has been found to be apt in the interest of proper assimilation. Inputs like improved seeds, fertilizers, agricultural implements, pesticides, irrigation, soil conservation, pedigree insemination of cattle, etc., are being arranged. The second important source of living of tribals is forest. They obtain fuel, timber, roots, wild fruits, flowers, etc., from forests which they partly consume at home and partly sell to earn little money. Hence, arrangements for marketing of minor forest produce form an important component of the programme of credit-cum-marketing structure. In the Sixth Plan period, higher priority has been attached to education than in the Fifth Plan period; more attention is being given to primary and adult education. Similarly, health is also receiving higher priority. Primary health centres and dispensaries based on the homoeopathic and indigenous systems of medicine are to be opened in larger numbers, while the accent is on preventive side. The third important feature of the sub-Plan is to see that the normal programmes, i.e. programmes which are in the process of implementation, particularly in the non-tribal areas, are not superimposed on the tribal areas without considering their suitability. It is well known that most of the tribal areas are on elevations and their topography comprises hills and slopes more often than flat plains. For this reason, the crops grown by the tribals are mostly millets, maize, oil-seeds, pulses, tubers and some paddy, wheat, etc. The agriculture programme has to take account of this variation. The tribals keep small animals like pigs, poultry, goats and less often cattle, though the opposite is the case with non-tribals. Hence, the programmes for tribals should be chosen carefully and the ongoing programmes should be adapted, as necessary. This would also oblige variation in experimentation and multiplication of farm programmes as well as training programmes. If we lose sight of this factor, there is a likelihood that the programmes might fail before they start. In other words, the tribals should be allowed to develop along the line of their own genius in the agricultural, horticultural, animal husbandry, small industries and forestry fields.

You might be aware that we had constituted a Working Group to lay down guidelines for tribal development during the Sixth Plan period, 1978-83, under the chairmanship of Shri D. L. Mandal, Minister of State for Home Affairs. Among the anthropologists and sociologists who were members of this Group were Prof. L. P. Vidyarthi, Dr. B. K. Roy Burman, Dr. Surjit Sinha, Dr. Sachchidananda and Shri L. M. Shrikant. On the State-level committees also, members of the academic profession are being invited to participate in various formulations. The Working Group went into details and submitted a report which covers nearly every facet of tribal development. I am glad to say that no small part was played by academicians in forging of the report.

Tribal development embraces expanding universe. Every little take-off of the tribal communities is expected to lead to higher urges and aspirations. While this is to be welcomed, it would also pose a problem in the sense that the situation is likely to become more complex in future. As such, it will require a greater measure of effort based on a bigger reservoir of collective wisdom of theoreticians and practitioners. I do not think anyone can have the courage to deny that only a close collaboration between the two can lead to satisfactory appraisal and lasting solutions of the myriad problems we face in the country. The cultural matrix of the nation, even now a crazy mosaic, is likely to become even more fine-grained. It is, therefore, likely to pose a greater challenge. In this noble venture, a partnership based on human values and mutual self-respect needs badly to be forged.

TWO

P.N. Gour

MAIN TRENDS OF ANTHROPOLOGICAL RESEARCHES IN BIHAR

I

THE STATE of Bihar presents a most fertile field for the study of anthropology and ethnology. Here we have a considerable number of tribes and castes exhibiting various stages of socio-cultural development. Of the two natural divisions of the State, viz., the alluvial plains of Bihar and the Hill Tracts comprising Chotanagpur and the Santhal Parganas, the Hill Tracts are clearly marked off from alluvial plains, north and south of the Ganges, ethnically. Again the Hill Tracts region besides being ethnically different is, geologically, among the earliest formations, and one of the earliest habitats of man in India.

It is, therefore, natural that aboriginal tribes of Bihar should attract, as they have always done, special attention of anthropologists. Numerically also they constitute one of the four main strongholds of the aborigines of India, the other three being Madhya Pradesh, the north-Eastern States and Orissa.

II

Bihar has the third largest concentration of tribal population numbering 4,932,767 persons according to 1971 census, which is 13 per cent of the total tribal population in India and 8.75 per cent of the State population. There are about 30 tribes, belonging to various cultural types, such as Munda, Ho, Santhal, Oraon, Kharia, Maler, etc., distributed in Chotanagpur division and Santhal Parganas district.

The beautiful Chotanagpur plateau in Bihar is the home of the great Oraon tribe, the Munda, the Ho, some Santhal, the Kharia, and a number of smaller tribes, including the very ancient Asur who have been traditional iron-smelters. The chief tribe in Bihar, however, is the Santhal, whose total population very much exceeds 1.5 million, mostly inhabiting the upland areas of Santhal Parganas, Dhanbad, Hazaribagh, Giridih, Singhbhum and Purnea.

These tribes have positively distinct characteristics so far as their physical features, material culture, languages and dialects, system of village and inter-village organization, kinship organization, marriage, birth and death rites and customs, social traditions of succession and inheritance, and religion are concerned. All these have naturally provided interesting and absorbing fields of study for anthropologists.

III

At the initial stage the tribal studies in Bihar, as well as in other parts of tribal India, were undertaken mainly by British administrators and scholars, foreign missionaries and travellers, for purposes of colonial administration, historical study of culture and society, expansion of Christianity and adventurous memoirs. British administrators like Dalton (1872), Hunter (1877), Risley (1891-1905), Reid (1902-10), O'Malley (1906-25) and others published reports on the tribes and castes of Bihar in various handbooks, census reports, district gazetteers and journals. The first detailed account of the land and people of Chotanagpur appeared in a book by F.P. Bradley-Birt in 1903. It was followed by the work of another British administrator, Bainbridge, on the Sauria-Paharia of the Raj Mahal hills, which was published in 1907 in the *Memoirs of the Asiatic Society of Bengal*. This work obviously remains the first monograph on the Sauria-Paharia and has been used by later anthropologists in India as the base-line data for studying culture change in this tribe.

While mentioning the anthropological works of British

administrators, the last one who needs a significant mention is W. G. Archer, who left India after independence, but whose love for anthropological studies made him pay repeated visits to this country even after 1947. He died recently.

Archer's most important work in which he was later assisted by his wife, Mildred Archer, consisted in compiling and translating tribal poetry. His two books, *Blue Grove* and *The Dove and the Leopard*, containing Oraon poetry, have been widely acclaimed by eminent anthropologists and scholars interested in folk-lore. His translations of tribal poetry are characterized by charm, simplicity and an unfailing sense of balance all his own. His latest book, *Hill of Flute*, gives a sympathetic account of Santhal life and culture as he saw it in the mid-forties. The reminiscences of his life in Bihar related so wistfully by him when I happened to meet him and his wife in London in 1963 were indeed touching. After his retirement from India, he held the prestigious post of the Curator of Victoria and Albert Museum for a number of years.

Amongst the foreign anthropologists who have left significant studies on Bihar tribals, the Rev. O. P. Bodding's name deserves special mention. His monumental work, *Santhal Dictionary*, is a careful and scientific study of the Santhal language, besides being a mine of information of all that concerns the Santhal people. His other writings relating to beliefs and religious practices of the Santhal and their folk-tales are no less scholarly.

Two other lexicographical works deserving special mention are the Rev. Hoffmann's *Encyclopaedia Mundarica* and the Rev. Campbell's *Santhal Dictionary*. The former is indeed a work of immense scholarship.

IV

The history of tribal studies in Bihar was given a turning point by keen interest in the subject by Sarat Chandra Roy, the first Indian national to produce detailed monographic studies of some of the tribes of Chotanagpur. Roy was a lawyer by profession and an anthropologist by interest. Being a lawyer, his first interest in anthropology emanated from a study of the customary laws of the Munda, Oraon and other tribes of

Chotanagpur. He gradually found it useful to learn the tribal languages. His monograph on *The Munda and Their Country* (1912) was the first such study of a tribe in Chotanagpur by an Indian scholar. This was followed by a series of monographs on the *Oraon* (1915), the *Birhor* (1925), *Oraon Religion and Customs* (1928), and the *Kharia of Chotanagpur Plateau* in two volumes (1937).

In these monographs, Roy presented an exhaustive account of the life, cultural changes and history of the respective tribes. He also attempted to examine the antiquity of the tribes in terms of certain archaeological evidences and the ancient scriptural sources, and modern Asuras were taken up as a case for study.

Roy started an exclusively anthropological journal, *Man in India*, in 1921 and was its first editor. This journal has attained international reputation and continues to be published even now. Roy also encouraged a large number of ethnographers in the field of anthropology. His son, R. C. Roy, collaborated with him in writing the monograph on the Kharia (1937)* Roy initiated S. S. Sarkar for undertaking an ethnological study of the Maler as early as 1935, and D. N. Majumdar to take up researches among the Ho of Kolhan which were published in 1937. Majumdar revisited the same tribe in 1947-49 with his students from Lucknow University and made a restudy of the Ho and published an analytical volume on the same subject in 1950.

The tribal studies in Bihar got further impetus with the establishment of the Department of Anthropology by Calcutta University in 1921. Several anthropologists like T. C. Das, S. S. Sarkar, G. S. Roy and their students made frequent visits to the tribal areas of Bihar and published a series of papers as well as a few monographs.

Another scholar, P. C. Biswas, also trained at Calcutta, worked among the Santhal of Santhal Parganas and, in the mid-thirties, wrote a few papers on them which were later published in a book form in 1956.

* For a detailed account of the contributions of S. C. Roy, see *Sarat Chandra Roy* by Sachchidananda, published in the Builders of Indian Anthropology Series, by the N. K. Bose Foundation, Varanasi, 1978.

Two later events gave a marked fillip to the anthropological studies in Bihar. One was the setting up of the Department of Anthropology in Ranchi University in 1953, under the leadership of Prof. Sachchidananda and the other was the inauguration of the Tribal Research Institute at Ranchi, under the guidance of Dr. B. S. Guha. With the opening of the Council of Social and Cultural Research, Bihar, in 1956, it gained a scholarly medium of study and research through its organ, *Journal of Social Research*, which was started in 1958. The Department of Anthropology of Ranchi University has conducted extensive social anthropological researches in tribal Bihar under the learned guidance of Prof. L. P. Vidyarthi. The research activities of the Department under Prof. Vidyarthi may be divided into four categories, viz., (a) research programmes of the individual teachers, (b) post-graduate students' field research programmes, (c) doctoral field research programmes, and (d) large-scale research projects sponsored and financed by outside agencies.

The Tribal Welfare Research Institute, Ranchi, too has undertaken some welfare-oriented research projects, and in addition to several Bulletins, it has published a few books like *Land and People of Tribal Bihar* (1964), *Life and Times of Birsa Bhagwan* (1964), *A Report on Land Alienation in Chotanagpur*, *Culture Change Studies on Chero and Pahariya Tribes*, etc.

In addition to the tribal studies conducted by the University Department of Anthropology and Tribal Research Institute at Ranchi, some other scholars with different affinities have made significant contributions in this field. K. K. Leuva, Assistant Commissioner of Scheduled Castes and Tribes, Bihar, published his study, *The Asur* in 1963. Another civil servant, Kumar Suresh Singh, has revived the tradition of the old administrators in Bihar and wrote the *Duststorm and Hanging Mist : Study of Birsa Munda and his Movement* (1966). Other administrators and missionaries like W. G. Archer (1974), mentioned earlier, Somers and Troisi have continued their studies of the different aspects of the Santhal way of life in Santhal Parganas. These later studies, however, differ from the earlier ones, in that they reflect the chief concern of the modern social anthropologists in the context of the tribal culture.

The census operations had undertaken preparation of monographs on 23 tribal villages in Bihar. S. D. Prasad, the Census Superintendent in Bihar, and his associates and L. P. Vidyarthi have brought out some of these village monographs. P. C. Roy Choudhary and D. K. Prasad worked among the Sauria, Mal Pahariya, and Kumar Bhaga Pahariya of Santhal Parganas and wrote on their economic conditions and spread of education. N. G. Nag published his work on the Pahariya tribe of Palamau in 1977.

Besides the Department of Anthropology, the Political Science Departments of Ranchi and Bhagalpur Universities have also shown keen interest in the tribal studies. The Political Science Department of Bhagalpur University has made some studies on the Santhal of Santhal Parganas.

At Patna also, in the A. N. S. Institute of Social Studies, its Director, Dr. Sachchidananda, has been engaged for long in anthropological studies in Bihar. He has recently finished the restudy of the Mundas of Chotanagpur. In addition, he has published a number of papers on the tribals of Chotanagpur in learned journals. His two earlier works, *Profiles of Tribal Culture in Bihar* and *The Tribal Village in Bihar* (his D. Litt. dissertation) are justly considered as some of the best studies on Bihar tribals. Another scholar of the A. N. Sinha Institute, K. K. Verma, has published his study *Culture, Ecology and Population of Santhals and Birhors* (1978). The Institute is currently engaged in a couple of studies of tribal Bihar, the results of which will soon be published.

The main credit, however, for enriching the anthropological studies of Bihar tribals must go to Dr. Sachchidananda of the A. N. Sinha Institute of Social Studies, Patna, and Prof. L. P. Vidyarthi, Head of the Department of Anthropology, Ranchi University, who are the two acknowledged doyens of the subject, and who have by their sustained scholarly interest in the tribal studies not only gained national but international reputation. It is gratifying that they are still busy producing more and more gainful tribal literature and also training a team of younger anthropologists, some of whom have already shown great promise.

V

The need for anthropological studies is most apparent when we consider the enormous attention that is now being paid to other branches of science. It is a pity that the study of man's material needs is getting much more attention by the scholars and scientists than the study of his psychological, moral, social and cultural necessities.

What, indeed, can be more rewarding than the sociological and anthropological studies regarding a people who were the original inhabitants of a country with moral claims and rights thousands of years old ? As Verrier Elwin says, "To study a people is to learn to love them, and to publish your studies is to make them widely loved."

Instead, the Indian tribals are looked down upon as a "benighted group of humanity" and are treated with ignorance and patronizing concern by all but the very best officials, politicians and members of the public.

It is, indeed, gratifying that gradually modern methods and ideas are influencing study of this subject in India and also in Bihar and a larger number of Indian scholars are coming forward to endure the tedious and exacting labour of research in the field.

But it is a pity that in our own State, where, as mentioned earlier, the concentration of tribal population is the largest in India, and where tribal life presents itself in all its varied and variegated colours, the study of tribal life, stupendous in all conscience, has so far been carried on by the scholars in an ad hoc way, lacking in proper planning and coordination. This has been, perhaps, mainly due to the absence of a centrally organized forum, which could plan, guide, coordinate and integrate the anthropological studies and researches. It is earnestly hoped that the present seminar will effectively help in drawing the serious attention of the authorities concerned towards removing this lacunae in the field of scholarly studies and research in the State.

THREE

M.R. Chakravarthi

INTERDISCIPLINARY ASPECTS OF ANTHROPOLOGICAL RESEARCH IN BIHAR

MAN, like other animal species, is evolving, but evolving under pressures very different from those that have shaped him during the million years of his existence on this planet. And these pressures are becoming every year more intense as movement is facilitated, as ethnic groups mix, as environment changes with urbanization, and food supplies dwindle. If the adaptation of man to his environment is to be measured, if we are to predict and eventually forestall, we must have a baseline. Recently we have been hearing about multidisciplinary collaborative research from various quarters. Probably it is a new approach of research taking into consideration a number of scientists or to accommodate a number of allied disciplines to undertake as well as to complete the proposed research systematically and meaningfully. Interdisciplinary research in physical anthropology or in medico-biology presents two difficulties : there is an enormous inertial mass to set in motion in the first place, and its motion demands paper as fuel. But once it is moving it behaves like a breeder reactor and generates paper in an increasing volume. I shall briefly mention below certain areas especially in the field of human biology and physical anthropology.

We are in a period when the biology of the human group is undergoing continuous change measured in terms of health, fitness and genetic constitution. The records for research in this field in Bihar are not many and are scattered through a wide range of periodicals and books; also, with a few exceptions these records are based upon fragmentary research.

I do not intend to attempt a review of these research investigations since most of these are incomplete and a reasonably true picture would not emerge. During 1964-65, a study on the two major tribal groups of Ranchi district was undertaken jointly by the Indian Statistical Institute, Calcutta, and the Anthropology Department, Ranchi University. By and large, two other faculties also joined the research project. This may be mentioned as the first or the only interdisciplinary research programme in physical and cultural anthropology in this part of the country. Here the statistical methodology and design played their proper role in making the survey more scientific and meaningful. While planning the survey, it was kept in mind that regional differences might exist between individuals with the same affiliation of caste or tribe, living in different parts of a State, and that no single region could provide a representative sample for the State as a whole. It was, therefore, considered necessary to classify groups by regions in addition to caste, tribe, etc., and to plan the survey at the district and block levels and not merely Statewise. An attempt was made to mark off the inbred populations, for which the sub-divisions of the tribes and their marriage regulations were studied. This study provided a model for future anthropological survey especially from an interdisciplinary aspect in India but, for obvious reasons, the research programme had to be stopped mid way.

The International Biological Programme (IBP) has recently mentioned the major problems in human population biology. At a number of its meetings with experienced human biologists in over 30 countries, discussions covered the topics of environmental physiology, population genetics, physiological fitness, growth and physique, including ancillary medical and nutritional aspects. If not exhaustively, four areas of interdisciplinary research programmes could be planned and carried out :(i) Intensive multidisciplinary regional studies; (ii) Intensive survey on growth, physique and genetic polymorphic systems; (iii) Investigations on selected population groups; (iv) Medico-geographical survey related to WHO. These were chosen to take account of (i) the need for urgent and rapid accumulation of certain biological data, (ii) the need for a multidisciplinary coordinated and sustained approach in certain "key" habitats for the solution of basic problems, (iii) the great variation in scientific personnel and other resources available through different research methodology, and (iv) the relevance of the programme to health and well-being. For these reasons, the categories have been suggested to provide different scientific groups with a maximum choice, and different topics can be combined in many different ways. Such contributions, obviously, national in nature, can thus take the form of either (a) participation in extensive coordinated surveys or (b) intensive and usually multidisciplinary, organized and coordinated regional studies, the latter to a large extent include the objectives of the extensive surveys.

In arriving at the present seminar, the set of proposals, the papers and discussions will be of immense value, not merely because many serious gaps in our knowledge will be made so clear; it will be possible to examine by reference to progress already made, what is required in terms of hypothesis, design, methodology and organization, as well as national/international collaboration, to cope with such fundamental questions of human ecology, as fitness, selection, and population balance, with physiological, developmental, polymorphic and other forms of adaptation, and with problems of genetic and environmental interaction, affinity and divergency.

How actual field work should be planned, its design and strategy, as well as the agreed basic methodology, is at the heart of any coordinated interdisciplinary research programme.

What purposes are likely to be served by interdisciplinary surveys ? The distributional pattern of genetic characters has been used, of course, for a long time, like other anthropological features, to elucidate the degrees of relationship between populations on a local, regional and area scale. To establish such relations on a secure basis, a knowledge of a large range of genetic markers is necessary. Studies of affinity can be carried out to a high degree of discrimination and this would be one desirable objective of intensive regional studies. There is still, however, much to be learnt on this question even from general genetic surveys.

Another significant outcome of surveys is the uncovering

of clines and gradients. The existence of these or of major discontinuities can only be substantiated and made meaningful as more and more gaps between populations are filled in. The distribution of particular genes in relation to certain geographical features or to climate may suggest the operation of some selective factor. We need a well-designed coordinated survey data to provide as complete a geographical picture as possible of those genes with a presumed relation to malarial resistance or sensitivity. And in order to do justice, a meaningful interdisciplinary study could thus be undertaken jointly by the faculties of geography, anthropology, statistics, biochemistry and pathology. The past and present distribution of many other diseases, lethal in the reproductive period of life, are known; a more detailed regional mapping of various blood group genes could well point out to the existence of a selective influence.

A multidisciplinary study may confidently be expected to reveal the existence in high frequency in certain communities of hitherto "rare" genes or to the discovery of new allelic variations and their modes of inheritance. The general genetic survey is an essential first step in all multidisciplinary studies, involving comparison between two or more communities. Some assessment of genetic similarity or dissimilarity is always of significance in such studies, whatever their special purposes might be.

Anthropometric descriptions of samples of adults and children have of course been carried out extensively. But undue concentration was directed to certain cranial and facial dimensions, body weight, etc. The available data give no answer to many other questions especially on growth and physique. Is there a definite effect of climate on the adolescent spurt or on the time of appearance of puberty ? Is the secular increase in body height a continuing and world-wide phenomenon and what are its causes? Do nutritional differences affect growth and body composition differently according to the genotype? The basic approach to all studies of growth and physique is summarized by Tanner (1966). In his paper Tanner provides clear guidance on the types of genetic study that are needed. Some of these are clearly a matter for intensive, sustained and multidisciplinary research. Standardized and well-conducted surveys would serve a number of purposes. In many countries it would provide a base-line for measuring progress in health and nutritional programmes, both over a period of time and by comparison, as in the results achieved in comparable social and environmental conditions elsewhere. Data giving a minimal but adequate assessment of physique especially on the relation between climate and growth, climate and puberty and climate and physique would be of immense value.

There is always a requirement for a comprehensive, multidisciplinary regional survey. Because every population chosen is to be studied by this comprehensive approach, the research programme will require preliminary and pilot stages before full-scale study by repeated visits by multidisciplinary teams can be undertaken. Over and above the background information, the particular problems posed by the ecological situation, the habitat and population contrasts, as well as the research design, will determine which elements are to receive special and sustained attention. The emphasis could fall on climate adjustments (physiological, morphological or biochemical), on genetic and demographic structure of the community, on intensive studies of growth and physique, on intensive studies of physical fitness or on various aspects of nutrition. As already mentioned, one fundamental aim would be to attempt to distinguish between genetic and non-genetic elements in adaptation, and another would be to detect the operation of selection.

There are many other important questions which only multidisciplinary, long-term, cooperative investigations can answer.

A start has been made at Ranchi recently. We have already been thinking of undertaking an interdisciplinary study on the aspects of certain human populational cytogenetics. The idea has emerged out of our earlier studies on ABO blood groups and selection in this area. Approximately 4-5 per cent of all marriages are found to be childless and it is expected that a significantly high proportion of the males will be infertile which might be due to chromosomal abnormalities. There is also a significantly high percentage of fetal loss due to ABO incompatibility, as detected by Chakravarti and Chakravarti (1977:1978) and it is generally accepted that about

25-35 per cent of all recognizable spontaneous abortions are caused due to chromosomal abnormalities. About 5-8 per cent of tribal women here suffer from primary amenorrhoea, which has been found to be due to chromosomal disturbance.

Human chromosome studies have become an essential component in the investigation and management of individuals presenting with disorders of differentiation and function of reproduction as well as for genetic counseling, which form an important integral part of family welfare planning. For the first time, a bio-medical research programme has been planned where the departments of anthropology, zoology, obstetrics and gynaecology, pathology and human cytogenetics of three universities have joined.

Another plan of research has also been mooted. A study on the biology of man in Ranchi district has been proposed by Dr. Mrs. Rama Chakravarti, an ex-student of this department and presently a UGC Research Associate of the Department of Zoology of Ranchi University. The objectives of the said project include the impact of environmental conditions on socio-economic factors, growth and development pattern, health status and genetic aspects of three groups of people under three different ecological settings. Obviously in order to carry out a meaningful study like this would require extended cooperation of various interdisciplinary teams and to our satisfaction, we could receive active interest of the very many faculties from Ranchi and other universities and institutes.

One basic idea in the proposed study is to establish measures of "genetic distance" between population groups. In fact, to do all this satisfactorily, for communities ranging from the very simple to the highly industrialized, requires an integrated approach and application of methods drawn from many fields, particularly those of cultural anthropology, environmental physiology, population genetics aided by auxiliary disciplines like medicine, ecology, demography, etc. Bihar still offers a very vast uncovered field for various interdisciplinary research schemes. Besides various tribal groups belonging to different ethnic strains, we are aware of climates and terrains where the people live in an absolutely primitive state.

Before this unique mass of material is lost, there is an urgent need for undertaking a multidisciplinary research programme to explore the man and environment in Ranchi—a study into the anthropo-eco-medical factors in this State.

FOUR

A.C. Sinha

PERSPECTIVE OF SOCIAL RESEARCH IN BIHAR

ON THE EVE of the Silver Jubilee of the Department of Anthropology in 1978, various facts of the anthropological research were surveyed and assessed by the competent authorities. I take them as a genuine effort to look back and evaluate the quality and types of research done so far in Bihar. These studies catalogued the achievements made so far in anthropological studies and provided an impressive bibliography as usual. And there lies my problem: What are we doing? How relevant are our academic exercise and expertise? Where do we go from here? In other words what I feel is that there is an urgent need for having a consensus on perspective and direction of anthropological research in Bihar. Firstly, I propose an analytical classification of the major research activities in Bihar. Secondly, this small note may throw some light on the rationale for the above researches. And lastly this exercise may end with some suggestive themes for the future researches where expertise from all the other social sciences may gainfully be utilized. As members of an elite and educated segment of the vast illiterate and impoverished society, I feel it is our sacred social responsibility to take our unknown patrons (the masses) into confidence. And in my considered opinion, this may possibly be done if we examine the context of our research activities as an instrument in improving the quality of life.

I

I invite the attention of the readers to Vidyarthi's survey of researches on the tribal dimension in Bihar (Vidyarthi, L.P., 1978 : 230-235). The 80 references may conveniently be reduced to 20 significant authors who have written handbooks, monographs and theme specific books. It will be enterprising to examine the social background of the authors and treatment they gave to their subjects. But before we come to it, let us have a view of the Ranchi Anthropology. Perspective of Anthropology at Ranchi may be termed as the generalist where physical anthropology, pre-history, and social-cultural anthropology are taught. However it goes without saying that the department of Anthropology at Ranchi has established its credentials in social-cultural anthropology in the most effective way. Thus, for me, anthropological research means research in social-cultural anthropology. The department activities may briefly be summarised as follows:

- Anthropology
  - Teaching
    - Teachers
    - Students
  - Research
    - Model Re-statement,
    - Thematic Probing or Investigative
    - Evaluative or Assessment

Teaching consists of the teachers and students. I wonder if it is relevant to examine the social background of the teachers. Also, it may be useful to establish the social characteristics of the students since 1953. Where are they working now, and with what accomplishments? Except for a few guesses, I have limited data to work on. Thus, I am not in a position to generalize. However, there are many ex-students of the Department who have become now members of the Faculty.

Anthropological research in Bihar is naturally concentrated at Ranchi and the Department of Anthropology in the University obviously plays the decisive role. Such research enterprises are being published for the last seven decades or so. The very obvious questions come to our mind. Research for what? What are the social phenomena to which the authors addressed? What happens to the research reports/books? Keeping the above in mind, we propose to classify the research works in Bihar into the above four categories. The classification needs further sharpening and many a time the proposed categories may not be mutually exclusive. However, our purpose of classifying is limited only to providing a thematic treatment to the subjects investigated.

Model researches may be those which are popularly known as pioneering, such as Roy (Roy, S. C.: 1912), Majumdar (Majumdar, D. N.: 1937) and Vidyarthi's (Vidyarthi, L. P.: 1961) in our present context. These were the trend setters for future research and for decades to come they shadowed the new trends to emerge. Normally, within a few years of their publication they are known as classics. Incidentally, such researches create more converts than innovators. It may also be because of the status, individual charm, persuasive appeal, and magnetic personality of the authors.

The second type of research in Bihar one comes across is what follows from the first. These are as if re-statements on different social contexts on the model of some previous works. They are re-applications of some conceptual, technical, methodological and even empirical context in a slightly different way. Such examples can easily be multiplied: Leuva's study of the Asurs (Leuva, K. K.: 1963), Sharan's study of crimes among the Munda and Oraon (Sharan, A. B.: 1975), Jha's study of Janakpur (Jha, M.: 1971). Contribution of such studies is in no way small. These are the types of researches which validate the relevance of the model research. They provide the literature on which broad generalizations can be made.

The third type of anthropological research in Bihar may be provisionally termed as thematic probing or investigative. The authors select the processes and examine their implications in a given community or region. These are in a way issue-specific researches. In many ways they are like the re-statement researches; but certain processes are unique and the way they are tackled make them all the more unique. Thus, they constitute a separate category by themselves. Sahay's study of Christianity in Chotanagpur (Sahay, K. N.; 1976), Sinha's study of market as an agent of culture change (Sinha, D. P.: 1968), Vidyarthi on implications of industrialization (Vidyarthi, L. P.: 1969) may serve as the best examples.

The next category of research in Bihar may be the evaluative one, in which specific problems are examined with a view to remedial suggestivity. These are the researches entrusted by the administration to the individuals or institutions so that solutions to some specific problems may be found out. This goes very close to what we know as the action, applied and operational research. Conceptual sophistication may be an asset, but normally policy recommendations with a bearing on solving the specific problems are expected from these studies. Singh's study of famine, scarcity and economic development (Singh, K. S.: 1972), Sinha's study of tribal indebtedness (Sinha, S. P.: undated), Gupta's study of the bonded labour (Gupta, S. P.: 1974) may serve as the best examples.

II

The above hurried survey presents a picture in which what Vidyarthi terms as "Indianness" is missing. (Vidyarthi, L. P.: 1968). Indian sociologists are similarly engaged in search for an authentic identity of their discipline. The growth and professionalization of sociology as an academic discipline in India led to two phases of inauthenticity. "The first phase is evidenced in the implantation of sociology in colonial countries by the Britain; the other is reflected in the Americanization of the discipline, with an excessive emphasis on an essentially ethnocentric and limited empiricism." (Momin, A. R.: 1978: 154-155).To the above state of affairs, Yogendra Singh finds that the Western reference model continues to flourish in the Indian social sciences today as much as under the colonial regime (Singh, Y.: 1973).

In a not very different context, Sabrawal is baffled with "the sociologists' lack of sensitivity, or at least their lack of intellectual response, to the magnitude of poverty and to the pressures making for increasing inequalities in India". Some possible explanations for our intellectual aloofness and maintaining of ivory tower researches away from the appalling social context may be discerned from the following: (1) The prevalent public ideology whose premises were drawn partly from the colonial public institutions, which in turn incorporated the premises of the British social and political thought, and partly from the ideology of the Indian national movement; I shall argue that both these strands served to desensitize the generation entering the academia in the 1940s and 1950s to issues of exploitation and of conflict of interest between different segments of society; and that this desensitization was aided by; (2) the theoretical, methodological and substantive interests of American cultural anthropology—which came to overwhelm Indian sociology in the 1950s—and the absence of countervailing insights in the other intellectual traditions to which Indian sociologists took recourse, and, finally, (3) the social backgrounds of Indian sociologists have been limited to relatively narrow strata and their social experiences to relatively narrow grooves; and therefore their resources of personal knowledge have been much too lean to generate much resistance to the desensitization caused by the first two factors (Sabrawal, S.: 1979:243).

In the light of the above statement our earlier questions become relevant. What is the social background of the anthropologists and what have been intellectual consequences of such an elitist approach to the common masses? Do we really want to concern ourselves with the issues such as social inequality, inter-ethnic violence, solidarity movement of the great religions, etc., or be contented with our traditional concern for the unique, exotic, distant, marginal, relatively stable and small words? There is no denying the fact that the "primitive" world of the tribesmen needs special attention and anthropologists in Bihar must not feel shy of fulfilling this obligation thrust upon them by themselves. But should this be the end of all? Do we propose to continue with the traditional concerns when the traditions themselves are on the verge of collapse? Do we feel the need for re-examination of our perspective, tasks, tools and relevance of our academic enterprises not only to the academic fraternity but also to the larger social context? What should we concern ourselves with? Should we have an introspection to uncover the system as to why certain types of researches have not been fashionable for the students of the Science of Man?

We, on our part, have few answers, but many a question to ask. With all modesty I propose to expose my ignorance to this audience. We feel the Science of Man may attempt to uncover the following:

(a) Understanding the process of social formation: How do the classes perpetuate themselves? How do the new social bases emerge? What is the equation between the class and the caste complexity? How does the feudal social structure in Bihar sustain itself? What roles do the factors like education, professionalization and communication play in disturbing the social equilibrium?

(b) Uncovering the culture of poverty: Have the State sponsored welfare programmes and special amenities been able to disturb the social equilibrium in favour of the poor section of the population? Who migrate from the impoverished village to the urban slums and why? How many monographs have we to prepare to understand the landless labour, urban labour in unorganized sector, building construction and brick-kiln workers, hawkers and petty shopkeepers, professional craftsmen such as carpenters, plumbers and professional service castemen such as barbers, washermen, etc.?

(c) Uncovering the ethnic identity and urban violence: It is believed that the urban-industrial centres are the melting pots where unique primordial loyalties are submerged into a type of cosmopolitanism. Urbanism brings about a universal world view in which small social worlds get themselves transformed. In spite of all these how uniquely are the ethnic identities maintained and to what effect? Why is it so that the worst inter-ethnic clashes (communal violence) occur in the industrial cities such as Ranchi, Jamshedpur, Rourkela, Ahmedabad, etc?

(d) Understanding the great solidarity movements: Tribal revivalist and solidarity movements have been studied. More than a decade back Kathleen Gougheven made the plea that anthropologists should study phenomenon such as war, rebellion, revolutions or other types of physical violence based on ethnic ideologies. In the Indian context an Australian has studied the Arya Samaj movement and another scholar the Dravida Kazagham movements in Tamilnadu. One wonders what stops our own Indian anthropologists from studying the solidarity movements such as the Ramakrishna Mission, the Anand Margis the Rashtriya Swayam Sevak Sangh, the Jamaat-e-Islami and the various denominational Christian movements?

Summing up we may restate that the four types of researches in Bihar are not exclusive to each other and are tentative at the moment. We have indicated a distinct gulf between the academic research and the social context and referred to some recent studies suggestive of the genesis of the problem. We feel that the themes suggested for the research are not entirely novel. We are aware that certain areas of the suggested themes might have been undertaken by scholars. However, these themes remain suggestive. Whether it is the search for "Indianness" in the Indian anthropology (Vidyarthi, L. P.: 1966) or the proposal for "a man-centred, critical and active science of society" (Momin, A. R.: 1978 : 169), the issue of our academic authenticity vis-a-vis social context remains a moot question.

SUGGESTED READINGS

Gupta, S. P., Tribal Indebtedness and Land Alienation in Dhanbad, in *Two Decades of Tribal Research in Bihar*, Welfare and Forest Department, Govt. of Bihar, 1974.

Jha, M., *The Sacred Complex of Janakpur*, The United Publishers, Allahabad, 1971.

Leuva, K.K., *The Asur : A Study of Primitive Iron-Smelters*, Bharatiya Addimjati Sevak Sangh, New Delhi, 1963.

Majumdar, D. N., *A Tribe in Transition : A Study in Culture Pattern*, Longman, London, 1937.

Momin, A. R., Indian Sociology, Search for Authentic Identity—*Sociological Bulletin*, 27 (2), 1978.

Roy, S.C., *The Munda and Their Country*, City Book Society, Calcutta, 1912.

Sabrawal, S., 'Sociologists and Inequality in India—The Historical Context,' *Economic and Political Weekly*, Annual Number, 1979.

Sharan, A.B., *Murder and Suicide among the Tribes of Chotanagpur*, National Publishing House, Delhi, 1975.

Singh, K.S., (ed), "Famine, Scarcity and Economic Development in Tribal Areas" in *Tribal Situation in India*, Simla, Indian Institute of Advanced Studies, 1972.

Singh, Yogendra, "The Role of Social Sciences in India : A Sociology of Knowledge," *Sociological Bulletin*, 22 (2), 1973.

Sinha, S. P., "Tribal Indebtedness in Singhbhum District", Tribal Research Institute, Ranchi, unpublished.

Sahay, K. N., *Under Shadow of the Cross*, Institute of Social Research and Applied Anthropology, Calcutta, 1976.

Sinha, D.P., *Cultural Change in an Inter-Tribal Market*, Asia Publishing House, Bombay, 1968.

Vidyarthi, L. P., *The Sacred Complex in Hindu Gaya*, Asia Publishing House, Bombay, 1961.

Vidyarthi, L. P. "Social Anthropological Researches in India, *Journal of SocialResearch*, IX (1), 1966.

Vidyarthi, L.P., *Socio-Cultural Implications of Industrialisation : A Case Study of Tribal Bihar*, Council of Social and Cultural Research, Bihar, Ranchi, 1969.

Vidyarthi et al (ed), "Special Number on Twenty-five years of Anthropology in Bihar", *Journal of Social Research*, 21 (iii), 1978.

Vidyarthi, L.P., *Rise of Anthropology in India*, two volumes, Concept, Publishing Company, New Delhi, 1979.

FIVE

V. S. Upadhyay

RESEARCHES IN SOCIAL ANTHROPOLOGY IN BIHAR
Problems and Prospects

THE DISCOVERY in our time that scientific methodology can be applied to human problems has revolutionized all branches of social science. As a consequence research in the field of anthropology has seen unparalleled growth. We have been too absorbed in doing research. This call for an effort to take stock of one's progress and select the new fields of social anthropological research. Though Sir William Jones broke the ice in 1774 by publishing a paper on linguistics, it was Rai Bahadur S. C. Roy of Ranchi who wrote the first anthropo-historical monograph on the Munda in 1912, and also delivered the Readership Lectures in Patna University on different branches of anthropology in 1915. Though the first teaching department was opened in Calcutta University only in 1921 the research tradition was continued by the Rai Bahadur, who published a full-length work on the Oraon on 1915. He held the banner of anthropological research aloft till his death in 1942 and was aptly rewarded during his life-time (Kaiser-i-Hind Silver Medal in 1913, title of Rai Bahadur and two certificates of honour in 1930, Honorary Member of Folklore Society of London in 1920, President, Anthropology and Archaeology Section, Indian Science Congress 1920, President, Anthropology and Folklore Section, All India Oriental Conference 1932 and 1933, Member, Conseil d'Honneur, ICAES) and was honoured by the title of "The Father of Indian Ethnology" as early as 1938. Besides these by Roy anthropological writings by Dalton, Bodding,

Hutton, Archer, Campbell, Bompass, Anderson, Cole and others appeared in different journals during the British administration in Bihar. It may be mentioned that these writings appeared in the form of papers or short essays primarily in two journals of Bihar—*Journal of Bihar and Orissa* (now only Bihar), *Research Society*, Patna and *Man in India*, Ranchi. The other journals in which papers on Bihar appeared, were *Journal of Anthropological Society of Bombay*, *Journal of Asiatic Society of Bengal*, *Transactions of Bose Research Institute*, *American Journal of Physical Anthropology*, *Indian Atiquary*, *Journal of Royal Asiatic Society of Bengal* and others. The standard of these publications has aptly led Prof. Vidyarthi (1973) to categorize them as belonging to the constructive period (preceded by the formative period). In Bihar the analytic phase of anthropological inquiry began when the Post-Graduate Department of Anthropology was opened in Ranchi College under Bihar University in 1953. This was followed by the establishment of Bihar Tribal (now Welfare) Research Institute in 1954 at Ranchi. Both these institutions under the guidance of trained anthropologists began to explore the fascinating life and culture of tribals of Chotanagpur and Santhal Parganas. Thus began the trends of analytic research in Bihar. The present paper is devoted to highlight the problems and prospects of social anthropological enquiry in Bihar. The scope covers training facilities, levels and institutions for research, reporting, research facilities, etc. The trend of researches has been analyzed on the basis of regions, ethnic groups, themes and subjects. A major part of the researches has been devoted to analyse the retrospects and prospects of research. As my main task is to look into the future, I have tried to visualize the problems before the young anthropologists before making concluding remarks.

Institutions for Training

There is only one post-graduate department in Ranchi University which is teaching anthropology as a full-fledged subject. It is also taught as a special paper under the Post-Graduate Departments of Sociology in Patna, Mithila and Bhagalpur Universities. Even at the Intermediate,

Bachelor and Honours levels only Ranchi University has it as an independent subject, while other Universities have made it a part of sociology. Apart from these two sister disciplines, the Post-Graduate Department of Psychology in Ranchi University has a special paper on Social Anthropology, under its courses of study. The B.Ed. trainees also study anthropology as paper. Similarly, post-Master's degree level course offering diploma in Psychiatric Social Work and Mental and Social Psychiatry at the Institute of Psychiatry, Kanke, offer courses in Cultural Anthropology. Even the trainees for the Civil Services are sometimes being acquainted with anthropological ideas. This makes it clear that these facilities are available for imparting basic ideas of anthropological knowledge from Intermediate to Master's level. At the Ph. D. Litt. level only Ranchi University trains the intending candidates. If one is allowed to stretch it further, the other universities, having post-graduate departments of sociology, and institutes are choosing subjects of social anthropological interest for doing research towards a doctorate or project level. Similar comparison can be made to name language departments of different universities which are doing work on different aspects of linguistics and folklore.

Research Standards

The first glimpse into the fields of anthropological research is provided to young students of the Bachelor Degree (pass as well as Honours course) in Ranchi University. They are expected to do a fortnight's field work and write a report based on the field material. The report, mainly descriptive in nature, can be noted as "formative phase" of individual training in anthropological inquiry. For a Master's degree a student is led through the "Constructive Phase" of training in field researches. He goes for a six-week field camp and produces a field report of considerable depth. The young trainee uses both descriptive and explanatory words to prepare his report. A brilliant student has the opportunity to test his mettle by writing his dissertation. He has mainly library sources for writing a critical analysis by revitalizing the published material on the subject concerned. After receiving his Master's degree the budding anthropologist can go to combine field work, library source and his own anthropological ideas to propose a thesis of doctorate standard, the analytic phase of his training. Sometimes this phase is preceded by an opportunity to work as research officer in a large-scale project. He is left to develop his ideas in new anthropological field which later may be further sharpened during his doctorate thesis. An anthropologist is not allowed to handle an independent research proposal on an empirical theme. He keeps his ideas or concepts before the members of the discipline to discuss, criticize, analyze and recognize. Though these levels of research are being followed in Ranchi University, the categories are universal, applicable to all engaged in anthropological or for that matter, social sciences research in Bihar.

Institutional Efforts

The canvas of anthropological enquiry is so large that it is difficult to limit and name specific institutions engaged only in anthropological research. There are instances where other institutions are working on their own but are touching the realm of anthropological subject or interest. In other words, the lack of trained anthropologists in particular fields or absence of research proposals by anthropologists in the particular subject compels one to use data gathered by other scientists while making a comprehensive report. Still, there are institutions whose personnel are engaged in such an inquiry which has some anthropological importance. Many of them have trained anthropologists on their role while others are making anthropological reporting. One may question their methodological approach being scientific or not, but the field of inquiry being anthropological arouses our interest. Naturally, the P.G. Department of Anthropology, Ranchi University, will head the list of such institutions followed by the Bihar Tribal Research Institute, Ranchi. The third name to recall is that of the A. N. Sinha Institute of Social Studies, Patna, and then comes the Anthropological Survey of India. (The contribution of A. N. Sinha Institute of Social Sciences has been reported elsewhere in this book.)

Records show that the Anthropological Survey of India has undertaken 73 research projects in Bihar between 1953 and 1975, showing an average of more than three projects a year. On ethnic basis, there were 63 projects covering tribes, and 10 concerning caste populations. From the point of scientific background, there were 54 ethnological studies, six of physical anthropological nature, four ethnographic films, and nine of linguistic and folklore category. Looking at the vast country under the Survey, it seems the share of research in Bihar is sufficient. Lately, the Survey has established a regional office for the Eastern Region, which may lead to enhancement of the research activities in Bihar in the near future.

Some other institutions are the Council of Social and Cultural Research, Bihar, Ranchi, C.D.P.R. Training Institute, Ranchi, Bihar Research Society, Patna, Adimjati Seva Mandal, Ranchi, Santhal and Paharia Seva Mandal, Deoghar, Regional Offices of Commissioner for Scheduled Castes and Scheduled Tribes and Commissioner, Backward Classes and Social Welfare Board. Apart from these there are the Sociology Department of Patna, Mithila and Bhagalpur Universities. A few Christian missionary organizations and Bihar Rashtra Bhasha Parishad, Patna, have also worked on proposals of anthropological leaning. Special mention may be made of the Institute of Ancient Culture, Singhbhum, Chaibasa, the personnel of which are devoted to investigate Ho life and culture. As already referred, this list can be enlarged by additing the departments/institutions of sister sciences, specially Archaeology, Linguistics, Psychology, Geography, Statistics (for Demography), Forensic Science (for Physical Anthropology), Hindi and English (for Linguistics and Folklore) and so on.

Circulation of Researched Materials

One of the greatest handicaps of anthropological research in India is financial support. But the crux of the problem is the reporting of the researched material. It is really unfortunate that there is no data bank or agency where one can be sure of having all about anthropological research even on the Bihar State level. In other words, printing/cyclostyling of all the researches is not being done, so its distribution is hampered. The ones we get today are usually in the form of books which are heavily edited to minimize the cost of printing. Therefore, the comparable form of research material—the raw data—is taken out. The other form is that of papers in journals. The most important once published in Bihar are the *Journal of Social Research*, *Research Journal of Ranchi University*, *Man in India* and *Bulletin of Bihar Tribal Welfare Research Institute*, all from Ranchi, *Journal of Bihar Research Society* and *Journal of Social and Economic Studies*, both from Patna. Journals, published outside the State, which publish anthropological papers concerning Bihar, are many. Important among them are: *Eastern Anthropologist*, Lucknow, *Indian Anthropologist*, Delhi, *Journal of Indian Anthropological Society*, Calcutta, *Society & Culture*, Calcutta, *Vanyajati*, Delhi, *Social Welfare*, Delhi, and *Indian Folklore*, Calcutta. Publications of interest have also appeared in District Gazetteers, Census of India, Reports of Commissioner, Scheduled Castes and Scheduled Tribes, and Commissioner, Backward Classes, and Journals like *Man* and *Adivasi* from Bhubaneswar, or *Geographical Society of India*, Calcutta. If one looks a little further, one can search in the Proceedings of Indian Science Congress, Folklore conference, Seminars held by different institutions including Post-graduate Department of Anthropology, Ranchi University, conferences on Tribe and Tribal Areas, Indian Anthropological Association, etc. Reports of Research Projects, sponsored by ASI, UGC, ICSSR, Home Ministry, Department of Social Welfare, etc., are some of the important treasures of anthropological materials. The greatest treasure can be reported from the unpublished Master's field reports submitted in P.G. Department of Anthropology during the last 25 years.

Facilities of Research

Unfortunately the research facilities had not drawn the attention of the Government till recently. For earlier efforts, the credit goes to individuals who devoted their time, energy and money to write and publish what we see today. Even in the beginning of the analytic phase of anthropological researches in Bihar, i.e., in the fiftees, the facilities were quite inadequate on institutional level. Perhaps only during the sixties and seventies, we noticed the growing pace of research activities.

(a) Finance is the first on the list of facilities. Today, UGC, ICSSR, ASI, IIAS, CSIR, Department of Social Welfare and Home Ministry are some of the institutions providing research funds for work on individual or projects level. There are Junior and Senior Research fellowships, Research Associateship, Teacher Fellowship, etc., for pursuing one's personal efforts. By establishing the Centre for Special Assistance in the P.G. Department of Anthropology, Ranchi University, the UGC has recognized its contribution in the field of anthropological researches. This has increased the opportunity for group and individual research for the social scientists in Bihar.

(b) Library facility could be noted as the next important need for researchers. Apart from the libraries and departments concerned, there are also many libraries, independent or associated with an organization, which attract the serious worker, for example the libraries of Bihar Research Society, Patna, ANSISS, Patna, BTWRI, CDPRTI and "Man in India" at Ranchi. On the national level, libraries of Anthropological Survey of India, Calcutta, Central Language Research Institute, Mysore, and National Library, Calcutta, are the most important. Moreover, the records available in some offices or institutions are of real anthropological importance, such as those of Commissioners for Scheduled Castes and Tribes and Backward Classes, Secretariat, Election Office, District Libraries and in the Commissioner's office. For particular type of anthropo-historical researches on Bihar, National Archives are of great value.

(c) After funds and library, are the personnel with training in methodology in anthropological or sociological researches. As referred to earlier, the prime centre for research training are the university departments and institutes, sometimes there are summer institutes for imparting training in research methodology. But none would touch the status and importance of such training in methodology as is imparted by the P.G. Department of Anthropology by teaching a complete paper on the subject in the Master's degree courses and giving practical training to the students through six-week compulsory field camps.

(d) So far as themes/trends of researches are concerned, much has been discussed later in this paper. The Silver Jubilee number of the Journal of Social Research on the 25 years of anthropology in Bihar has enumerated to a great extent the researches done till date, specially by the Department of Anthropology, Ranchi University. Two broad categorizations can be attempted, problematic or theoretical. But above all, the Indianization of the themes, better to say Indian themes, is the latest hue and cry in the field of anthropological analysis. Prof. Vidyarthi (1978) in his presidential address at the Xth ICAES, New Delhi, and Dr. B.N. Saraswati in his paper, "Behavioural Scientist", has drawn our attention to the want of Indian tradition in the anthropological researches. Dr. Saraswati has put forward the Indian themes of "Maryada", "Parampara" for future researches. Dr. Agarwal (1978) has also put forward a study of *Jajmani* as model of research analysis.

Research Projects

As referred elsewhere in this paper, there are numerous areas —geographical, ethnic and thematic—for the future anthropologists to probe. They are to select from innumerable problem of anthropological research a fresh one or even select to do a restudy on the areas already done. They have the advantage to use latest methodological approaches to the problem. The multiplicity of problems in the State of Bihar is really fantastic.

Geographical Area

Anthropologically the State of Bihar has been categorized into four linguistic cultural zones with some marginal cultural areas. From the point of view of anthropological researches, the tribal zone of Chotanagpur and Santhal Parganas will top the list of highly researched area. The life and culture of the tribals have fascinated and attracted a number of amateurs, scholars, travellers, administrators, missionaries, and others to describe them for a long time. It may not be wrong to guess that 80 per cent of the anthropological literature concerns this zone. Next comes the zone of Bhojpuri culture. As it crosses the

State boundary into U.P., it has been studied by the scholars of this State too, hence we have literature on this cultural zone. The third on the list is the region of Mithila. As the area has the tradition of study and learning, the local scholars have written on some aspects of Mithila life and culture, which they found unique for their area.

The Magahi zone is one where very few studies had been done. Similarly the marginal cultures of Angika and Panch Pargania draw our attention as the future areas of research. It must be pointed out here that if the researches by trained anthropologists are to be counted, all others except tribal area, have very few important studies. I want to draw the attention to these zones as future prospects.

Ethnic Groups

The major categorization of people of Bihar is done as Tribal and Non-Tribal populations. While the tribals have their specific names to identify, the non-tribals can be categorized on the basis of caste. There are 30 scheduled tribes in Bihar, eight of them major having more than one lakh population. Five of them have been studied well: Oraon, Munda, Santhal, Ho and Kharia. Surprisingly enough we do not have much on the Lohra, Kharwar and Bhumij, who are numerically quite strong. Of the remaining 22, eight have a population of around 25,000 and above, we have a good amount of knowledge on the Chero and Mal Paharia, the remaining six—Sauria-Paharia, Mahali, Karmali, Gond, Chick Baraik and Bedia—are still to be explored of the 14 minor tribes, we have data on the Birhor, Korwa, Parahiya while Kisan, Birjia and Asurs are under study. The remaining eight are least studied. There are groups like Gorait, Kora and Savar about whom we have negligible anthropological data.

Among the non-tribal population, the Scheduled Castes have drawn the attention of anthropologists because of their being traditional downtrodden, socially. Among the 23 population groups classified as Scheduled Castes, we know something about Ghasi and Bhoktas (Jayswal,1976), Chamar (Dwivedi, 1976) and Dusadh (Mishra, 1975). Some Master-level reports are also available on Dhobis, Pasis, Mehtars and Musahars in the Department of Anthropology, Ranchi University. Apart from that besides some general studies on the Scheduled Castes have been done by Prasad (1959), Sachchidananda (1975-76), Mishra (1975, 1977 and 1978), Mukherjee (1975 and 1977) and Vidyarthi (1959, 1975, 1976 and 1977). Thus, on individual level, we are to know much about the 16 other Scheduled Castes in future. Talking about backward and higher castes, we have very little data on them. Some studies on Yadavs or Ahirs, Kurmis, Brahmins, Bhumihars and Kayasthas are available. But a lot is yet to be done.

Themes

Researches at the Doctorate and Project levels have been taken up since the inception of P.G. Department of Anthropology in 1953. Several themes have been put forward by different anthropologists which are being strengthened by further studies. To begin with the concept of Sacred Complex studies was advanced by Prof. Vidyarthi which was followed by M. Jha (1971), S. Narayan (1932) and M. N. Jha (1979). Thesis on some aspects of Sacred Complex is being actively attempted by B. N. Sahay, A. P. Sinha, A. Das Gupta, V. P. Sharma and others. K. N. Sahay has put forward a completely new dimension on civilizational study by talking about the impact of Christianity on the tribals. To study the primitive societies a framework of Nature-Man-Spirit Complex has been propounded by Prof. Vidyarthi (1963). This has led to a spate of studies on the tribal life and culture by S. Prasad (1967), R. K. Prasad (1968) and A. N. Sandhwar (1973). There are still more: V. S. Sahay, S. Birbora, A. C. Sahu, S. S. Jarai, N. C. Samaiyar, S. Srivastava, Ajit K. Sahay, D. Prasad, N. K. Horo and others. The third theme has covered the scope of Industrial Anthropology. Prof. Vidyarthi (1969-70) chose Ranchi and its industrialisation as the field of research. He was followed by Rajendra Singh (1967), J. K. Sarkar (1970), G. R. Sharma (1971), P. K. Roy (1974), G. N. Choudhary (1978), A. K. Haldar (1978) and M. P. Srivastava (1979). At present A. C. Mishra is following the line of research. Then came the spate of studies in Developmental Anthropology. The scholars made a critical appraisal of the welfare measures as found among the Scheduled Tribes. Pioneers of such work are V.S. Upadhyay (1967), N. K. Ambasth (1967), L. R. N. Srivastava, B. K. Rai (1967),

Sita Toppo (1976) and B. Kumar (1978). The tradition is being continued by Mr A. K. Singh, S. Bhattacharya, S. N. Ridra. Another theme taken up for research by the anthropologists is on the Scheduled Castes. These downtrodden groups are of special interest to anthropologists. The trend was started by Y. K. Jayswal (1976) and R. K. Dwivedi (1977), and is followed by A. K. Sahay and R. N. Mukherjee. Apart from these, researches on Unity and Extension (Sachchidananda, 1961), Women (Kala Rani, 1975, and A. Srivastava 1977), Demography (K. K. Verma, 1970), Social Structure and Change (N. K. Shukla, 1968, N. Mishra, 1971, P. Verma, 1971, R. R. Sinha, 1973), Leadership (B. N. Sahay, 1967) and Potters and Pottery (H. N. Saraswati, 1968) have been done on doctorate level. Another unique research project on socio-cultural background of mental disorders is in progress under the guidance of the author.

On the level of large-scale project themes like Urban Pattern, Industrialisation, Tribal Indebtedness, Harijan, Action Research, Tribal Leadership, Voters and Elections, Student Unrest, Sacred Complex, Cultural Linguistic Zones, Gastronomy Restudy of Tribes and many others have been taken up. New projects on the lines of Urgent Anthropology, Anthropo-Geography, Exploitation are on the anvil as future prospects. Other ideas like changes in villages through Electrification, Package Programme, Televization, Education of Scheduled Tribes and Castes have also formed the basis of large-scale projects.

Subjects

A few years ago a *Bibliography of Social Studies in India* was edited by Prof. B. K. Roy Burman (1968). It gave a broad classification of papers/books published on different aspects of social anthropology. For the State of Bihar, it has listed 65 publications on prehistory and archaeology, more than 300 on castes and tribes, about 175 on magic and religion, only 60 socio-economic studies, almost 30 publications on material culture, more than 200 on folklore and folk art, fairs and festivals, about 120 on languages and linguistics and over 200 notes in Gazetteers and Census reports. It must be noted that after the publication of the bibliography, there has been a spate of new additions, which must have increased this total of 940 to more than 1,500 by now. But having with tribal, rural, urban and industrial dimensions of 30 tribes, 23 Scheduled Castes and numerous other castes in the four cultural linguistic zones, this number is also very meagre.

PROBLEMS AND PROSPECTS

Looking from the retrospective angle one finds the list of researches shorter while the prospects for future research planning interesting and attracting. Here an attempt is made to list out the major areas (basic postulates) of researches done, and to be done, in Bihar, though every time the State and individuals have not being quoted. This has been done deliberately to use the idea for better planning of research proposal according to one's choice of area, theme and people. The IXth ICBES at Chicago had made an excellent categorization of anthropological subjects of research which has been used here for basic classifications.

Cultural Anthropology

Excellent work has been done in this field of religion, specially Hindu and tribal, in Bihar. All its aspects like ideas, actions, its agents and its audiences have been researched into. The great traditions of Hinduism and Christianity and little traditions of the primitive, religion, and festivals on caste levels have been noted. Data is also available on gastronomical researches in the State. A large-scale project on food and food habits has been completed by the Department of Anthropology. The language and culture have also come under the focus while completing the study of distinctive life and culture among the four cultural linguistic zones of Bihar.

The future plans for cultural, anthropological studies can safely include other great traditions of Islam, Jainism, Buddhism and Sikhism because every one of these has centres of national importance in Bihar. The impact of Hinduism on these religions and vice versa could be interesting to look into. Even the gastronomical studies could be added to the studies of culinary practices, ethnography of food, kitchen culture and food in relation to human growth. A study of rite-de-passage or life cycle with special reference to the cult of purity and pollution at the time of birth, marriage and death can be made. Little details are available on ancestor worship. Similarly the study of the cultural-linguistic zones of Bihar can be developed by adding cross-cultural dimensions. A mental test and cultural adaptation study will be most interesting. The one idea which has remained completely untouched till date is about Art and Anthropology. Actually art is taken to be a method of affective response for man, hence a study of visual arts, both plastic and graphic, and the performing arts like music and dance, can be attempted. Even in the case of folk religion, religiosity of folk population is quite an interesting feature.

Social Anthropology

This branch of anthropology has received the maximum attention of the research personnel in the past. We have studies on the developmental process of urbanization and industrialization, human interaction and social structure in tribal and rural societies, caste politics with details of equality and inequality, conflicts and tensions, social change, land tenure, scarcity and rural tensions and so on. In case of tribal Bihar, we have data on women, polity and political change, continuity and change among ethnic groups, social prerequisites for economic and educational development and other socio-cultural developmental studies. There have been works on multi-caste villages and social mobility of some of the castes/tribes in Bihar.

The prospects of future researches in social anthropology are as big as its captivating character. One can look for socio-cultural identity or ethnicity and resource competition in the plural societies of Bihar. Fact-finding can be done in the fields of religion and politics, social stratification and urban development, tribalism and casteism, modernization of a village community, etc. A study of women of non-tribal societies and comparisons of their status, role, achievements and struggles can be done. There are few kinship studies in Bihar. A multilateral approach to study the socio-economic change and population vis-a-vis the economy is in demand. One can also do an anthropological analysis of regional development, such as Meso projects, in Bihar. The caste and state politics could be another important theme to study political development at State level, and political changes in non-tribal societies could also be looked into. A study of continuity and change of a non-tribal ethnic group would also be fascinating. Further, the implications of urban development can be found out through migrations and ethnicity. The changing family structure and relations, including marriage, can throw new light on the oldest subject of anthropological research. The values in a changing society or anthropology of intoxicants and/or prohibition need immediate attention. A rare subject could be an anthropological analysis of famine.

Ethno-Studies

The author had the privilege to make a comprehensive survey of researches in linguistics and folklore in Bihar (Upadhyay, 1978). So far as linguistics is concerned, we are still at infancy stage. Very few researches by some language departments of different universities of Bihar can be noted but none by trained anthropologists or linguists. The exception is provided by Ram Dayal Munda's study of the Mundari language. All the materials on folklore are of Master's level which includes a collection and nominal content analysis of folktales, folksongs, riddles and myths. The only study of Munda dance and music at Master's level can be listed under ethno-musicology.

The list of prospective subjects in this field is quite large. The important aspects are the description and classification of languages, meanings in languages, grammar, text and vocabulary, suffix and prefix, etc. There could be comparative study of dialects of Hindi and Mundari dialectic geography, comparative phonology, lexicography and semantic studies. Special mention can be made of studies on non-oral communication systems like gesture or sign language or Braille literature from anthropological angle.

Similarly, there are many aspects of folklore still untouched by any of the researchers. The folklore can be studied on the level of performance and also communication. Many aspects like motifs, customs and mores, proverbs and sayings, popular beliefs and superstitions, oracles, ballads and folk-drama, abuses, etc., are yet to be noted. The folk literature and the oral traditions can be studied as an aid to anthropological history. Ethno-musicology has yet to open its account properly in the field of anthropological inquiry.

Another branch of ethno-studies which draws our attention is ethno-aesthetics. We have nominal data on pilgrimage and ancestor worship as part of religious studies. But many more details are required on the two important aspects of human aesthetics. Then there is the attraction to study art as an element of culture, totemic symbols and the culture-complex of handicraft under this heading.

General Anthropology

The cultural history of Bihar has been studied in detail under various disciplines. We have data on social, economic, linguistic and cultural classifications of the people of Bihar in general and tribals in particular. Some studies on demography and early men are also available. The unique part of anthropological researches covers the trend or rise of social anthropology by Prof.. Vidyarthi. Not long ago anthropologists were branded as tribalists, and this was so because majority of them engaged themselves in studying tribal culture. The studies were more focused on the problematic angle, for the anthropological knowledge was being used to solve the problems of tribal world on individual and ethnic bases. Hence the applied anthropological researches have been done thoroughly.

The coming generation has the privilege to witness the development of anthropology in its major interdisciplinary role. Hence new terms have been coined to classify the in-roads of anthropology in other sciences, such as Psychological Anthropology, Urgent Anthropology, Industrial Anthropology, Linguistic Anthropology, etc. Medical anthropology has also shown its importance in judging parentage and forensic science. Again bio-social researches are coming to fore. Apart from these ultra-modern concepts are being put forward for future use, e.g., Visual Anthropology, Island Anthropology, Literary Anthropology, Marxist Anthropology, Adaptational Anthropology, Communication Anthropology, Symbolic Anthropology, Spiritual Anthropology and so on. Scholars have come to study anthropology of gerontology, richness, poverty, etc.

PROBLEMS BEFORE YOUNG ANTHROPOLOGISTS

The future of any discipline rests on the shoulders of the younger generation. And only Ranchi University has the proper training facility. Its intake is limited to 32 students. Even at lower levels of training, no other university offers such an opportunity. There has been a long-standing controversy between the methodological approaches of sociologists and social anthropologists. At many levels, the two come very near each other, at times even overlap in their identity, but still there are many aspects of social anthropology which have not been under the scope of sociology. Hence training by the Sociology Departments of different Universities has somewhat limited scope in anthropological inquiry.

Apart from training, the young anthropologists face lack of incentives. The idea and expectation of a permanent occupancy in a young mind is natural. Hence a longer continuance in project works or research activity is an avoidable phenomenon. Except for the Anthropological Survey of India, no other institution has come up with permanent research jobs. Some other institutes like BTWRI, Ranchi, or ANSISS, Patna, or CDPRTI, Ranchi, have perhaps reached a point of saturation. So they continue to offer only project works. Even the teaching departments in universities and colleges have not offered a solid background by offering permanency to future anthropologists. Lastly, the young are always in search of new pastures. Lack of new models of research dampen their inquiring minds. It is high time that new models to study the Indian cultural phenomenon should be brought in the field. Encouragement to bring in new concepts is the demand of future anthropologists, and sincerity on their part is the expectation of the elders in the field.

The paper is a humble attempt to enlist prospects of anthropological researches in Bihar. Something has deen done and a lot is to be done. The various problems of research activities have been discussed to enable those who matter to do something for the development of anthropology in the State of Bihar. More funds, more jobs, more research models, more training centres are required to fill in the gaps and open of new avenues of researches. On the part of young anthropologists, devotion, as said above for search and research, is expected.

SIX

William Ekka

SOME PROPOSALS FOR ANTHROPOLOGICAL RESEARCH IN TRIBAL BIHAR

TRIBAL BIHAR, roughly comprising Santhal Parganas, Dhanbad, Hazaribagh, Palamau, Ranchi and Singhbhum Districts, offers a vast scope for anthropological studies. Almost all the 30 tribes of Bihar, listed in the 1971 Census, are found in large numbers in this area. At present their study is important both for practical and academic purposes because of the emergence of certain situations. Vidyarthi (1969) has rightly laid emphasis on the need for urgent anthropological research among them. Giving reasons for this urgent necessity he states that great changes having ramifying implications are occurring in the folk and traditional societies due to technological advancement and industrial development. Besides, several other factors of culture change are operating simultaneously accelerating the change in their culture. Hence, in this context his proposal for studying the cultures of different tribes on a priority basis before they change beyond recognition or vanish completely, and the present economic and religious phases of certain societies before their total transformation, appears to be very much to the point.

A lot of anthropological studies have been made on the tribes of Bihar. These have been amply referred for by several authors such as Vidyarthi and Rai (1977) and Sandhwar (1978). Taking the large number of books and articles on the tribes of Bihar Vidyarthi and Rai state without any exaggeration that "... tribal Bihar ranks as one of the most extensively studied areas in India from the point of view of basic ethnography" (ibid: 50). It is all the more true when a few other books and articles, published recently on the tribes of Bihar are included in the long list of already published anthropological material. Of the books, mention may be made of the ones written by Mukherjee et al. (1973) on the Chero, Choudhury (1971) on the social structure of the Munda, and Das Gupta (1978) on the Birjhia. These books are ethnographic in nature. In addition to these, there is a book by Das Gupta (1978) which deals with the impact of industrialization on the Ho. There are two other books on the tribes of Bihar which have not been written by anthropologists but they do have anthropological relevance. One of them has been written by Virottam (1972) which gives a historical account of the Nagbansi and the Chero. The other, by Singh (1978), deals with resistance to British rule in Singhbhum by the Ho. Both these authors are historians; and their works manifest the usefulness of interdisciplinary approach to the study of the tribals.

Proposal for Further Research

In spite of the substantial amount of anthropological work there are needs and areas for further research in tribal Bihar. Briefly they are:

Basic Ethnographic Study

Some of the tribes of Bihar have received very scant attention of the anthropologists. Their thorough study will help fill up the gaps in the ethnographic map of tribal Bihar. The tribes such as Bedia, Bhumij, Binjhia, Karmali, Kharwar, Kisan and Lohra have not been studied in detail. They have been briefly described by Narmedeshwar Prasad (1961); and a few articles may be found on them in some anthropological journals. The study of some other tribes such as Chik Baraik and Mahli may be taken up urgently as there is practically no published material on their societies and culture.

Re-study of the Tribes

Re-study of the tribes which have been studied long back is needed for the purpose of knowing the comparative change in their culture and recording their present way of life. In fact many such tribes have been studied later on. But only certain aspects of their societies have been studied by different persons at different places. These studies have appeared in the form of articles in different anthropological journals. But the lack of coordination among the individual workers and different areas of their field work make it rather difficult to get a comprehensive or composite picture of the changing society and culture of any particular tribe.

Some such tribes also need re-study which were studied long ago but the findings on them were published much later or very recently. Such works do not lose their value in any way because of their late publication, but by the time they are brought out many traits are already changed.

Study of Large Tribes over a Wide Area

The distribution of numerically large tribes such as the Oraon, Munda, Kharia, Santhal, etc., over a very vast area has naturally created variation in their customs and practices. Hence, on the basis of the study of a particular tribe at one place no generalization can be made for the whole of the tribe spread over many places. It is, therefore, necessary to study these tribes in different areas to find out the similarities and to record, at least, regional variation in their respective customs and practices prevalent at different places.

Study of the Oraon of Rohtas Hill

There has been extensive study of the Oraon in Chotanagpur and elsewhere. But no study on them has been attempted on the Rohtas Hill and in the villages at its foot. Such study would be worthwhile for comparing their customs and traditions with those of their tribesmen living in other places.

Use of Anthropology in Tribal Bihar

The ultimate aim of all branches of knowledge is the betterment of human life. Anthropology must also contribute to this noble cause. The time has come when it cannot afford to lag behind as its practical utility can go a long way in this respect. It has to apply its vast store of knowledge of the tribals to the understanding of their various problems and endeavour to find out suitable solutions for the betterment of the lot of the tribals. In a developing country like India anthropological study without having some practical utility is a luxury rather than a necessity. In the context of tribal Bihar the following points may be taken up for consideration for making better use of anthropological knowledge:

Study of tribal unrest: A note of urgency has been rung by Sachchidananda (1969) for the study of tribal unrest in Bihar. But this problem has received practically no attention of the anthropologists. There is a greater need for this study at present as there is a seething tribal unrest in tribal Bihar which has found expression in their growing demand for a separate Jharkhand State. Their unrest is intensifying in Bihar and at the same time extending over to the neighbouring areas of other States. The demand for Jharkhand state in quite old. But they were never so persistent in their demand as they are now. It indicates that the grievances of the tribals, which appear to be mainly economic in nature, have been aggravated. They have waited long enough and with patience to get a better or fair deal. But now they feel that they are economically more deprived. Hence, they themselves want to redress their grievances through an effective control over political power. When things have come to such a pass anthropologists may undertake the study of the problems of tribal unrest with a view to helping the tribals achieve their economic and political aspirations in the best possible way and by peaceful means or to giving practically useful suggestions to the Government to deal with this situation judiciously and prudently for the good of the tribals as well as of other people.

Study of the problems of tribal education: The absence of education among the tribals is quite conspicuous. It partly accounts for their general backwardness. As they have a special socio-economic status the Government has been trying to spread education among them by providing certain facilities and giving financial assistance. In spite of this the overall response of the tribals to this effort of the Government is far from satisfactory. But at present there is great necessity for educating the tribals. In case of certain tribals whose traditional economy has lost its sustaining capacity tribal education with associated avenues of gainful employment is all the more necessary. Through education the tribals can be economically diversified and assured of better economic life. Taking these things into consideration some of the tribes of Bihar may be studied for finding out the cultural, economic and any other constraints which prevent the spread of education among the tribals. Ambasht (1970) has dealt with the educational problems of a few tribes of Ranchi District. But some more such studies are needed for suitable suggestions for the education of the tribals.

Study of the tribal welfare schemes: It is high time that some studies were done on the tribal welfare schemes of the Government to assess their outcome. It is quite astonishing that though vast sums of money are spent on tribal welfare desired results are not visible. Anthropologists, with their deep knowledge of tribal society and culture, could be helpful in formulating the welfare plans and executing the programmes in a systematic and sound way.

Study of the effect of industrialization on the tribals: There is consensus regarding the industrialization of tribal areas, that national development has often not coincided with the economic development of the tribals. Their land has been taken away from them on which they depend mainly for their subsistence. The money they received as compensation for their land was not spent wisely for their lack of knowledge of its proper investment in profitable business. Semi-skilled and skilled jobs have been denied to them on the plea that they are not found suitable for them. Even for the non-skilled jobs the outsiders are recruited. This has left the tribals frustrated and discontented. Besides there has been an influx of non-tribals into tribal areas as a result of the establishment of industries there. This has had an unwholesome effect on the different aspects of the society of the tribals. It is a fact that the tribals cannot develop in isolation. They have to come in contact with the non-tribals. But for their gradual development and for avoiding psychological, economic and other strains they need planned socio-economic change. Anthropologists can be very useful in this task of bringing about such socio-economic change among the tribals. Keeping this in view, and also the fact that the tribals can develop primarily in their own area rather than anywhere else, more such studies as have been done by Vidyarthi (1970) with reference to tribal economy and culture are needed.

The areas and needs which this paper contains for anthropological studies are not exhaustive. Many others can be added to them. But this is a pointer in the direction of desired research and the application of its findings.

SUGGESTED READINGS

Ambasht, N. K., *A Critical Study of Tribal Education*, S. Chand & Co., New Delhi, 1970.

Choudhury, N. C., *Munda Social Structure*, Firma KSM Pvt. Ltd., Calcutta, 1977.

Das Gupta, P. K., *Impact of Industrialisation on a Tribe in South Bihar*, Anthropological Survey of India, Calcutta, 1978.

Das Gupta, S. B., *Birjhia*, K. P. Bagchi and Company, Calcutta, 1978.

Mukherjee, B., et al., *The Chero of Palamau*, Anthropological Survey of India, Calcutta, 1973.

Narmedeshwar Prasad, *Land and People of Tribal Bihar*, Bihar Tribal Research Institute, Ranchi, 1961.

Sachchidananda, "Some Urgent Anthropological Problems in Bihar," in *Urgent Research in Social Anthropology*, ed. by Behari L. Abbi & Satish Saberwal, Indian Institute of Advanced Study, Simla, 1969, pp. 137-143.

Sandhwar, A. N., "Studies on Tribal Ethnography in Bihar", *Journal of Social Research*, Vol. 21, No. 2, 1978, 129-147.

Singh, C. P., *The Ho Tribe of Singhbhum*, Classical Publication, New Delhi, 1970.

Vidyarthi, L. P., "Urgent anthropology for tribal Bihar", in *Urgent Research in Social Anthropology*, ed. by Behari L. Abbi & Satish Saberwal, Indian Institute of Advanced Study, Simla, 1969, 175-186.

Vidyarthi, L. P., and Rai, B. K., *The Tribal Culture of India*, Concept Publishing Company, Delhi, 1977.

Vidyarthi, L. P., *Socio-Cultural Implications of Industrialisation in India: A Case Study of Tribal Bihar*, Research Programme Committee, Planning Commission, New Delhi, 1970.

Virottam, B., *The Nagbanshis and the Cheros*, Munshiram Manoharlal, New Delhi, 1972.

SEVEN

Ratish Srivastava

METHODOLOGICAL ORIENTATIONS OF SOCIAL-CULTURAL ANTHROPOLOGICAL RESEARCHES IN BIHAR, 1953-1979

A STRIKING feature of the field of anthropology in India is its rapid growth and professionalization. The increase in the number of anthropologists in the country has been accomplished by expanding opportunities in the job market. Credit goes to the living anthropologists of the first generation whose efforts have made anthropology a recognized discipline both at the Central and State level. In this paper, unless otherwise stated, I shall limit my observation only to the Anthropology Department of Anthropology, Ranchi University, which is the main production centre of anthropologists and their works and to a few allied distributive centres of anthropological discourse.

Paper by K. N. Sahay and others give excellent summaries of researches done in Bihar. These review papers encourage me to emphasize the recent period and to look at the methodological aspect of social-cultural anthropological researches completed in Bihar since 1953.

An index of growth and professionalization is the number of Ph.D. degrees in anthropology granted by Ranchi University. The first such degree was awarded in 1962. During the period 1964-69 12 dissertations had been accepted, rising, by 1975, to 10 and to 11 by mid-1979. Nearly six dissertations are under submission and over a dozen well under process. Of the 34 recipients of Ph.D degrees, 27 were the regular students of this Department. Eight members of this Department have had the privilege of receiving higher training in anthropology in the U.K. and the U.S.A. By and large, anthropology in Bihar is dominated by young people who entered the profession between 1953 and 1973.

In an effort to give some idea of current interest and methodological orientations of researches I have made an analysis of the titles and contents of doctoral dissertations accepted by Ranchi University, and other universities of India and abroad during the past 25 years. In addition, I have examined small and large-scale projects undertaken by the Department of this university and by research institute of this State, viz,, Bihar Tribal Research and Welfare Institute of Ranchi and A.N. Sinha Research Institute of Social Science, Patna. In some cases, major works done in Bihar by the scholars affiliated to the institutions other than noted above have also been examined. In the light of these works we can evaluate the status of anthropology in Bihar.

Both space and time do not permit me to review individual works completed between the period 1953 and 1979. And I find it more convenient to put them together in a tabular form (see Table and Bibliography).

What in fact the Table tells us are the methodological approaches and fields of interest covered by 65 major works completed during the period under consideration. Following are my general observations:

Category 1

In this are included those six studies whose primary approaches are historical in orientation. This category also includes interests about a single tribe/caste usually tracing its relationships with other groups in the same cultural area. Of the six, two are Ph.D. and one D.Lit. dissertations.

Category 2

Works with non-historical orientations may be classified in many ways. According to my criteria, included in this are the works concerned with social structure, function, studies of social institutions, analysis of tribe and caste, aspects of social interaction, role, status and stratification. Ten studies (out of 65) form this category.

Category 3

A large number of researchers have shown their interest in dynamics of change. This includes problem-oriented studies dealing with tribes and castes of Bihar. Problem-oriented studies include the impact of Hinduism on the tribes (3), of Christianity on the tribes (1), of modern education on the tribes (3), and the impact of mixed forces on the tribes/castes (12). Some studies are focused on applied problems (directed social change), viz., impact of welfare schemes on the tribes (4). Included in this category is one action research programme in tribal areas. Of the 24 studies represented by this category, 14 are Ph.D. projects and the rest individual projects.

Category 4

This is represented by 11 studies directly related to urban-industrial phenomena in Bihar. Of these, eight are Ph.D. works on various aspects of industrialization and three on the problems and prospects of non-skilled industrial (tribal and non-tribal) workers.

Category 5

Studies related to what the Ranchi anthropologists call "sacred complex" which, in fact, is an approach to study Indian civilization, form another major category and this is represented by five studies (four Ph.D. works and one large-scale project).

Category 6

Under this are included four studies involving the interaction of two or more variables, such as people and forest, people and economy, and population and other aspects of society. While two works are related to Ph.D. projects the remaining are individual projects.

Category 7

In this two Ph.D. works are related to the role of individual in culture, to socialization and to specific psychological processes.

Category 8

This category includes one comparative study of crime among the tribals, one social pathology of domestic relations and one on food intake system of the traditional societies in Bihar. The first two are Ph.D. works.

With regard to the methodologies of the above works, except for three, all are the result of intensive field work varying from a few months to a few years employing the popular anthropological techniques of data collection: participant observation, informal interview, record of household census, genealogies, map making, life and case studies; and techniques of other allied disciplines: sampling, structured questionnaires, rating scale, etc. Of these studies, two Ph.D. works are based on field studies and rigorous analysis of population data, one large-scale project is based on formal questionnaire method and computer analysis. Further, three are the product of use of documented sources combined with field work. All the 12 large-scale projects are the outcome of team work under the supervision of an expert.

In short, (1) Descriptive and analytical studies dealing with either structure, function or dynamics of change dominate current research in anthropology in Bihar; (2) Understanding Hindu civilization in the general frame of reference of sacred complex is entirely a new trend started by Prof. L.P. Vidyarthi and maintained by his partisans of this university; (3) Urbanism and applied anthropology is a major area of interest among the anthropologists of Bihar; (4) Research interests are heavily focused on cultural and linguistic zones of Bihar; (5) Studies concerned with the relationships between culture and individual are very few. Perhaps this field of cultural anthropology does not interest the researchers of this area. Beyond the Master's level explicit study on culture and personality is entirely lacking. Similar is the case with the study on material culture, folklore and languages of tribal Bihar. One can feel this kind of apathy. Unqestionably, the subjects of Ph.D. projects, to a large extent, represent the interest of the supervisors in charge rather than of the students. Post-doctoral research of those who are professionally active will bear same relation to their dissertations; (6) "In recent years, much has been talked about the rigorous (quantitative) ana-

TABLE 7.1 : **Approaches and Fields of Interest**

(Researches done in social-cultural anthropology in Bihar, 1953-79)

Categories of researches	Dissertations: Ranchi University	Dissertations: Elsewhere: India, U.K. U.S.A.	Large-Scale Research Projects	Individual Projects Ranchi University	Others	Total No.	Total %
1. *Historical* :							
Descriptive/Analytical							
a. Case Study	1	2	—	—	1	6	9%
b. Area Study	—	—	—	—	2		
2. *Social Structure*							
Social Interaction Non-Historical							
a. Case Studies	6	—	—	1	1	10	16%
b. Comparative	1	—	—	1	—		
3. *Dynamics of Change*							
a. Problem Oriented	9	2	3	1	5	24	36%
b. Applied Oriented	2	1	—	1	—		
4. *Urbanism/Industrial*							
a. Case Studies	7	1	1	—	—	11	17%
b. Area Studies	—	—	2	—	—		

(Contd.)

5. *Sacred Complexes*							
a. Case Studies	3	—	—	—	—	5	8%
b. Area Studies	—	1	1	—	—		
6. *Ecology, Economy, Population*							
a. Case Studies	—	1	—	—	2	4	6%
b. Comparative	1	—	—	—	—		
7. *Individual and Culture* Role of Individual & Psychological Processes	2	—	—	—	—	2	3%
8. *Others*	2	—	1	—	—	3	5%
Total Projects	34	8	8	4	11	65	100%

Notes : (1) Many works are classifiable in more than one category. They are classified according to the criteria suited to the above category. See text for further description and bibliographic references for individual entry with code number.

(2) Except for three, all works are based upon or related to field work in Bihar.

(3) Above works are distributed among the Anthropologists (40), Sociologists (4), Historians (2) and Educationists (1)

Source : Compiled by the author from various sources which included Ph.D. dissertations of Ranchi University and elsewhere, published works and personal contacts.

lysis of anthropological data. While I do not suggest that this is the only royal path of anthropological discourse, still, with some confidence, I can say that following a "non-deductive" (as opposed to deductive)* both we can have a deeper analysis and understanding of the social reality. Relatively, few works have been done in this direction so far (see, for example, Williams, 1973, and Srivastava, 1975); (7) Majority of the research projects are the outcome of field investigation. In these works interdisciplinary techniques of collection and treatment of data are rarely used. This is, I feel, because of heavy emphasis on field studies in the training of graduate and post-graduate studies of this department.

To be sure enough, academically and professionally, anthropology in Bihar is only 25 years old. Within this period of time the quantum of researches done in Bihar mostly by the scholars of this Department is much higher than the total production of any individual university department in this country during the same period (see Table 7.1). Keeping this fact in view, it is propitious to remark that anthropology in Bihar has occupied an important position not only in Indian anthropology but also in world anthropology.

*'Two routes of establishing a scientific law are deduction and non-deduction (induction). The former proceeds from numerous particular instances to universal statement', the latter from some a priori universal proposition to statements about a particular event. In deduction, the methodologists maintain, there is little scope of truth of validity so the emphasis is on non-deductive system which involves the use of probability statements within a deductive system.

SUGGESTED READINGS

Ambasht, N. K., *A Critical Study of Tribal Education*, Ph.D. dissertation (1966), Ranchi Univ., Published by S. Chand, Delhi, 1970 (3a).

Choudhury, G. N., Impact of Industrialisation in India, A re-study of Three Tribal Villages, Near H.E.C., Hatia, Ph.D. Thesis (1978), Ranchi Univ., (unpublished) (4a).

Choudhry, N. C., *Munda Social Structure*, Calcutta (2a), 1974.

Dasgupta, P. K., The Impact of Industrialisation on the Hos, Ph.D. thesis (1973), Calcutta Univ. (unpublished) (4a).

Datta-Majumdar, N., *The Santhal: A Study in Culture Change*, New Delhi (1956), (3a).

Dhan, O. R., *These are my Tribesmen : The Oraon*, G.E.L. Church, Ranchi, 1967, (3a).

Dongall, John M., Agrarian Reform vs. Religious Revitalization. The Sardar and Kherwar Movements among the Tribes of Bihar 1858+795, Ph.D. Dissertation, (1974) Harvard Univ. (unpublished) (1ba).

Dwivedi, R. K., The Chamars of Palamau, Ph.D. thesis, (1977) Ranchi Univ. (unpublished), (2a).

Haldar, A.K., Milling Labourers of Chotanagpur: A Comparative Study of Coal and Iron-ore Mining Laboures, Ph.D. thesis (1978), Ranchi Univ. (unpublished) (4a).

Harimohan, *The Chero: A Study in Acculturation*, B. T. Welfare Research Institute, Ranchi 1973, (3a).

Jaiswas, Y. K., The Pathology of Domestic Relationship among the Ghasis, and Bhogtus of Ranchi District, 1976, Ph.D. dissertation (unpublished) (8).

Jha Makhan, *The Sacred Complex of Janakpur* (in Nepal), Ph.D. thesis (1969), Ranchi Univ., published by United Publishers, Allahabad, (5a) 1971.

Jha, M. N., Social Organisation of the Temple of Viswanath, Ph.D. thesis (1978), Ranchi Univ., (unpublished) (5a).

Kala Rani, *Role of Conflict in Working Women*, Ph.D. thesis (1975), Ranchi Univ., published by Chetan Publishers, Delhi, 1976 (7a).

Kumar Vijoy, *Higher Education among the Scheduled Tribes: An Evaluative Study*, Ph.D. thesis (1978), Ranchi Univ., (unpublished) (3b).

Majumdar, D. N., *Affairs of a Tribe: A Study in Tribal Dynamics*, 1953, Universal Publishers, Lucknow, (3a).

Mishra, N., *Cultural Persistence and Change in a Chotanagpur Village*, Ph.D. thesis (1971), Ranchi Univ., published by Classical Publishers, Delhi, 1978 (3a).

Narayan, S., Sacred Complex of Deoghar, Ph.D. thesis (1973), Ranchi Univ., (unpublished) (5a).

Orans, Martin., *The Santhal: A Tribe in Search of a Great Tradition*, Detroit, Wayne State University Press, 1965 (3a).

Prasad, R. K., *Economic and Social Change among the Parahiyas of Palamau: A Study in the Tribal Dynamics*, Ph.D. thesis (1968), Ranchi Univ., published by Ethnological Institute, Vienna, 1978 (2a).

Prasad, S., *Where the Three Tribes Meet: A Study in Tribal Interaction*, Ph.D. dissertation (1967), Ranchi Univ., Indian International Publishers, Allahabad, 1974 (2a).
"Maler, Malpahera and Santhal of Bihar", This study gives an insight into the processes of cultural adaptation and social dynamics.

Rai, B. K., "Nature and Man: A Study of Interaction between Man and Forest in Bihar", Ph.D. thesis (1967), Ranchi Univ., (unpublished) (3a).

Roy, P. K., Socio-Economic impact of Industrialization on the Indian Family. A Case Study in Hatia, India, Ph.D. thesis (1974), (unpublished) (4a).

Sachchidananda, *Culture Change in Two Tribes of Bihar: Munda and Oraon*, published by Bookland, Calcutta, 1964 (4a).

Sachchidananda, *Tribal Villages in Bihar*, D.Litt. thesis (1968), submitted to Patna University, published by Munshi Ram, Delhi, 1968 (3b).

Sachchidananda, *Educational Problems of Scheduled Castes and Scheduled Tribes in Bihar* (1973-75), mimeographed, A. N. Sinha Institute of Social Sciences, Patna, 1975 (3a).

Sachchidananda, *City of Patna: A Study*, Ministry of Home Affairs, Govt. of India, 1977 (6a).

Sachchidananda, "Harijan Educated Elite", (1971-72), published as the *Harijan Elite*, Thompson Press, Delhi, 1977 (3a).

Sachchidananda, Re-study of the Munda, A. N. Sinha Institute of Social Sciences, Patna, 1976-77 (unpublished) (3a).

Sahay, B. N., "Changes in the Leadership pattern among the Maler and the Santhals of Santhal Parganas (Bihar)," Ph.D. thesis (1967), Ranchi Univ., published as *Dynamics of Leadership*, Book-live, Delhi, 1969 (3a).

Sahay, K. N., "Impact of Christianity on the Oraons of the three villages in Chotanagpur", Ph.D. dissertation (1964), Ranchi Univ., published as *Under the Shadow of the Cross: A Study of the Nature and Processes of Christianization among the Oraon of Central India*, Institute of Social Research and Applied Anthropology, Calcutta, 1976 (3a).

Sahay, K. N., *Hindu Shrines of Chotanagpur*, I.I.A.S., Simla, 1975 (1b).

Sandhwar, A. N., *The Korwa of Palamau: A Study of their Society and Economy*, Ph.D. thesis (1973), Ranchi Univ., published by Ethnological Institute, Vienna, 1978 (3a).

Saran, A. B., *Murder and Suicide Among the Tribes of Chotanagpur*, Ph.D. thesis (1962), Ranchi Univ., published by National Publishing House, Delhi, 1973 (8).

Saraswati, B.N., *The Peasant Potters of North India*, Ph.D. dissertation (1968), Ranchi Univ., published by Anthropological Survey of India, 1970 (2b).

Sarkar, J., "Uprooted Families in Bokaro Industrial Complex: A Study of Impact of Industrialization", Ph.D. thesis (1970), Ranchi Univ., (unpublished) (4a).

Sharma, G. R., "Living Conditions of Colliery Workers in Jharia Coalfield", Ph.D. thesis (1971), Ranchi Univ., (unpublished) (4a).

Shukla, N. K., *Social Structure of a Village in Bihar*, Ph.D. thesis (1968), published by D. K. Publishers, Delhi, 1973 (2a).

Singh, R., "Impact of Industrialisation on Patratu and four other Villages", Ph.D. dissertation (1967), Ranchi Univ., (unpublished) (4a).

Sinha, D. P., "The Role of the Benari Inter-Tribal Market among the Hill Tribes of Chotanagpur: A Study of Culture Change", Ph.D. thesis (1964), Southern Illinois University, published as *Culture Change in an Industrial Market*, Asia Publishing House, Bombay, 1968 (3a).

Sinha, R. K., "Social Structure of Munda and Oraon Villages", Ph.D. thesis (1973), Ranchi Univ., (unpublished) (2a).

Sinha, S. P., *Life and time of Birsa Bhagwan Birsa*, B.T.R.W.I., Ranchi, 1963 (1a).

Sinha, R. K., "A Study of Nature-Man-Spirit Complex among the Pendo Tribes of Chattisgarh", Ph.D. thesis (1977), Ranchi Univ., (unpublished) (2a).

Sinha, S. P., Conflict and Tension in the Tribes of Chotanagpur and Santhal Parganas (1858 A.D.-1978-A.D.): A Case Study in Social Perspective, D.Litt. thesis (1978), Ranchi Univ., (unpublished) (1a).

Srivastava, Aruna, "Tribal Women of Central India", Ph.D. dissertation" (1977), Ranchi Univ., (unpublished) (7a).

Srivastava, A. R. N., "Modelling Developmental Cycles in Domestic Groups: A Case Study from the Korwa of Palamau, South Bihar", Ph.D. dissertation (1975), Arizona State University, Tempe, U.S.A. (in press, titled as *Developmental Dimension of Domestic Group Organization in India*, (6a).

Srivastava, B. K., "Social Structure and Social Organisation of the Oraons of North Central India: A Study in Change and Stability", Ph.D. dissertation (1967), Univ. of Summer, Illinois, U.S.A. (3a).

Srivastava, N. P., "Coal miners of Jharia", Ph.D. thesis (1979), Ranchi Univ., (unpublished) (4a).

Toppo Sita, "Education Then and Now among the Oraon", Ph.D. thesis (1974), Ranchi Univ., published in *Tribal India*, Classical, Delhi, 1977 (3a).

Upadhyay, V. S., Tribal Rehabilitation Schemes: A Study in Directed Social Change in Chotanagpur, Ph.D. thesis (1966), Ranchi Univ., (unpublished) (3b).

Vidyarthi, L. P., *Sacred Complex in Hindu Gaya*, Ph.D. dissertation (1958), University of Chicago, published by Asia Publishing House, Bombay, 1961 (5b).

Vidyarthi, L. P., "From Simpler Economy to Industrialization, A Techno-Cultural Implication of Change in India", (1958-68), published as *Socio-cultural Implications of Industrialization: A Case study of Tribal Bihar*, Ranchi, 1970 (4b).

Vidyarthi, L. P. and others, "The Urban Pattern of Ranchi" (1960-62), published as *Cultural Configuration of Ranchi: A Study of Pre-industrial city of Tribal Bihar, Ranchi*, 1969 (4b).

Vidyarthi, L. P., "Monographic study of a Munda village, Ghaghra", (1965), published as *Gaghra: A Village in Chotanagpur*, Delhi, 1966 (2a).

Vidyarthi, L. P., "Changes in Leadership Pattern in Tribal Society in India", (1964-68), published as *Dynamics of Tribal Leadership in Bihar*, Allahabad, 1976 (3a).

Vidyarthi, L. P. and others, *The Sacred Complex of Kashi* (1972-76), published by Concept Publishing Company, Delhi, 1978 (5b).

Vidyarthi, L. P., "The Scheduled Castes Studies in Bihar", (1973-75), published as *Harijan Today*, Classical Publishers, Delhi, 1977 (2b).

Vidyarthi, L. P., *Revival of Indigenous Nutritive Dietary Habits and Recipes in the Four Culture-linguistic Zones of Bihar*, 1975-77 (8).

Vidyarthi, L. P., *Re-study of Kharia Tribe* (1975-77), 1979 (3a).

Vidyarthi, L. P., *The Birhor Action Research Project*, (1976-77) (3b).

Vidyarthi, L. P., *The Peasant Organisation in India: A Case Study of a Voluntary Organisation in Tribal Bihar*, (1977), Council of Social and Cultural Research, Bihar, Ranchi (3a).

Varma, Poornima, *Social Structure of Chotanagpur Village*, Ph.D. thesis (1971), Ranchi Univ., published by the Institute of Social Research and Applied Anthropology, Calcutta, 1977, (2a).

Varma, K. K., "Anthro-Demographic Study of Two Tribes of Bihar", Ph.D. dissertation (1970), Ranchi Univ., published as *Culture Ecology and Population*, National Publishing House, Delhi, 1977 (6b).

Williams, B. J., "A Model of Band Society: (Birhor of Hazaribagh)", (1973), *Memoirs of the Society for American Archaeology*, No. 29 (6a).

EIGHT

Ajit K. Danda

AN ANTHROPOLOGIST LOOKS AT BIHAR

I

AN EXAMINATION of facts from Bihar in terms of their spatial distribution as well as through time presents a picture of its variegated character and multiple personalities. They are at times not only discrete due to their characteristic special attributes, some of them are even contradictory to one another in selected respects.

As a political state, contemporary Bihar has a distinct autonomous entity though, as a linguistic area, it forms part of a major Hindi-speaking belt. At the level of linguistic families, however, Bihar is represented by at least Indo-Aryan Mundari and Dravidian languages, most of which in turn are represented by multiple dialects. And even when only its important dialects are taken into account, the apparent homogeneity of Bihar recedes to the background and differences do appear on the surface.* In terms of other items of culture, Bihar forms part of other major areas with whom it is linked through cultural as well as civilizational fabrics. There is a considerable amount of overlap between the areas though they

*There are at least three distinct units of Hindi spoken in Bihar, namely, Maithili in the east, Magahi in the south and Bhojpuri in the west. All of them belong to the Eastern group of modern Indo-Aryan languages. There is a large number of tribal dialects belonging to the Mundari and Dravidian families. (For details, vide Grierson: 1903.)

are never exactly alike. In fact, culture areas identified on the basis of specific cultural items constitute more or less an interlocking chain that delineates the broader area of which Bihar forms a part.

So far as the ethnic composition is concerned, the tribal and non-tribal population of Bihar representing various levels of economy occupy its distinct eco-cultural niches consisting of hills, plateaux and river valleys. During ancient times Bihar has been populated in phases though, due to differential exposures and eco-cultural constraints, they have come to develop and maintain their special characteristics a great deal.

Tribals who occupy the river valleys have come within the fold of peasantry like the Santhal, Munda, Oraon and Ho. They are generally large in population size. Small tribes like the Paharia and Birhor are still at the threshold of hunting-gathering stage. The bulk of the population in general are, however, agriculturists, who divide themselves into various castes, communities, and religious groups.[1]

II

When looked through time, Bihar presents a picture of extraordinary glory which any other region or state of the country would cherish with envy.[2] In ancient India, Bihar distinguished itself for its spiritual outlook. It has been the birth-place of some of the greatest seers, pious kings, scholars, philosophers, and founders of haterodox faiths. Even during the pre-Mauryan period famous seers like Yajnavalkya and Gautama grew and flourished here. Yajnavalkya's explanation of the nature of ultimate reality had earned vast acclaim that transcended over centuries. Gautama's logic of Naya Sutra also survived the test of time. King Janaka of Mithila is generally regarded as an emblem of perfect wisdom and it is said that the great sage Sukadava and many others travelled across the country to meet Janaka for acquiring Brahmajnana or knowledge of the highest reality from him.

Parsva, the 23rd Jaina Tirthankara, was not born in Bihar though his sect grew and flourished in both the north and south Bihar.

Mahavira, the founder of the present-day Jainism, hailed

from Vaisali and mostly operated in and around Bihar, until he attained Nirvana at Pavapuri near Patna. Buddha had not only his enlightenment in Bihar, he also operated his missionary activities from there. The Jaina philosophy of extreme self-mortification as well as the pragmatic philosophy of the Charvakas grew in Bihar. Gargi, Maitrayi and Ahalya are also believed to have had their association with Bihar, particularly with Mithila.

Urban life had not grown during the period and the communication system was poor. Even then Bihar had attracted a large number of immigrants who come for the fulfilment of their mundane as well as spiritual desires.

During the Maurya period, Magadha of Bihar came to a level of eminence which may be considered an all-time best. The Maurya rulers could establish not only an extraordinary political solidarity and stability for India, this was perhaps for the first time that the state authority dedicated itself to the cause of welfare of the people. Kautilya, the friend, philosopher and guide of Chandragupta Maurya, architect of the Mauryan empire, wrote his famous *Arthashastra* while at Magadha. Even today this is counted as one of the most important treatises on political economy. The extraordinary eminence of the Mauryan empire attracted the Greek scholar Megasthenes to Magadha who wrote extensively on the glory of the then India.

The period between 325 B.C. and 320 A.D., when the Mauryas, Sungas, Kanvas, and Kushanas ruled India, is specifically famous for the development of the *Puranas* and the epics. Upavarsha, a commentator of the *Mimamsa* and *Vedanta Sutra*, and Varsha, the teacher of Panini, had associations with Pataliputra. *Ashtadhyayi* of Panini was also composed there. Other scholars like Pingala, Vyadi, Vararuchi, and Patanjali also grew during this period and had associations with Pataliputra.

Agriculture was the mainstay of the economy during the period. Model farming for seeds and commercial crops, employment of irrigation and development of state farm for cattle are the special characteristics of the era. Cotton and jute were the principal commercial crops which circulated through inland as well as foreign trade.

Mauryan, Sunga and Kanva arts had set in an era of magnificent monuments executed in stone. Asoken columns, Stupas, Yakshas and Nagas may be cited as the characteristic examples of the era.

Between A.D. 319 and 750 the Guptas ruled from Pataliputra. Although dynasties rose and fell, the tradition of excellence continued and Pataliputra went on radiating its influence over India and also over most of Asia, particularly over China, Korea, Tibet and Nepal. Having two famous universities, namely, Nalanda and Vikramsila, Bihar remained the most important centre of learning and culture that attracted eminent visitors like Fa-Hien and students like Yuan Chwang and I. Tsing.

In philosophical tradition Varahamihir's *Brihat Samhita* and *Panchasiddhantika* made important landmarks during the period. The literary contributions of poet Kalidasa also earned eminence. It is generally believed that the treatise of Aryabhatta was written at Pataliputra around A.D. 499, which besides dealing with arithmetical progression, described geometrical characteristics of the circle, discovered the rotation of earth on its axis, explained planetary motions, and accurately predicted duration of eclipses. The Gupta period is also famous for artistic excellence, particularly sculpture.

During 750 A.D. to A.D. 1200 Bihar came under the rule of the Palas, Senas and the Gahedvalas when the seat of the principality shifted from Bihar to Bengal. In spite of these changes in the dynasties and the shifting of the capital, Bihar's leadership in academic excellence and contributions to the Indian thought and philosophy continued unhindered. Contributions of Mandana Misra of the 8th century, Vachaspati of the 9th century and Udayana of the 10th century are particularly important in this respect. It is said that the fame of Mandana Misra spread far and wide and attracted even Adi Sankaracharya to Bihar. The high tradition of scholarship of the universities of Bihar also attracted students from far-off places like China and Tibet. Writings of the Siddha poets of Bihar developed a tradition of their own that left a permanent impression on the literary traditions of those days and of the later. Vidyapati, Surdas, Tulsidas and Kabir are considered to have been highly influenced by the Siddha poets.

Bronze and copper castings developed as new art traditions during the period and along with stone sculpture bronze sculpture also grew.

Agriculture, however, continued to be the mainstay of economy. As media of trade cowrie and coins came in circulation. Although metal was used, particularly as media of art objects, large-scale exploration or exploitation of it did not grow.

Around A.D. 1206 Bihar came under the Turko-Afghan rule and the capital periodically shifted back and forth between Bihar and Bengal. The development of Brahmanical culture which received special patronage during the Gupta period lost its support and consequently the importance. In fact, throughout the medieval period Bihar lost a great deal of its sovereign status and the tradition of glory. During the 320 years of Turko-Afghan rule, only during the rule of Sher Shah Bihar recovered some of its ancient eminence. A bulk of the administrative reforms introduced by him have stood the test of time and are found relevant even today.

However, in spite of the periodic political eclipses, the tradition of scholarship of Bihar did not totally die out. Even during this period Gangesa Upadhaya founded his Navya Nyaya philosophy and Pakshadhara Misra established himself as a renowned scholar. Writer-saint Sharf-ud-din Ahmad of Maner also lived during this period.

A new architectural style based on arches, vaults, and domes developed during the period.

Agriculture, however, remained the mainstay of economy and textile manufacturing developed as the household industry. Interest in cattle farming, particularly for milk products received special attention and metal extractions took place only for making art objects.

With the establishment of the Mughal power around 1526, the centres of Islamic learning received state patronage and the Hindu system of education became a public charge kept up by voluntary contributions. While this contributed toward a healthy growth of Islamic tradition in India, this also accelerated the retrogressive transformation of the Brahmanical traditions of Bihar that had already set in particularly with the shifting to the capital during the Pala rule and quick change of dynasties.

Loss of state patronage of the Hindu system of education appears to have made the Hindu scholars introvert who, as a result, concentrated their attention mostly on theoretical and theological issues which were of little practical significance to the Muslim rulers. The Muslim scholars, on the other hand, encouraged by the state patronage, directed their energy toward the development of applied sciences.

During the Mughal period (1526-1756), Bihar had the first contact with the European mercantile nations. Around 1620 the British Commercial Mission was established at Patna for exporting salt patre. While this should have boosted Bihar's commercial importance and revitalized its economy, relative political instability, due to lack of a well-knit centralized authority, had a tremendous demoralizing effect. As a result, in spite of the exposure to and contact with the outside world no new economic initiative was visible.

Around the end of the Mughal rule the political instability turned into political chaos. Then followed invasions, famine, uprisings and revolt. Rivalry between the Dane and English made the situation worse. Thus whatever healthy tradition and glory were yet left went into oblivion.

Establishment of British rule did not bring about any new economic initiative and no concerted efforts were made to restore its eminence to Bihar. Instead, by 1773 it was made a part of the Bengal Subah and thus Bihar's stature was further reduced. Since then Bihar remained a part of the Bengal Presidency until 1911, when along with Orissa it constituted a separate administrative unit. Only in 1936 Bihar attained the recognition of an independent state. But the spirit of righteousness that had developed over the centuries had still some energy left for initiating action. The revolt of Rudu and Kantu Munda of 1820; Sidhu, Kanhu, Chand, and Bhoirab of 1855-57; Birsa Munda of 1895; and the courage and organizing ability displayed by the eminent freedom fighters like Mazhar-ul-Haque, Sachchidananda Sinha, Rajendra Prasad and Jaiprakash Narain are only a few illustrations.

III

Contemporary Bihar forms almost a mirror image of what it was in the ancient times. Once the foremost region it has turned into one of the most backward states of India. A great majority of its present 31 districts[3] have been declared backward and approximately 22 per cent of the total area of Bihar had to be separated as Scheduled Area. Nearly 14 per cent of its total population belong to the Scheduled Castes who divide themselves into 23 specific and unclassified categories[4]. The Scheduled Tribes comprise 30 communities and are an unclassified cluster forming nearly nine per cent of the total population of the state.[5] Only about 20 per cent of the total population of Bihar is literate when the all-India average is approximately 30 per cent. The per capita income at current prices is Rs. 604, which is one of the lowest in the country as a whole.[6] Agriculture still provides livelihood to 77 per cent of the people.

One posted with the full facts of the historical Bihar would scarcely believe that the above statistics are of the Bihar that has many a glorious achievements on its record. Pataliputra of ancient Bihar was not only the political capital of India, but was the cultural capital of most of Asia and the foremost seat of learning.[7]

What then could be the reasons for this extraordinary retrogressive transformation? We have already discussed how periodic shifting of the seat of principality, change of dynasties, withdrawal of state patronage to the traditional system of education and similar happenings adversely affected the continuity of supremacy of Bihar. At the same time we have also become aware from the facts of history that such periodic eclipses could not totally crush the tradition of extraordinary spirit that grew there over the centuries. Further, we are also aware that the fleeting events have had practically very little impact upon the firm economic potential of Bihar which has the largest mineral resources and mineral production in India. Under the circumstances, for a plausible explanation of the phenomena of history an even more comprehensive approach to the facts of Bihar seems essential. For the present, however, in view of the constraints of space, we will have only a brief examination of physiography, historical sites, mineral deposits, and pre-historic sites of Bihar which may provide a relatively better appreciation of the events of history.

IV

Contemporary Bihar can be divided into three broad but distinct physiographic divisions : 1. Himalayan foot-hills, 2. Gangetic Plains, and 3. Chotanagpur plateau. (Map 8.1)

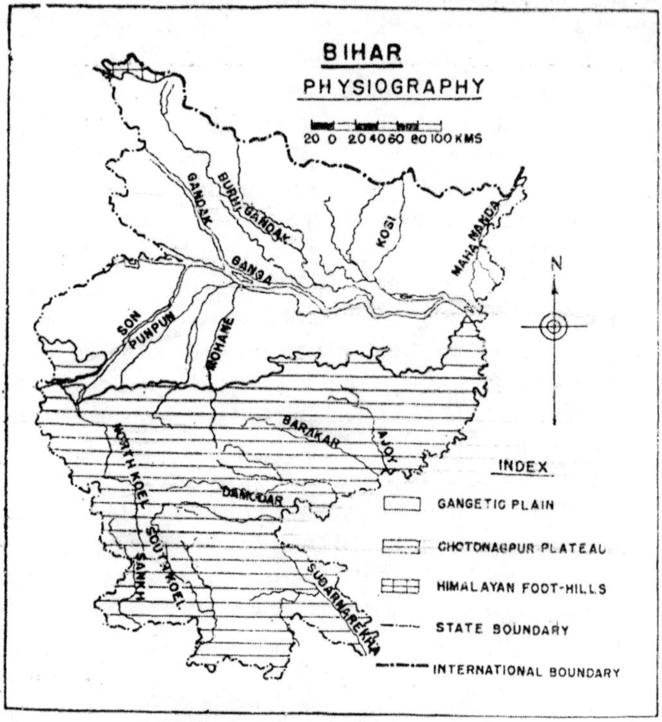

MAP. 8.1 : *Bihar : Physiography*

Source: The External Boundary of India on the map agrees with the Record Copy certified by the Survey of India.

The second and the third physiographic divisions in comparison with the first are of gigantic proportions. The Himalayan foot-hills consist of rather a narrow strip situated at the north-west corner of the State. The Gangetic Plain comprises the vast alluvial plains of the Ganga and her tributaries. It has two sections, namely, extensive plains interspersed with rivers of North Bihar and the plains of South Bihar. The geological formations belong to the well-known groups of the lower Gondwana, the Vindhyan, Bharwar and the Aravalli.[8] The plains of Bihar form part of the middle and lower Gangetic Plain. The Aravalli formations that mostly flank the Chotanagpur plateau on the north and south contain the most valuable iron ore of India. In fact, most of the mineral deposits of Bihar are concentrated in the Chotanagpur plateau (Map 8.2)

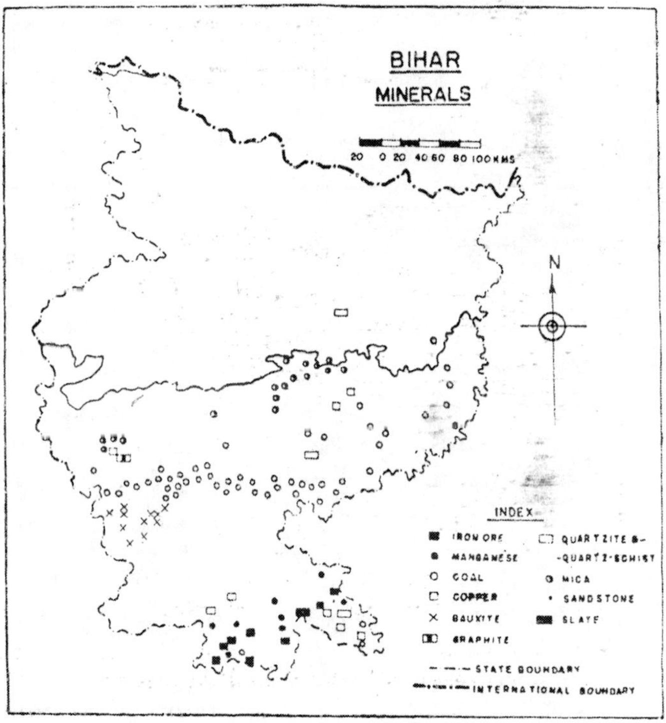

MAP. 8.2 : *Bihar Minerals*

Source: The External Boundary of India on the map agrees with the Record Copy certified by the Survey of India.

In this context it may be worthwhile to make a reference to the important pre-historic sites of Bihar. Map 8.3 gives the distribution of major neolithic, mesolithic and palaeolithic sites have been discovered so far.* As it could be seen from the distribution, the concentration of the palaeolithic sites is in the districts of Palamau, Ranchi, Hazaribagh and Singhbhum. The mesolithic sites are also found concentrated in the same set of four districts as well as at Dhanbad. A rather relatively isolated palaeolithic site has been discovered at Munger which is the northernmost and so far the only palaeolithic site discovered beyond the Chotanagpur plateau of Bihar. The neolithic sites have been discovered from Saran, Patna and Aurangabad dis-

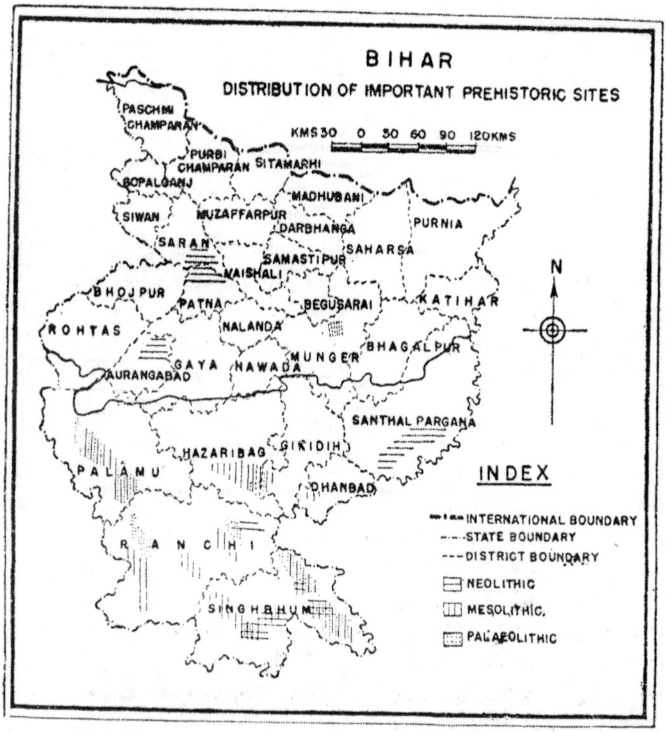

MAP. 8.3 : *Bihar Distribution of Important Pre-historic Sites*

Source: The External Boundary of India on the map agrees with the Record Copy certified by the Survey of India.

* The author thankfully acknowledges the valuable help rendered by Dr. A. K. Ghosh of the Department of Anthropology, University of Calcutta, in preparation of the map showing distribution of prehistoric sites of Bihar.

tricts of the Gangetic Plain as well as from the Santhal Pargana, Ranchi and Singhbhum districts of the Chotanagpur plateau. On the whole, however, the great majority of the pre-historic sites of Bihar are concentrated on the Chotanagpur plateau. It is, therefore, perhaps not for nothing that the pre-historic sites of Bihar had to be from the mineral-bearing Chotanagpur plateau. I would rather venture to presume in this respect that the early inhabitants of Bihar had a fair knowledge about the extraordinary industrial potential of the area.

A close examination of the distribution of pre-historic sites indicates a possible migration of population from the Chotanagpur plateau to the Gangetic Plain along with the development of neolithic culture of which agricultural farming is an important constituent. This, however, does not rule out the possibility for a fresh inflow of migrants from outside Bihar through the Gangetic Plain with the advanced knowledge of agriculture. Whatever it may be, during the pre-historic and early historic period there had been a gradual shift of focus of attention from the Chotanagpur plateau to the Gangetic Plain. The civilization that grew centring around Pataliputra and the adjoining areas was primarily an agro-based civilization.*

With the development of agriculture the fertile Gangetic Plain having facilities for natural irrigation had attracted the early innovators. Thus, the arena of major human activities shifted from the plateau to the plains and a series of public utility centres grew there (Map 8.4)** and whatever capital formation had taken place was more or less entirely ploughed back into the Gangetic Plain.

* Agro-based civilizations in general, by their very nature of being subject to exploitation of their resources, suffer from certain built-in constraints. Such civilizations, coupled with the feudalistic order of social development being face to face with the industrial revolution, usually suffer from stagnation and consequential decadence. The kingdom of Magadha was no exception in this respect.

** The author thankfully acknowledges the help rendered by Shri K. M. Srivastava, Superintending Archaeologist of the Archaeological Survey of India, Shri Sudhengshu Ganguly and Shrimati Archana Datta, both of the Anthropological Survey of India, in the preparation of the map.

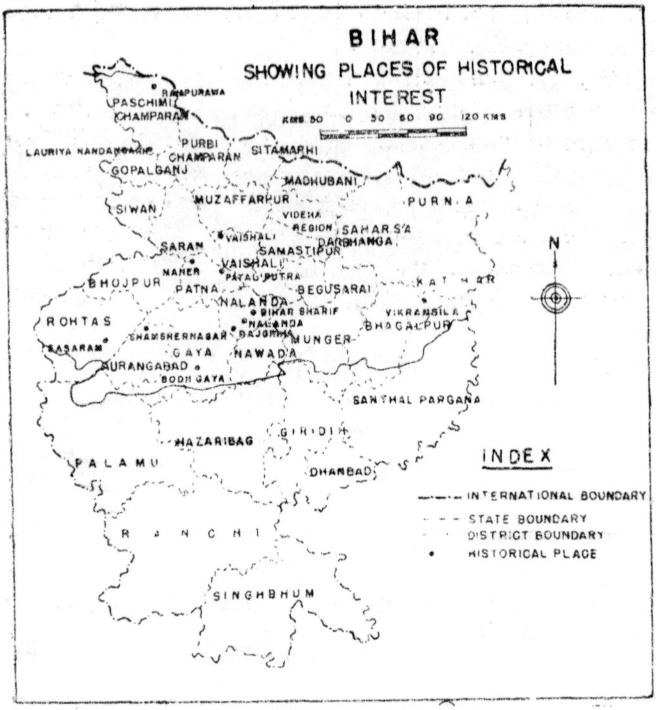

MAP. 8.4 : *Bihar : Showing Places of Historical Interest*

Source: The External Boundary of India on the map agrees with the Record Copy certified by Survey of India.

In spite of various adversaries, Pataliputra of Magadha could somehow maintain a lead until the on-set of the industrial revolution. Exposure to modern technology as such had initially reduced the importance of agriculture as well as the agro-based civilization. Over and above, having no major mineral deposits around for participating in the industrial revolution there was a need for the shift of focus of attention from the plains to the plateau. But once the pragmatic elite, who with the establishment of the Mughal rule and due to state apathy toward their scholarship, turned introvert they were neither quick in their appreciation of the development that necessitated a shift of focus of attention, nor could they perhaps provide the required leadership for preparing the people to absorb benefits from the new innovations. As a result, in spite of the extraordinary resource potential of Bihar as a whole the process of decadence could not altogether be checked.

During the post-independence decades the wheel seems to have turned the full circle and the focus of attention has again been turned to the Chotanagpur plateau but with a difference that unlike the previous almost total attention there is an attempt for harmonic, balanced and integrated development of both the plateau and the plains. And with the existing industrial and agricultural potential, and some retrieval of its centuries-old tradition of scholarship I do not see any reason why with some concerted effort by its elite and the committed citizens, Bihar should not be able to regain a place of eminence among the various states, sub-states and union territories of India.

REFERENCES

1. For details, see Roy Chaudhury, 1974.
2. For details, see Diwakar, 1959.
3. *Survey of India*, 1974.
4. For details, see *Census of India*, 1961, Special Tables for Scheduled Castes.
5. For details, see *Census of India*, 1961, Special Tables for Scheduled Tribes.
6. *Times of India Directory and Year Book*, 1979.
7. Prasad, 1959.
8. For details, see Singh, 1971.

SUGGESTED READINGS

Basham, A. L., *The Wonder that was India*, Grove Press, Inc., New York, 1959.

Bose, N. K., Pabitra Gupta, and Arbinda Bose, "Palaeoliths from Monghyr District, Bihar", *Man in India*, Vol. 40, 1960.

Census of India, *Census of India 1961*, Vol. 1, Part VA(I), Special Tables for Scheduled Castes, Office of the Registrar General of India, Delhi, 1966.

Census of India, *Census of India 1961*, Vol. 1, Part VA(II), Special Tables for Scheduled Tribes, Office of the Registrar General of India, Delhi, 1966.

Dani, Ahmad Hasan, *Prehistory and Protohistory of Eastern India*, Firma K. L. Mukhopadyay, Calcutta, 1960.

Datta, Kalikinkar, *The Life and Thought of the People of Bihar*, Scientific Book Agency, Calcutta, 1967.

Dobray, Wm. Theodore (ed), *Sources of Indian Tradition*, Vols. I and II, Columbia University Press, New York, 1958.

Diwakar, R. R., (ed), *Bihar Through the Ages*, Orient Longmans, Bombay, 1959.

Ghose, A. K., 'Implementiferous Laterite in Eastern India' in *Studies in Prehistory*, Firma K.L. Mukhopadhyay, Calcutta, 1966.

Grierson, G. A., *Linguistic Survey of India*, Vol. V, Indo-Aryan Family Eastern Group Part II, Motilal Banarasidass, Delhi, 1903.

Houlton, Sir John, *Bihar: The Heart of India*, Orient Longmans, Ltd., Calcutta, 1949.

Krishnaswami, V. D., "Stone Age India", *Ancient India*, No. 3, 1947.

Lamb, Beatrice P., *India: A World in Transition*, Frederiet A. Prager, New York, 1966.

Prasad, Rajendra, 'Message', *Bihar Through the Ages* by R. R. Diwakar (ed), Orient Longmans, Calcutta, 1959.

Roy Chaudhury, P. C., *Bihar*, Publications Division, Ministry of Information and Broadcasting, Government of India, New York, 1974.

Sankalia, H. D., *Prehistory and Protohistory in India and Pakistan*, University of Bombay, Bombay, 1962.

Sen, D., "Lower Pelaeolithic Culture Complex and Chronology in India", *Man in India*, Vol. 34, 1954.

Singh, R. L. (ed), *India: A Regional Geography*, National Geographical Society of India, Varanasi, 1971.

Survey of India, *Survey of India Maps*, Survey of India, Dehra Dun, 1974.

Times of India, *The Times of India Directory and Year Book*, Times of India Press, Bombay, 1979.

Tyler, Stephen, *India: An Anthropological Perspective*, Goodyear Publishing Company, Inc., California, 1973.

Upadhyay, V. S., 'Studies on Pre-historic Archaeology in Bihar', *Journal of Social Research*, Vol. 21, No. 2, 1978.

PART II

INSTITUTIONAL EFFORTS TOWARDS RESEARCH

NINE

Sachchidananda

ANTHROPOLOGICAL STUDIES IN THE A.N. SINHA INSTITUTE OF SOCIAL STUDIES

THE A.N. Sinha Institute has a division for sociological and anthropological studies. Of the five members in the faculty in the division, only two are trained anthropologists. In spite of this, during the last decade a number of projects were taken up, some on behalf of the Institute and the rest financed by outside agencies. Some Ph.D. dissertations were also written under the guidance of the members of the faculty dealing with tribal Bihar.

In 1966 the Institute sponsored a study of the Khutkatti system of which relics are to be found only in the Erki Block of the Khunti sub-division. The work was done by Satish Kumar, Junior Research Fellow, at the Institute. He stayed in a village in that Block where an unbroken Khutkatti system still prevails in over 100 villages. On the basis of field investigations Kumar presented a short report on the present structure of the Khutkatti system. He also noted the changes that had taken place in it.

Another study sponsored by the Institute dealt with the phenomenon of transformation of tribes into castes. The author studied this in the context of the concept of tribe-caste continuum with particular reference to the Gond tribe. The study was conducted in six districts, three in Chotanagpur, one in the South Bihar plains and two in North Bihar. A total study of Gond culture in Bihar, as it existed at the six different places, was made. The frequency of Hindu traits among the Gond was examined in the different areas of study.

It was found that Gond groups in Bihar are at different levels of assimilation in the fold of Hinduism. The Gond of Ranchi and Palamau are nearest to the tribal end of the scale and stand between two competing traditions in the regions they inhabit. In Singhbhum, the influence of Hinduism is stronger. In Shahabad they are recognized as one of the Hindu castes of craftsmen. There is nothing tribal about them, except their dance. The Gonds of Saran and Champaran are nearest to the caste end of continuum and have taken up a number of professions the most important of which is parching of grains. It is remarkable that on entry into the Hindu fold, the Gond groups do not necessarily occupy the lowest position. They have been recognised as a ritually clean Hindu caste. Ownership of land and possession of wealth determines their status. In cases where these two qualifications—status resources—are lacking the tribal group identified itself with the caste group that was compatible with its economic and occupational level.

In the early seventies, as part of the nationwide study of the educational problems of the Scheduled Castes and Scheduled Tribes, the Institute took up a study commissioned in Bihar by the Indian Council of Social Science Research. The study covered both school and college students. The school samples were taken from the top two classes, while the college samples included students in the under-graduate classes. The sample was carefully chosen on the basis of a uniform frame devised by the Coordinating Committee of the project. The study considered the demographic characteristic of the students, their family background and economic environment. Importance was given in the study to an analysis of the tribal students as scholars. This included the distribution of students by courses of study, reason for the choice of a particular college for admission, influence of father on education and their financial position, study habits, the educational career of students, their participation in extra-curricular activities, their educational and occupational aspirations and the support that they received from home. The social life and outlook of students included their exposure to mass media, political participation and outlook on marriage and authority of parents. Thus, students' perception of their status as a scheduled community, awareness of reservation of jobs, working of the scholarship scheme, choice of first employment, etc., were also looked into. The special problems of students residing in hotels were also considered along with the image of the tribal students in the eyes of the teacher and vice versa. A comparison was made between hostelers and non-hostelers in regard to their educational aspirations, degree of politicization and decision-making in regard to selection of spouse. A section of the study was devoted to a consideration of the problems of girls and how these differed from those of boys. The impressions of the teachers regarding their Scheduled Tribe students were also collected.

A study of the educated Harijan elite was conducted under the auspices of the ICSSR. It was based on 200 case studies of educated Harijans taken from the ranks of politicians, social workers and public servants. The sample was drawn both from the urban and rural areas and covered the five most populous scheduled castes, viz., Dusadh, Chamar, Dhobi, Pasi and Musahar. The study dealt with mobility, networks, perception of change and the role of the elite in social transformation in their own community. It brings out clearly the winds of change among the Harijans, the gap between the elite and the masses, the differential impact of development among the five castes. The results of the study have already been published in book form.

One of the most significant developments in India since independence is the politicization of the tribal scene. It is a natural and logical culmination of the democratic process. But the study of the voting behaviour in tribal areas is a terra incognita. To fill in this gap a study of the Assembly elections in tribal areas in three districts was made in 1972. The studied covered the Munda, Oraon, Santhal and Ho tribes distributed over six constituencies. The work, in a short campass, traces the growth of the political consciousness among Chotanagpur tribes as a backdrop of their voting behaviour. It deals with the political awareness of the tribals, participation in the electoral process, decision-making in respect of choosing party and candidates and the communication channels through which election message reach the electorate. The study is rounded off with a picture of the electoral campaign in the different constituencies. It makes it clear that there are no significant differences in the voting patterns in tribal and non-tribal areas since the same factors are at work in both places. However, the importance of each factor differs from one constituency to another. The results of the study have been published in book form.

At the request of the Space Application Centre in Ahmedabad the Institute participated in a holistic study programme to assess the impact of the Satellite Instructional Television Experiment which was in operation for a year in 1975-76. Two villages were selected for this study, one in Rajasthan and the other in Bihar. In Bihar, the study was made in Barahser village in Saharsa district. The study delineates the village profile and deals with traditional channels of communication as well as modern developmental communication. The messages communicated through TV programmes in different fields and their impact on the people have been studied in some detail. The study was done in three stages, i.e., the period before the introduction of TV, the period with TV and the period after the withdrawal of TV. There is a chapter dealing with the life of the people in that village after TV had been withdrawn. The study is an effort in the little explored field of communication anthropology.

In pursuance of a decision taken by the Indian Council of Social Science Research restudies of some tribes were commissioned. The author was given the responsibility of making a restudy of the Munda. The study was not confined only to those aspects which had been studied by S.C. Roy in his book *Mundas and Their Country*, published in 1912, but sought to include some more aspects with which social anthropologists of the present day are concerned. It also took into account the various other studies made of different aspects of Munda culture by such scholars as Hoffmann, N.C. Choudhury, Koichi Sugiama, Kumar Suresh Singh and others. Field work for the project was done in their sub-culture areas of the Munda country, i.e., Hasda area, Panch Pargana and the Christian-dominated area in Torpa. An attempt has been made to present a rounded picture of important aspects of Munda life and culture. The scope as well as the direction of change clearly delineated.

A short study of tribal participation in Panchayati Raj

with special reference to Ranchi district has also been taken up by the Institute. The objective of the study is to explore the extent of tribal participation, both in the political and economic fields. The purpose is to examine the hypothesis that the greater the participation, the better would be the development work in the area.

This year, 1979, International Children's Year, a study of tribal children has been undertaken as part of a larger study of the problems of children in the region. The study is located in the Oraon area. An attempt is also being made to find out the role of the Dhumkuria in the socialization process of Oraon children.

Some Ph.D. research projects were taken up by students working under the guidance of our faculty. Some of these dealt with tribal life and culture. Binay Kumar Rai made a study of the interaction between man and forest in Chotanagpur. He examined forest policy and management of forests in Bihar and the role of forest in the life of agricultural tribes, shifting cultivators and hunting and food-gathering tribes. He also detailed the role of the forest in their economic and socio-cultural life and the place of the forest in tribal belief and ritual. The Panchayat management of the forest, the forest co-operative societies, the forest villages, established by the Forest Department, were also studied. The tension and the conflict between the tribals and the Forest Department was also considered in all aspects in the thesis.

L.R.N. Srivastava dealt with the problem of education and modernization among the Mnnda and Oraon of Ranchi. He sought to examine the extent to which education is the key that unlocks the door to modernization. He made a comparative study of the educated and uneducated sections of the two tribes. Modernization was tested with reference to six indices, i.e., mobility, empathy, rational choice, participation, achievement motivation and media of mass communication. Six villages, three each from Munda and Oraon areas were selected for the study. Besides using the questionnaire, case histories for a large number of respondents were also collected. Both participant and non-participant observations enriched the data. Thematic apperception tests were also administered to forty Munda and forty Oraon students. This was in the context of the measurement of achievement motivation. Srivastava came to the conclusion that educated persons are more empathic, more rational, have a high level of participation and achievement motivation. They are more exposed to mass media and are more mobile.

Dr. S. M. Raz studied the process of socialization in a multi-ethnic village in Ranchi district. Three communities, the tribal Oraon, Brahmins and Muslims weaver families have lived together for a long time in that village. Dr. Raz has delineated the process of growing up in each of these communities and tried to explore if there were any common principles that held true for the entire village community. The communities played different roles in the village set up. The Oraon are small peasant proprietors, the Muslims weavers and the Brahmins erstwhile landlords and comparatively better off than the other two communities. As such, the children in the three communities do not interact on levels of equality. The socialization process, however, prepares the child in each community for its adult role. The drive behind toilet training in each community differs. Similarly, attitude differs in regard to obedience and in the observance of Purda. The author tries to explain the differences among the three communities in their attitudes towards some of the essential ingredients of the socialization process.

Another Ph.D. study, which is half-way, is focused on the Munda elite. The author has identified 150 elite on the basis of responses of 50 judges. He tries to explore their personal characteristics, avenues to elitehood, mobility, networks and their role in social transformation of their own community. (The thesis is expected to be ready in a couple of months)

The Institute has taken up and completed a number of applied studies in tribal areas. At the instance of the Chotanagpur and Santhal Parganas Autonomous Development Authority, the Institute prepared project reports for three integrated development projects in the district of Singhbhum, namely, Saraikela, Dalbhum, Chaibasa. It was indeed an effort to make anthropological inputs in the planning process for these areas.

At the instance of the Rural Electrification Corporation the Institute took up a study of the evaluation of the rural electrification in tribal areas. Two schemes each in Ranchi district and Santhal Parganas were taken up for a detailed study. The study would try to find out the impact of electrification in tribal areas, the reasons why the tribals are not enthusiastic about the programme and identify the administrative bottlenecks in the delivery of electricity services in tribal areas. The report of the study is expected to be submitted by August 1979.

SUGGESTED READINGS

Rai, B. K., Man and Forest in Chotanagpur, unpublished Ph.D. dissertation, Ranchi University, 1967.

Raz, S.M., *The Socialization Process,* Chetna Publications, New Delhi, 1976.

Sachchidananda, "Tribe Caste Continuum: A Case Study of the Gond in Bihar", *Anthropos*, Vol. 65, 1970.

Sachchidananda, *Harijan Elite*, Thomson Press, New Delhi, 1977.

Sachchidananda, *Tribal Voter in Bihar*, National Publishing House, Delhi, 1976.

Sachchidananda, *The Changing Munda*, Concept Publishing Company, New Delhi, 1979.

Sachchidananda, A. K. Lal et al, Educational Problems of Scheduled Caste and Scheduled Tribe Students, 2 Volumes (unpublished Report).

Sachchidananda and M N. Jha, Communication in a Bihar Village, (unpublished Report, 1979).

Srivastava, L. R. N., Education and Modernization among the Munda and Oraon, unpublished Ph.D. dissertation, Patna University, 1968.

TEN

S. P. Gupta

STUDIES BY TRIBAL WELFARE RESEARCH INSTITUTE, RANCHI

TRIBAL STUDY is one of the main objectives of anthropologists and the value of anthropological research in administration has heen recognized by Governments. British administrators initiated anthropological investigations in India as early as in 1774 under the auspices of the Asiatic Society of Bengal. Since then the British administrators, missionaries, travellers and a few other anthropologically oriented individuals collected data on tribal and rural groups about their life and culture and published them in the *Journals of Asiatic Society of Bengal* (1784), *Indian Antiquary* (1872) and later on the *Journal of Bihar and Orissa Research Society* (1915) and *Man in India* (1921). Owing to their early efforts we come across basic material about tribes and castes of the different parts of India published in a series of hand-books, gazetteers, census reports and a number of tribal monographs. With the increasing governmental concern to obtain desired studies on the tribals and the aim of direct or ultimate assistance to the administrators and the people of the area concerned the question of establishing tribal research institutes inevitably arose.

The Union Government realized the need for such institutes as early as 1953. The Commissioner for Scheduled Castes and Scheduled Tribes recommended to the President of India that tribal research institutes be established in those States which have a substantial tribal population. Bihar has the third largest concentration of tribal population next to

Madhya Pradesh and Orissa. The thirty Scheduled Tribes in Bihar State present varied aspects of their culture and economic development from settled agriculturists, shifting cultivators, the artisan communities to the nomadic group of tribals living on hunting and food-gathering.

The varied and complex tribal problems call for a scientific study to understand them. With this aim the State Government under its Welfare Department established the Bihar Tribal Research Institute at Ranchi in 1953 which started functioning from 25th January 1954 "for conducting researches on right lines into the customs, manners, languages, culture, etc., of the tribes inhabiting different parts of the State."

For the first two years the Institute had a skeleton staff. However they carried out investigations on the specific problems of the Bihar tribes as assigned by the Government.

Later, in August 1957, with a view to effecting a multi-disciplinary approach the Institute was reorganized under the able directorship of late Dr. B. S. Guha, formerly Director of the Anthropological Survey of India and Anthropological Adviser to the Government of India. Dr. Guha could reorganise the Institute and initiated detailed surveys among the Paharias in Santhal Parganas, the Hos of Sawanda in Singhbhum and the Tana Bhagats of Ranchi District.

Highlights of Tribal Studies

The Institute has now completed 25 years of its existence. During this period, salient gains have been achieved in the field of tribal studies. It published a volume in 1961 entitled *Land and People of Tribal Bihar*. In this volume, as the title suggests, the tribal region, its flora and fauna and tribal people along with their major social and economic institutions have been analyzed on the basis of available literature and field work. It also gives short accounts of all the Scheduled Tribes in Bihar together with relevant maps and statistics. The information compiled in it may serve as bench-mark data as for as the Bihar tribes are concerned. But as the volume was prepared about two decades ago, it needs revision and updating.

Tribes of Chotanagpur Plateau (Bihar): An Ethno-Nutritional and Pharmacological Cross-Section, another publication of the Institute, attempts a new approach in human biology and is based partly on field researches and partly on theoretical studies. The indigenous ethnic types based on ABO blood groups inhabiting the Chotanagpur Plateau, their foods, dietary habits, fire-making and preparation of food and drink, consumption of certain foodstuffs, sufficiency or otherwise of foodgrains, methods of meeting the deficiencies, general deficiency diseases and some of their medical practices constitute the theme of this monograph. This work is of direct interest in fields like racial anthropology, biology, medicines and the social organizations that are concerned with tribal welfare and betterment of the people. However, in analyzing this study, several gaps in our knowledge have been found to exist and attention is drawn to them in the hope that further studies in these fields would be stimulated.

The racial origin and affinities of the Asur tribe, which has been identified as a primitive group in Bihar, their population pattern and reproductive performance, their food habits and nutritional state, diseases prevalent among them and indigenous herbal cures resorted to by them have been discussed in the monographic study entitled *The Asur: An Ethno-Biological Profile*.

Then the institute has also completed studies on three little known tribes of Palamau district in Bihar, viz, Chero, Parhaiya and Korwa. Separate short monographs in culture change and acculturation have been brought out and are hoped to be of great value to workers in the tribal areas.

Life and Times of Birsa Bhagwan is a biography of Birsa Munda, a great tribal hero who shook the foundations of British rule in this part of India and left the zamindars, jagirdars and Christian missionaries exasperated at the close of the last century by leading and organizing his people for the establishment of a Munda Raj in place of British Government. He propagated a religion, gave a code of life to his followers. His people acclaimed him as "Dharti Aba", Father of the Earth. This study has been further analyzed by K.S. Singh (1966) in his book *The Dust-Storm and the Hanging Mist*.

Impact of Industrialization on Bihar Tribes

At the suggestion of the late Sri U. N. Dhebar, the then Chairman of the Commission on Scheduled Tribes a small project on an experimental basis was undertaken in 1960-61 to study the impact of industrialization on the tribal communities of Bihar. The general picture that emerged from the study at Jamshedpur, Noamandi and Ranchi was one of chaotic development in different ways—meagre employment opportunities and no clear policy regarding personnel. The anchor of life had drifted. People had become landless without gaining anything in return. The intermediate stage of commercialization was non-existent. Non-tribal immigrants filled up the gaps. The tribal was out of place in his own country. Consequently, social organization of tribals disintegrated. The new situation is drab and dull.

Tribal Indebtedness in Bihar

The study of tribal indebtedness in five districts of Chotanagpur and Santhal Parganas was taken up in 1969-70. The survey was conducted on one per cent sample of tribal households and the whole village was the lowest unit of the sample. Altogether material on 9,599 families distributed over 153 villages was compiled and tabulated. The report contains figures of family assets, income and expenditure, loans outstanding, current loans and average indebtedness in relation to tribal and non-tribal families, cultivators and non-cultivators, etc. The report is in two volumes, the first has recommendations and the second statistical tables.

Currently fresh studies are being undertaken in all the seven districts of Chotanagpur and Santhal Parganas with a view to studying tribal indebtedness and land alienation as well as other dimensions like exploitation, harassment, etc.

Specific Survey of Tribal Development Blocks

The Institute carried out specific surveys in four tribal development blocks in four different districts, viz. Karra (Ranchi district), Boarijor (Santhal Parganas district), Manjhari (Singhbhum district) and Bhavdaria (Palamau district) comprising different tribal communities like the Munda, Santhal, Paharia, Ho, Oraon, Kherwar and Korwa. The surveys were intended to enable the Block people to know the difficulties of the area, the needs of the people and to allot priorities in their work. Currently the Institute is undertaking evaluation of the Chakradharpur Tribal Development Agency.

Linguistic Studies

The linguistic unit of the Institute has undertaken the important task of preparing dictionaries. Six of them, viz., Mundari-Hindi, Hindi-Mundari, Kurukh-Hindi, Hindi-Kurukh, Santali-Hindi and Hindi-Santali have been prepared so far. These dictionaries are useful tools in the hands of administrators, research and social workers in the tribal areas.

Other Important Studies

From time to time the Institute is called upon to study some of the pressing problems of the Scheduled Tribes and Castes which come to the notice of the State and Central Governments. Socio-economic studies of Gangai, Markande, Khatwe, Kaibratta, Tanti, Khangar, Domai, Bhuiyan, Pujhar, Namsudra, Bharkiar, Nonia, Muriari, Rautias, Rangwa, Gow, Gond, Tharu, Pahan, Senduria, Kharwar, Loharia, Maghaiya, Dhangar, etc., communities were made with a view to advising the Government of their position.

The Institute made a study of the bonded labour in Palamau district and its recommendations have been found quite helpful by the State Government in streamlining the working of the Minimum Wages Act as well as the Bihar Money Lending Act.

The Institute is playing a vital role in the formulation of the "sub-plan for the tribal regions of Bihar". The Institute has also prepared integrated tribal development projects like the Latehar Meso Area Project (Palamau district), Lohardaga and Gumla Meso Area Projects (Ranchi district) and Pirtanr Micro Area Project (Giridih district).

Other problems like shifting cultivation, Bataidari, unemployment, impact of modernization, rehabilitation of nomadic tribes, etc., have been studied. The various study reports, which have been published or are in the process of publication in the *Bulletin of the Bihar Tribal Welfare Research Institute*, have been incorporated in *Two Decades of Tribal Research in Bihar* (1954-1974).

Anthropology as a Core Discipline

Man has always been interested in studying himself and therefore some branches of knowledge like physical, biological, cultural, psychological, social, etc., have become more specialized and yet there remains a central common field for Anthropology as the Science of Man for professionals in all its branches. The administrators have at times questioned the researches done by the Tribal Research Institutes. Their contention is that these institutes should confine themselves to applied research only and that the fundamental researches should be the concern of the universities. But it is not always easy to draw a line between pure and applied research. Only known facts could be applied. So, thorough research in all aspects of tribal life is an indispensable prerequisite. It is not difficult to cite numerous instances in which well-intentioned measures were nullified because of being found to be incompatible with the tribal social institutions or some religious or magical prejudice, which had not been known earlier.

One of the complaints of administrators or planners is that researchers take too much time to produce results and the schemes for the people's benefit cannot wait so long. It may be argued that if the schemes are planned well in advance, researchers could get sufficient time to produce the necessary background information. No good work could be expected out of pressure research. One who is devoted to the subject has a sense of time and urgency and given the necessary facilities he would not be failing in his duty. The Government should allow the Anthropologist freedom of research and pay due attention to his findings.

An anthropologist, as a scientist cannot judge good and evil but he can make a distinction between an objective fact and its implications. There is no scientific ideal of human welfare, there can be no authoritative direction of events. The task of an anthropologist in a tribal research institute is to make scientific and objective study. He should make it clear that he cannot be utilized for supporting a particular policy or scheme. It is the business of the Government to make use of his findings.

The role of an anthropologist, at the planning stage of

welfare programmes, is extremely vital. This has three facets. Firstly, the basic data regarding socio-economic conditions of the community as well as their arts and handicrafts, health and nutrition has to be collected. Factual and statistical information thus collected would help in the formulation of schemes with a tribal bias. Secondly, there should be a resource inventory of a particular area so that the economic potentialities are known. It would enable us to plan how local talent and local resources could be exploited in the best interest of the people when the welfare measures have been in operation for some time; they may be monitored to see the extent to which they have been successful. If the measures are found wanting, ways and means have to be suggested for their improvement.

SUGGESTED READINGS

Gupta, S. P., *Tribes of Chotanagpur Plateau: An Ethno-Nutritional and Pharmacological Cross-Section*, Bihar Tribal Welfare Research Institute, Ranchi, Welfare Department, Government of Bihar, 1974.

Gupta, S. P., *The Asur: Ethno-Biological Profile*, Bihar Tribal Welfare Research Institute, Ranchi, Welfare Department, Government of Bihar, 1976.

Gupta, S. P., *Two Decades of Tribals Research in Bihar (1954-74)*, Compiled, Bihar Tribal Welfare Research Institute, Ranchi, Welfare Department, Government of Bihar, 1976.

Mohan, H., *Chero: A Study in Acculturation*, Bihar Tribal Welfare Research Institute, Ranchi, Welfare Department, Government of Bihar, 1973.

Mohan, H., *The Parhaiya: A Study in Culture Change*, Bihar Tribal Welfare Research Institute, Ranchi, Welfare Department, Government of Bihar, 1975.

Prasad, N., *Land and People of Tribal Bihar*, Bihar Tribal Welfare Research Institute, Ranchi, Welfare Department, Government of Bihar, 1961,

Prasad, N. & A. Sahaya, *Impact of Industrialisation on Bihar Tribes*, Bihar Tribal Welfare Research Institute, Ranchi, Welfare Department, Government of Bihar, 1962.

Prasad, S., *Mundari-Hindi Sabdakosh*, Bihar Tribal Welfare Research Institute, Ranchi, Welfare Department, Government of Bihar, 1973.

Prasad, S., *Hindi-Mundari Sabdakosh*, Bihar Tribal Welfare Research Institute, Ranchi, Welfare Department, Government of Bihar, 1976.

Sinha, S. P., *Life and Times of Birsa Bhagwan*, Bihar Tribal Welfare Research Institute, Ranchi, Welfare Department, Government of Bihar, 1964.

Singh, K. S., *The Dust-Storm and the Hanging Mist*, Firma K. L. Mudhopadhyay, Calcutta.

ELEVEN

V.S. Upadhyay

STUDIES BY ANTHROPOLOGICAL SURVEY OF INDIA IN BIHAR

THE ANTHROPOLOGICAL Survey of India was established in 1945 with headquarters at Calcutta. Its work includes social, psychological, economic, linguistic, physical and genetic research throughout the sub-continent. The Survey is organized into divisions, regions and field stations. The divisions include Cultural and Physical Anthropology; scientific sections include Bio-chemistry, Human Ecology, Linguistics, Psychology and Radiology. It is divided into seven regions: Northern Region with headquarters at Dehra Dun, Southern Region with headquarters at Mysore, Central Region with headquarters at Nagpur, North-Eastern Region with headquarters at Shillong, Eastern Region (which includes Bihar) with headquarters at Calcutta, Western Region with headquarters at Udaipur; and a special region in Andaman and Nicobar Islands with headquarters at Port Blair.

The Anthropological Survey of India was created out of the Anthropological Section of Indian Museum at Calcutta. Earlier it was a part of the Zoological Survey of India. In December, 1945, it started its independent establishment with Dr. B. S. Guha as its first Director. Its objectives include inter-disciplinary field investigations in remote tribal areas like the Andaman and Nicobar Islands, NEFA, Nagaland, Tripura, Bastar, Himalayan regions and the hill regions of Kerala. The Survey publishes memoirs, monographs, besides its own *Bulletin* which carries reports of its research activities.

Researches in Bihar

At the outset it must be pointed out that various unavoidable circumstances have restricted the author to secure a complete list of the research projects by the A.S.I. Hence a categorization has been attempted on the list appended, which shows that about 72 projects have been undertaken by the Survey in about 22 years (1953-1975). As has been classified in another paper by the author, the record shows that on the ethnic basis, there were 60 projects covering tribes and 10 covering caste populations. On the basis of the nature of study, these are: 54 (75%) ethnological studies, six physical anthropological, four of ethnographic films category and nine of linguistic and folklore nature. The year 1967 was the most rewarding for Bihar as about 10 projects were undertaken. The other important ethnological works, themes like caste panchayats, Kol rebellion, village judiciary, Jharkhand Movement, impact of industrialization and urbanization, personality formation, dietary nutrition and welfare works were chosen. There are surveys of tribes like Birhor, Pahariya, Santhal, Munda, Asur, Chero, Oraon, and a few others. Comparing this to the list of the 30 Scheduled Tribes, it seems much is still to be covered by the Survey. Mention may be made of the solitary study of Muslims by Hasan Ali. Similarly most unusual subject like Concept of sexual union for spiritual quest among the Vaishnava Preachers had been selected by Dr. S. C. Sinha.

Turning towards physical anthropological studies, one finds the major themes like genetic survey, blood group survey, growth study, skin colour, fertility survey, skeletal variations, etc. Under these studies, only a few tribes have been covered. A lot has to be done on other tribes and on non-tribal population groups

About half-a-dozen tribal groups have been covered under linguistic and folklore studies. Mention must be made about the studies of dance forms by Smt. Bisaka Gupta Roy.

Apart from all these, the Anthropological Survey of India has undertaken a photographic survey of various tribes in between the years 1964-1967. Mention may be made about the films on the Birhor and Chait-Parab.

Looking at the record of work done by the Survey, one feels that the State of Bihar has not been neglected. Recently, the Survey has established a separate region, namely, Eastern Region, under the able guidance of Dr. A. K. Danda, which, undoubtedly, will strengthen, both numerically and financially, the researches in this area in general, and Bihar in particular.

Research Projects undertaken in Bihar by the Anthropological Survey of India

1.	Bhattacharyya, A.	1953	The Binjia of Palamau.
2.	Bhattacharyya, A.	1953	An Account of Birhor of Palamau.
3.	Banerjee, H. N. Dasgupta, B. K.	1959	The Santhal of Modlurpur, Purulia district.
4.	Banerjee, H. N.	1959	The Kharia of Modlurpur, Singhbhum district and neighbouring regions.
5.	Dasgupta, B. K.	1959	The Piharas of Khokro, Singhbhum district.
6.	Sen, Jyoti	1960	Investigation of Tribal Welfare work done by the Christian Missionaries of Chotanagpur.
7.	Nandi, S. B.	1960	Cultural Changes in an Oraon Village.
8.	Banerjee, H. N. with Sinha & Dasgupta	1961	Agriculture Crafts and weekly markets of South Manbhum.
9.	Sinha, S. C.	1961	A Note on the Concept of Sexual Union for spiritual quest among the Vaishnava Preachers in the Bhumij Belt of Purulia and Singhbhum.
10.	Ganguli, S. K.	1962	All India Pottery Survey among Kurmi Mahatos of Chotanagpur.
11.	Goswami, B. B.	1962	Study of Caste Panchayats in Bihar.

12.	Banerjee, H. N. Dasgupta, B. K.	1962	Chhatra Parab of South Manbhum.
13.	Choudhury, N. C.	1962	Munda Settlement in Lower Bengal: A study in tribal migration.
14.	Dasgupta, B. K.	1962	A short ethnographic note on the Pahiras of Khokro.
15.	—	1962	Caste mobility among the Mahato of South Manbhum.
16.	Sen, Jyoti	1964	Ethnographic notes on Birhor.
17.	Sinha Bela and Roy Sriparna	1964	Fertility Survey among Oraons of Ranchi District.
18.	Chattopadhyay, S. K.	1964	Photographic Survey of Tribes in various districts of Bihar and Orissa.
19.	Das, P. R.	1964	Photographic Survey of the tribes of Birhor, Ho, Kharia, Munda, Korhan, Oraon and Bhumij of Bihar.
20.	Sen, Jyoti	1964	Study of the Birhors of Hazaribagh.
21.	Choudhury, N. C. Ghosh, Tapash Sam Topno	1965	Ethnographic Survey of the Munda of Ranchi.
22.	Mukherjee, B. Roychoudhury, B., Danda, Dipali	1965	Ethnographic Survey of the Cheros of Palamau Dist., Bihar.
23.	Prasad, R. K. Fellow	1965	The Parchiyas of Palamau: A tribe in transition.
24.	Dasgupta, D.	1965	Linguistic work on Kharia Thar of Manbhum Dist., Bihar.
25.	Chattopadhyay, S. K., Nandan, A. P., Sen, Jyoti	1965	Documentary cine-film on the life and activities of Birhor of Hazaribagh.
26.	Dasgupta, D.	1965	Socio-linguistic study of Saraki (language of Sarwak) of Ranchi and Purulia.

27.	Choudhury, N. C.	1966	Culture Types & Levels among the Tribes of Chotanagpur.
28.	Roy Choudhury, B.C., Mukherjee, B. C., Ghosh, Dipali	1966	The Chero of Palamau.
29.	Bose, Nivedita	1966	Socio-linguistic study of Kurmali (Language of Kurmi) of Manbhum Dist., Bihar.
30.	Negi, R. S., Kumar, N., Bhattacharya, P. N., Maitra, A.	1966	Genetic Survey among the various tribal populations of South Bihar—Munda, Ho, Kharia, Kharwa.
31.	Sen, Jyoti Panchbhai, S. C.	1967	Anthropological Study of the Jharkhand Movement as a case study in inter-tribal solidarity movement in post-Independent India, Ranchi and Singhbhum.
32.	Dasgupta, D.	1967	Linguistic field work on Malpahayer of Santhal Pargana, Bihar.
33.	Chattopadhyay, S. K.	1967	Documentary film on Chait-Parab of Manbhum, Bihar.
34.	Hasim Ali	1967	Study of the Muslims of Rural & Urban Ranchi: Study of Minority Community.
35.	Mahato, S. N.	1967	Study of the trading community of Ranchi Dist.
36.	Kochar, V. K. with Siddiquis, M. K., Banerjee, S.	1967	Strategy and framework for ethnographic research in India.
37.	Goswami, B. B.	1967	Working of a Caste Panchayat in Bihar.
38.	Goswami, B. B.	1967	Caste Panchayat among the Hindu Nai (Barbar) of Patna city.

39.	Goswami, B. B.	1967	Tribal Panchayat in Rural & Urban setting.
40.	Mahapatra, B. P.	1967	Study of the language of the Maler in Bihar.
41.	Dasgupta, D.	1967	Study of Malpaharia dialect.
42.	Sen, D. K., Gupta, P. Dutta, P. C.	1968	Anthropological Investigation of Asur of Ranchi Dist.
43.	Dasgupta, P. K.	1969	Impact of industrialisation on the life of tribals of Singhbhum, Bihar.
44.	Banerjee, S.	1969	Impact of industrialisation among the tribals, Raniganj and Jharia Coalfields, Dhanbad.
45.	Kumar, N. Dey, D. C.	1969	Blood group genetic survey in Palamau.
46.	Mukherjee, D. P.	1969	Skin colour survey in Palamau Dist.
47.	Gupta, P., Pal, A.	1969	Study of skeletal variation: Collection of skeletal materials from Chotanagpur and adjoining areas.
48.	Gupta, P., Dutta, P. C., Pal, A.	1969	Study of skeletal variation: Chotanagpur & adjoining areas.
49.	Chakravorty, D. K.	1970	Kol rebellion in Manbhum.
50.	Lal, R. B.	1970	Problems of nutrition among Mundas and Oraons.
51.	—	1970	A study of tribal myths in Bihar.
52.	Spencer, D. M.	1970	The recruitment of Shamans among the Mundas.
53.	Bisaka Gupta Roy	1970	Study of tribal, folk and relatively advanced dance forms of Barabhum, Singhbhum, Bihar.
54.	Topno, Sen	1971	System and land tenure and land revenue administration among Chotanagpur tribes.

		(Ranchi and Singhbhum districts).
55. Sen, Jyoti	1971	Jharkhand movement and a study of the Concept of Dikus among the Chotanagpur Tribes.
56. Basu, Nivedita	1971	Kurmali Dialect of the Kurmis of Purulia Dist., Formerly Bihar.
57. Roy, Bisakha Gupta	1971	Core Pattern of Group Dances of Munda of Khuti area, Ranchi Dist.
58. Panchbhai, S. C.	1971	Inter-group Stereotypes and Social Tension in Relation to Jharkhand Movement.
59. Singh, V. K.	1971	Acculturation and Change in Personality structure of the Munda of Ranchi.
60. Nair, P. T.	1971	Birsa Munda.
61. Priya, S.	1971	Study of Stereotypes of Munda boys and girls towards three Castes of Bihar.
62. Rai, H. and Prasad, S. B.	1971	Village judiciary at work: A Case Study in the Working of Gram Cutcherie in Bihar.
63. Chatterjee, P. N.	1971	Dhalbhum.
64. Kumar, N.	1971	Distribution and displacement of Population in Bihar.
65. Mukherjee, D. P.	1972	A Growth Study on Tribal groups in Santhal Parganas.
66. Biswas, S. K., Bhattacharya, K. K.	1972	Dietary and Nutrition Survey in Tribal India: Palamau district of Bihar.
67. Kumar, N.	1972	Serological Investigations among the Santhal and Sauria Paharia, Santhal Pargana.
68. Ahmed, S. I	1975	A Comparative Study of Socialisation and Personality

			Structure among the Harijans and Adivasis, Chotanagpur, Bihar.
69.	Dasgupta, D.	1975	On the Lodha of Midnapur and the Pahira of Singhbhum.
70.	—	1975	Comparative Study of Mal-pahariya and Gharoali.
71.	Maitra, Archana	1975	Impact of Urbanization on Ecology and Geography of the Tribes in Raniganj-Asansol Industrial Belt.
72.	Mahato, P. P.	1975	The position of the Kurmi Mahato of Purulia in tribe-caste peasant continuum.

PART III

MAJOR THEMES OF STUDIES

TWELVE

Guru Charan Ghosh

RESEARCH STATUS OF PHYSICAL ANTHROPOLOGY IN TRIBAL BIHAR

TRIBAL POPULATION in Bihar is mainly concentrated in south and south-eastern portion covering the area of Chotanagpur and its adjacent district of Santhal Parganas. In numerical strength as well as in ethnic plurality this area represents a holistic picture of tribal Bihar. Most of these tribes linguistically belong to Austroasiatic family excepting the Oraon, Maler, Pahira, Chero, etc., who speak Dravidian tongue. There is a good deal of controversy regarding the original homeland of these tribal groups. There are quite a few thesis and antithesis. But the fact is still obscure. S. C. Roy (1912) opined that "whether the Mundas immigrated into India from now submerged hypothetical continent of Lamuria which has been supposed to have once connected India with Madagascar and Africa or whether they entered India from north-east as has been sometimes supposed or whether they originated from a mixture of colonists from Eastern Tibet or Western China across the Himalayas with Austro-Dravidians to the south of the range or whether indeed they are genuine autochthons of Indian soil, as the Mundas and their congeners in India assert, we have, in the present state of our knowledge, hardly any material to ascertain. Though a few decades have passed, we are still in the same darkness as we were in the days of Roy. The problem has become more complex because of continuous and steady changes of physical characters and cultural values of these aborigines due to multiple processes of fusion and fission as well as effective interaction with the neighbouring population. Attempts have been made since earlier times to represent the morphogenetic features of the tribes living in Chotanagpur and Santhal Parganas. But in most of the cases, attempts are sporadic and ultimately failed to serve any meaningful purpose. Sometimes the data are too scanty to arrive at a definite conclusion. Some tribes have been studied repeatedly while quite a few are left untouched.

The present communication is aimed at furnishing a report on the aspect of physical anthropology of tribal Bihar on the basis of recorded material. This would eventually indicate the unexplored chapter which is the base line for implementing future programme.

In quantity and variety Santhal Parganas and Chotanagpur represents a full length picture of tribal Bihar. Since 1892, the tribes of this area have been studied from the angle of physical anthropology. These studies were mostly centred round three major fields of physical anthropology, such as anthropometry, blood group (ABO) and dermatoglyphics. Again a good number of scholars were interested in anthropometry and less so in blood groups. There are only a few reports on dermatoglyphics probably because of the fact that the interest in this particular aspect developed at a very late stage. The districts of Ranchi, Palamau and Santhal Parganas were the major areas of field investigation. There are a few tribes on which investigations have been carried out repeatedly while others remained untouched. In some cases the data are very scanty to arrive at a definite conclusion. The primary object of most of these studies was to represent the morphogenetic characters of individual tribes and to find out the inter-tribal biogenetic relationship. At the same time some scholars have tried to interpret the data in terms of ethnic origins and to evaluate the biological distinction between the Dravidian and Mundari speakers. From the recorded information it appears that the tribes of Chotanagpur are comparatively taller than those of the Santhal Parganas. Cephalic index indicates a more or less homogeneous situation and they are dolichocephalic. With respect to nose shape they are mostly platyrrhiny while a few tribes represent mesorrhine nose. Serological studies indicate that there is preponderance of *q* gene among the tribes of Santhal Pargana in comparison to *p* gene. But among the tribes of Chotanagpur there are quite a number of tribes who show a higher frequency of *p* gene. Dermatoglyphic studies bring forth a clear distinction between the tribes of Dravidian and Austric speakers. The Dravidian speakers are characterized to have a higher frequency of whorl than loop. But the situation is reversed in case of the Mundari speakers. It requires further investigation to arrive at any general conclusion

To evaluate the researches in physical anthropology of tribal Bihar, it may be stated, at first instance, that a considerable number of tribes have been left untouched which require immediate attention. Most of the researchers were mainly engaged in three major fields of physical anthropology while there is immense scope for studying these people with modern know-how and thereby representing a comprehensive picture of the genetic composition of the groups concerned. A systematic study may also be oriented to start with the problem of original homeland of those tribes which is still not clear since the time of S. C. Roy (1912). Multiple forces of fission and fusion are in operation in this particular field and provides a unique base to study some of the processes of evolution. Differences between the Dravidian and Austric speakers in terms of language and culture are very much apparent. But clearly enough there is no convincing evidence to indicate their differences in terms of physical characters. Digital dermatoglyphics of course reflect some idea of differentiation between the members of these two divisions. But it requires further probing with adequate data on a wider coverage of tribal groups. There could be other programmes to initiate such as on demographic pattern and mating system which would give the idea of the breeding unit and it is perhaps the basic information of any kind of genetic studies. Because of rapid industrialization in this region, the aborigines are exposed to new socio-economic environments which might have some impact on their socio-physical aspect. Therefore an integrated approach in this regard is urgently needed. These developments, on the other hand, have induced some ecological changes. Deforestation has compelled the aborigines to adapt to new situations with some changes in habits and behaviour. This would have some effect, as it is expected, on the physical aspect of the people concerned. Therefore, a detailed programme in this regard, specially on the aspect of health and nutrition, promises to throw some light which may be utilized for a planned development.

THIRTEEN

N. K. Sinha

STATUS OF RESEARCH AND TEACHING OF LINGUISTICS IN BIHAR

IT WAS in Bihar that the idea of a *Linguistic Survey of India* was first conceived by George A. Grierson and the work was initiated by him at the turn of this century. Although primitive modern standards, his methodology was basically descriptive. It was a significant departure from the hitherto employed comparative historical methods of the comparative philologists. This voluminous work was completed by 1921. It is here that we find the first reliable and systematic description of all the dialects along with their genetic classification. Although Grierson's classification of Bihari dialects has not been acceptable to present-day scholars, however, no body has yet come out with an appropriate alternative classification. Grierson has utilized and mentioned in the bibliography all the works done on these dialects prior to him, howsoever scanty some of them might have been. In the case of the tribal languages, linguistic works were initiated by the different Christian missions. They had to learn their languages in furtherance of their missionary works among them. Out of such contacts have emerged commendable works on Mundari by Rev. J. Hoffman and on Santali by P.O. Bodding. Other minor articles or treatises are scattered in the Journals of Asiatic Society or in booklet forms which have their own significance by virtue of being pioneering attempts.

Grierson himself made other contributions like Seven Grammars of Bihari Languages and Bihar Peasants Life, both of which are works of great interest. There are several limitations with the LSI right from data collection to their analyses and descriptions, but no institution has yet dared to undertake a parallel work to correct and improve upon it.

The post-Grierson era, which is still continuing in one way or the other, may be termed as the era of dissertations. To show the path Dr. U. N. Tiwary and Dr. B.N. Prasad submitted their dissertations on Bhojpuri and Dr. S. Jha on Maithili. And then, a number of attempts on the descriptive study of different dialects of Bihar were made in this process. Dr. H. S. Biligiri and Mr Dungdung worked on Kharia, Dr. S. K. Goswami on Nagpuria, Dr. S. Aryani Magahi, Dr. Cook on or Mundari and so on. Mrs S. Prasad has completed a comparative study of six major dialects of Bihar. There are a number of other dissertations which claim to be linguistic in approach or which include one or more chapters on linguistic treatment of the subject specially in the case of folklorist or vocabulary studies. It will be found that most of such dissertations follow a generalized pattern of formula in order to fit into the requirements of a Ph.D. or a D.Litt. degree. In the case of the non-tribal languages the data come from the researcher's own speech habits while in the case of the tribal languages there is generally a rearrangement of some previously collected data. Very little or practically no field works are undertaken in order to get actual present-day data from the informants. As a result, the dissertation work, in general, does not contribute anything in the sense of field studies.

There are some institutions like the Central Institute of Indian Languages at Mysore and the Tribal Research Institute of Bihar and Ranchi which pursue the Government policy of studying tribal languages and preparing instructional materials in them. From CIIL, Mysore, for example, Dr. N.K. Sinha completed *Mundari Grammar and Mundari Phonetic Reader* and also prepared the active vocabulary of Mundari children. At TRI, Ranchi, Mrs S. Prasad has produced Mundari-Hindi and Hindi-Mundari dictionaries and is presenly working on conversational guides to tribal dialects. Rashtra Bhasha Parishad, Bihar, at Patna, I am told, had some time back planned to undertake a linguistic survey of Bihar but the plan could not be executed. In collaboration with the Department of Anthropology, Ranchi University, the author is now conducting a study of Bilingualism among the Santhals of Bengal and Bihar.

There are some individuals who are working in the area of linguistics out of their own personal interest. Dr. D. N. Sharma is quite active in this area in many ways by contributing personally in linguistics, by supervision researches in linguistics and also by influencing the policy of the University Grants Commission and the Government in furthering the cause of linguistic studies in Bihar. Again, Dr. K. M. Tiwary has been interested in the study of Panini's methodology by applying modern linguistic techniques. Dr. R.K. Sharma of Sanskrit University, Darbhanga, is himself a traditional scholar of Sanskrit grammar and is one of the exponents of modern methods in linguistics in Bihar. But the ones of furthering the cause of anthropological linguistics naturally falls upon Prof. L. P. Vidyarthi of the Department of Anthropology, Ranchi University. Among the names of individuals, the list cannot be complete without mentioning the significant contribution of Norman H. Zide of the University of Chicago who, in recent times, has made the most organized attempt to study the Munda languages.

The biggest impediment to any systematic and well-directed linguistic study in this part of the country in the total and deplorable lack of teaching facilities in linguistics in any of the universities in Bihar. A number of times attempts were made to provide such facilities at one or the other university but as the results so far indicate all such attempts were half-hearted and abortive. Patna University was given funds by the UGC and even now some of the universities have got funds for setting up a phonetic laboratory, in Hindi departments, but obviously there is no utility of such a laboratory until and unless courses in linguistics and phonetics are introduced and there are qualified people to handle and make use of such laboratories. There has even been a paper on philology at the Master's degree level in all the literature courses, but this paper is not being taken care of to the extent that it has become a nightmare for the students of literature. Again, this paper is wrongly supposed to be a paper in linguistics and worse confusion is being created among the students and research scholars. It is understood that some of the universities have been sanctioned additional posts for professorships for language and linguistics in the Departments of Hindi but no qualified person is available to take up the job. So, the situation has become cyclic, no qualified person is available because there is no department to produce one and no department can be sanctioned because of lack of qualified personnel. Somewhere this cycle has to be broken.

Keeping in view such a neglect of teaching facilities in linguistics and extremely poor quality of whatever research work is being carried out in this area, the task before us becomes obvious. A consolidated plan for teaching and research in the area has to be taken up. Linguistics has become a very wide subject and has both theoretical and applied aspects. As it may not be possible to locate all the linguistic studies at one place or include them in one curriculum, a phased programme for covering them may be taken up. I would like to suggest the following:

(1) The Department of Anthropology at Ranchi University may take up the entire responsibility of introducing courses in Anthropological Linguistics with some general background in the theories and providing research facilities in the area. This may also cover such allied topics like socio-linguistics and biological study of language phenomena.

(2) In pursuance of the recent circular from the UGC suggesting for language-oriented curriculum as an alternative choice in literature courses for M.A. degrees, some of the Departments of Hindi could opt for this and introduce four papers in languages and linguistics which could cover philology, dialectology, textual criticism, stylistics, folkloristics, etc., which would be of immediate interest to the students of literature.

(3) At least one Department of Linguistics must be opened in the State of Bihar. This department, then, will mainly concentrate on theoretical linguistics, phonetics and such topics as psycholinguistics. The department could also introduce Diploma and M. Phil courses in order to provide guidance to such students of literature as would be interested in pursuing research in linguistics. Such a department will cater to the need of linguistic studies in the state and will keep a watch on the quality of research work in the area.

(4) Even other Departments of Hindi or other literature which cannot introduce completely language-oriented course in four papers could slowly have, at least two papers, one in philology and textual criticism and the other in linguistics and stylistics. This would be possible after some students complete language-oriented courses and are thus provided employment opportunities.

As for research programmes which have to be goal-oriented and must be of utility to the people, a number of projects have to be taken up as soon as the facilities are made available. Such projects would require team-work and would be exclusive of individual work at doctoral or post-doctoral levels. Some of such projects are enumerated below:

(1) A socio-linguistic survey of the State of Bihar would be of great significance not only improving upon the survey work conducted by George Grierson but also in including the sociological phenomena in language variance and change and also the factor of inter-communicability. Such a survey will provide a grammar of language usages in the different areas and highlight the cultural elements in speech habits of the community. This survey will not be a survey of language competence, it would be a survey of language performance in actual speech situation. This background would be useful for orientation of language-teaching programmes in school and college curriculum according to individual need and capability. This will also have value for theoretical purposes like study of language change, convergence and divergence of languages, language classification, etc.

(2) Associated with the above will be the study of bilingualism and diglossia among the different communities with tens of language change or language maintenance whatever be the situation. Such studies along with the study of language attitude will be of help in evolving satisfactory language policy and planning in different parts of the State.

(3) Study of language acquisition at different age levels among different communities will help in fixing up norms of language development in an individual which would in turn go a long way in developing language courses, language tests, working out of verbal I.Q. and evaluating the cases of mental retardation or delayed language development, etc.

(4) Compilation of different kinds of vocabularies with different specializations like agricultural tools and techniques, flora and fauna, professional and concerning business, day-to-day use, etc., will be useful for enriching the standard language and the literature as well as for adult education.

(5) Production of material for teaching through the mother tongue and for adult education, for teaching second or foreign language and production of translated material are certain areas where the language-oriented research would be of great help to the pedagogists.

The above projects are just an illustration, because linguistic researches may be of applicational value for innumerable language related problems. This only shows that we are actually in great need of linguistically trained men and, for some time to come a number of them may be employed both for teaching and for research if work in the right direction begins.

SUGGESTED READINGS

Aryani, Sampatti, *Magahi Bhasha aur Sahitya ka Adhyayan*, Patna, 1965.

Biligiri, H. S., *Kharia: Grammar and Vocabulary*, Poona, 1965.

Cook, W. A., A Descriptive Analysis of Mundari: A Study of Structure, Ann Arban, (unpub.), 1965.

Dungdung, M., Hindi aur Kharia: Ek Tulnatmak aur Vishleshnatmak Adhyayan, Ranchi University, (unpub.), 1976.

Flex, Oscar, *Introduction to Oraon Language*, 1974.

Jha, Subhadra, *Maithili Bhasha ka Vikas*, Patna, 1948.

Jha, Tribhuwan, Pramukh Bihari Boliyon ka Tulnatmak Adhyayan, Ranchi Univ. (unpub.), 1966.

Jha, Vidyapati, Santhali aur Maithili ka Tulnatmak Adhyayan, Bhagalpur University (unpub.),1975.

Mishra, H. N., Uttar Monghyr ki Boli: Ek Bhashavaigyanik Adhyayan, Bh. Univ. (unpub.), 1969.

Mishra, M., Bhojpuri Kriyapadon ka Vivaranatmak Adhyayan, Patna Univ. (unpub.), 1973.

Nawarangi, P. S., *Simple Sadari Grammar*, Ranchi, 1956.

Nawarangi, P. S., *Nagpuria Sadari Boli ka Vyakaran*, Ranchi, 1965.

Prasad, S., A Descriptive Study of Magahi Phonology, P. Univ. (unpub.), 1967.

Prasad, S. (Mrs), *A Study of Ho Dialect*, Ranchi, 1961.

Prasad, S. (Mrs), *Mundari-Hindi Vocabulary*, Tribal Research Institute, Ranchi, 1961.

Prasad, S. (Mrs), *Hindi-Mundari Vocabulary*, TRI, Ranchi, 1961.
Prasad, Vishwanath, Bhojpuri Dhawniyon aur Dhwani-Prakriya ka Adhyayan, London (unpub.), 1950.
Sanyal, N. M., *Bihari Bhashaon ki Utpatti aur Vikas*, Calcutta, 1969.
Sharma, K., Bhagalpur Jile ki Boli ka Bhashavaigyanik Adhyayan, Bihar University (unpub.), 1965.
Sharma, Y. N, Vaishali Kshetra ki Bhasha aur Sahitya, Bihar University (unpub.), 1968.
Shastri, A. B., *Evolution of Magahi*, Calcutta, 1932.
Singh, A. K., Begusarai ki Boli ka Bhashavaigyanik Adhyayan, Bihar Univ. (unpub.), 1972.
Singh, K. S., Bhojpuri ka Sanrachnatmak Adhyayan, Delhi (unpub.), 1970.
Singh, L. P., Pad-Vigyan ki Drishti se Magahi aur Bhojpuri ka Tulnatmak Adhyayan, Punjab Univ. (unpub.), 1973.
Singh, Vakil, Champaran ki Boli: Ek Bhasha-Shashtriya Adhyayan, Bihar Univ. (unpub.), 1969.
Sinha, N. K., *Mundari Phonetic Reader*, CIIL, Mysore, 1974.
Sinha, N. K., *Mundari Grammar*, CIIL, Mysore, 1975.
Tiwary, U. N., *Bhojpuri Bhasha ki Utpatti aur Vikas*, Allahabad, 1954.
Tiwary, Y. N., *Nagpuria Bhasha ka Sankshipta Parichaya*, Ranchi, 1971.
Vidyarthi, L. P., *Languages of Bihar*, Ranchi, 1959.

FOURTEEN

A. K. Haldar

STUDIES ON URBAN AND INDUSTRIAL CENTRES IN BIHAR

URBANIZATION in India is linked with the development of various types of towns and cities in the regional context. So there has been a continuous tendency to explain urban phenomena in that limited context. The scholars on the subject have taken similar examples with regard to collection and analysis of data, based on census and demographic figures. Some scholars also look upon pre-industrial and industrial societies as closed and mutually exclusive systems and then try to build sustaining generalisations on the nature of urbanization as a process of change. It is true to say that urbanization and industrialization are linked in certain parts of the country and have a definite relationship. At present the rapid growth of population in an urban centre occurs due to the growth of technological development. Yet industrial urbanization and the natural process of urbanization are different phenomena.

It is for this reason that this paper has been divided into two parts. Firstly, with the background of the census data on urban development in Chotanagpur, it will deal with the studies related to urbanization at different time levels and then with the studies on the process of industrialization in Chotanagpur. Then on the basis of these and other studies an attempt has been made to justify the development of the new discipline of urban and industrial anthropology and the present state of research on this subject in Chotanagpur.

II

In Chotanagpur most of the urban developments are linked with the technological impact.

In Bihar the urban population in 1971 was 10.04 per cent as against 8.43 per cent in 1961 (Census). Chotanagpur seems to be more urbanized as regards its precentage of urban population in 1971 which was 11.97 per cent. In 1961 (Census) it was 13.33 per cent.

At the level of growth of urban centres and the corresponding industry a positive correlation seems inevitable in Chotanagpur. Chotanagpur could not witness the development of large-scale urban centres till the rapid development of the mining and manufacturing industries. The 1882 Census declared six towns in Chotanagpur out of 48 in Bihar. These were administrative centres. The 1901 Census recorded 13 towns in Chotanagpur while the 1911 and 1921 censuses returned two towns each on the urban map of Chotanagpur. Among these Ranchi was declared a town in 1872 and Jamshedpur (Sakchi) in 1911. A significant urban development in Chotanagpur took place during the decade 1931-41 as it added 11 new towns. These towns developed due to accelerated development of the mining industries relating to coal, iron ore and mica. Eight new towns were added by the 1951 Census. Five of these were associated with industry, one with road nodality and two others were regional marketing as well as administrative centres. The tempo of rapid industrialization during the decade 1951-1961 added 29 new towns. Of these 16 were located in Dhanbad district. The economic forces that earned urban status for these settlements fell in four major groups: towns associated with mining, manufacturing, communication and power projects. Twent-ynine new towns were again recorded in the 1971 Census. Out of these 12 are in Hazaribagh and eight in Singhbhum districts. Most of these are mining towns.

From this brief appraisal it is evident that urbanization in Chotanagpur took place mainly due to rapid exploitation of mineral resources and consequent development of related industries in different parts of the area.

III

The Indian anthropologists originally gained an impetus to study the urban centres in India from Redfield's concept of the rural-urban continuum. His joint paper with Singer (India 1956) provided further stimulus and direction to urban studies in India. Madras (Singer: 1955, 1958), Gaya (Vidyarthi: 1961) and Wai (Marriott) were studied by a group of scholars trained at Chicago. These urban centres were studied as the "Great Traditional" centres of Indian civilization.

Under the same influence Oraon (1958) studied the new industrial city of Jamshedpur and examined the changing life ways of the Santhal in this industrial setting. He found Jamshedpur to be "one of the most modernised and the least "traditional" of India's major cities. But the neighbouring *bustees* continue to maintain their "distinctiveness and identity". The city Santhals according to him, have not come in the Hindu fold at all, and in the light of their sensitiveness, beliefs, practices and criticism of the general Indian society, their aim is to raise their own society to a level where it will command the respect of the non-Santhal world".

Jamshedpur tribals were also studied by Sharma (1962). He finds that "at Jamshedpur tribal communities have been found to be mostly settled in exclusive sub-urban slum areas. Even among the tribals who, for one reason or the other, first settled in composite urban areas, there is a tendency to migrate to sub-urban slum areas. In other words, the tribals in the urban context seem to prefer self-social segregation. Also the basic formal Mundari socio-cultural system has been found to be still functioning in the industrial milieu" (P.I). However, it appears that city planning might have a contributory role in this. Dutta (1962) points that Koeningsberger in drawing up his plan in 1943 for Jamshedpur city was not "courageous enough to introduce a new society of different classes in one particular neighbourhood unit".

The Research Programmes Committee

The next source of city survey come under the sponsorship of the Research Programme Committee (RPC) of the Planning Commission of India. It was felt that the rapid urbanization reflected in the 1951 Census resulted in a number of urban problems, particularly those relating to rural-urban migration and employment opportunities. So during 1954 and onwards the RPC sponsored a number of socio-economic surveys in various cities in India. Under this scheme a number of social scientists, mostly economists, conducted researches on Indian cities on the set pattern. Jamshedpur (Mishra: 1959) and Ranchi (Vidyarthi: 1969), the two premier cities of Chotanagpur, were also covered in this programme.

The socio-economic survey of Jamshedpur city conducted by an economist (B. R. Mishra: 1957-59) takes into consideration exclusively the economic variables. He focuses attention on the economic consequences of rapid urbanization and presents data on the features of urbanization like increasing population, commercial and industrial establishments, employment opportunities, extent and nature of migration, unemployment and, lastly, the factors promoting or hampering the developmental facilities like housing, transport, power, water supply and social amenities. He bases his survey on a stratified systematic random sample of five per cent of the total families. The study systematically ignores the consideration of social variables and fails to mention even in the background of the culture of the tribals which provided the base for the emergence of the city.

The anthropologists took time to gain the confidence of the RPC about their ability to conduct urban studies as they were mainly concerned with the study of simpler societies. The study of the Urban Pattern of Ranchi was assigned to a trained social anthropologist from Chicago (L. P. Vidyarthi: 1969). Because of the importance of Ranchi as a tribal city his approach was to study the role of Ranchi as a regional urban centre for the transformation of various tribal societies in the midst of which it is located. Along with this it was felt necessary to present a monographic study as there was no written account of Ranchi. For this it was necessary to bring out the geographical, historical, socio-economic and religio-political characteristics of the city as a whole.

From the methodological point of view he has combined sample survey techniques with intensive anthropological researches in four typical localities of the city, and four neighbouring villages. Microcosmic studies of these localities were made to get a clear picture of urban influence on the indigenous and convert tribal and other non-tribal communities. The field materials were collected on the basis of 10 per cent sample of the selected localities, urban institutions and selected villages. These were combined with literary data to bring out a holistic picture of the urban pattern of Ranchi. This study is also different from other RPC publications in that along with economic, demographic topics it has included chapters on religion and festivals leisure and recreation, political role of the city, class and caste in the city, the urban impact on the tribal's social life, the rural-urban continuum and women in the city, their social attitudes, etc., which are of social and cultural interest and at theoretical level help in understanding the cultural roles of the city (Redfield and Singer: 1956).

The UNESCO Report

The UNESCO report on the steel city of Jamshedpur on the basis of indirect sources first of all provides material about the city on physical, demographic, economic, social, cultural and personal aspects. Entire historical developments of the city have been divided into five phases. The social implications are understood under the titles of social differentiation and solidarity, social stratification, social (municipal) administration and social welfare.

A number of active and dormant tribal organizations have been discussed in its own way. It also indicates the lines on which studies can be undertaken to assist the growth of human personality under the impact of large-scale industry and a rapidly growing town. In the light of the concept of basic personality structure it also suggests that the characteristic of the "steel man" may be analysed. On the whole it is one of the authentic, wisely analysed and systematically conceived books on the social implications of industrialization in a steel city. It is unique from theoretical, methodological and practical points of view.

From these studies it is evident that the urban pattern in Chotanagpur is linked with industrialization and its ramifications in inter-ethnic relations. This will also be evident from the studies on industrialization.

IV

A large number of industrial units have sprung up all over Chotanagpur during the recent decades. The entire coal production in Bihar comes from Chotanagpur. Out of 651 other types of mining enterprises, e.g. iron ore, chromite, copper, and mica in Bihar, 571 (86.6 per cent) are in this region. In Chotanagpur the per capita consumption of electricity (201.90 KW) during 1971-72 was high because of the iron and steel, coal and other mining industries (Roy Burman 1975: 65).

Among iron and steel industries, the important are Tata Iron and Steel Company (estd. 1907), Tata Engineering and Locomotive Works (estd. 1921) at Jamshedpur, Bokaro Steel Ltd., with a capacity of 1 to 2 million tonnes. Then there are Indian Copper Corporation, Superphosphate Factory near Dhanbad, Hindustan General Electrical Corporation, Heavy Engineering Corporation, Ranchi, and so on. On the whole this region is marked by mining, power and industrial complexes.

Mining Labourer

In coal mining the tribal labourer had a certain advantageous position in comparison with the plain people, because of the paired working. After the 1937 legislation banning employment of female labour for underground mining the number of tribal labourers in the collieries has progressively declined. In other mines also, their number is tending to come down. The prevalence of a high degree of absenteeism among them is one of the reasons (Sharma: 1960). Mechanization of mines, lack of technical skill and availability of other jobs are the main reasons. (Haldar: 1977), G. R. Sharma (1970) and M. P. Srivastava's research on the coal mining labourers of Jharia and Bermo field have been devoted to the socio-economic life and problems of labourers. A rapid study of the iron-ore mining areas of Noamundi, Barajamda and Gua by the Anthropological Survey of India (Choudhury and Das Gupta: 1970) and Kiriburu and Ghatkuri (Nuia Camp) by the Department of Anthropology, Ranchi University (Haldar: 1977), have brought out some interesting facts.

Power Project

Patratu Thermal Power Project is located in a more or less Hinduised and agriculturally advanced area of Chotanagpur. The impact of industrialization with the installation of this power project was studied by R. Singh (1966). He finds that the impact so far felt can be judged only in terms of the disintegration of the traditional culture, the rehabilitation of the uprooted villagers and the trends of the emerging industrial society. His study reveals that the communities at Patratu under the process of industrialization have shown a considerable degree of change in their occupational structure and other spheres of their economic activities. There is a decline in agricultural occupation but the traditional core of the social structure of the neighbouring villages has not been affected so far. Religious beliefs and practices also reflect the minimum transformation.

Industrial Complexes

The full length study of the Hatia industrial complex by Vidyarthi (1970) provides a case study for the understanding of form and process of culture change caused due to the emergence of factories in an underdeveloped area. It was also planned to provide a case for longitudinal analysis of the various phases of industrialization from the very inception of the social and cultural base of the tribal people—the formulatory phase of industrialization including the uprooting of their folk and peasant society, the problem of their rehabilitation and reactions in the constructive phase of installation of the factory, the township and communication network, etc.; the productive and the elaborative phases of the full-fledged development of the industrial style of living. But the study only covers the first two stages. In addition he selected eight industrially affected villages within a radius of 20 miles to evaluate the impact of industrialization. Two villages were within a radius of five miles, and the remaining six villages were selected from the three concentric circles covering a radius of 6 to 10, 11, 15 and 16 to 20 miles distance from the core. Two villages were taken from each circle. The field data were collected mainly with the help of a number of schedules and questionnaires. However, some casual interviews were taken and the changing ways of life of the people were observed. The study, however, discusses in a series of three parts the industrial setting, the society of the migrants, and the industrialized village.

At the level of re-study G. N. Choudhury (1978) has restudied some of the industrialized villages in his Ph. D. thesis studied earlier by Vidyarthi. P. K. Ray (1974) has studied the impact of industrialization on the Indian family taking case studies from the Hatia Industrial Complex.

Bokaro Steel Complex was studied by J. K. Sarkar (1970). He has focused his attention on the uprooted families. The members of these families visit various work sites in search of jobs under contractors whc, in turn, prefer to employ experienced workers. This is also reflected in the wages of the local displaced labourers which result in the formation of very low income groups of local labourers. They have started disposing of their cattle and utensils to make both ends meet. The traditional village institutions have disintegrated and all round depression and despair seem to have affected the life of the uprooted villagers.

Choudhury and Dasgupta (1970) studied Chaibasa Cement Factory located at Jhinkpani. They are of the opinion that most of the local Ho are piece-and time-rated workers and their levels of aspiration are very low. Though the educated tribals are more eager to get jobs in the industries opportunities to rise in an industry are very limited for a tribal.

Dasgupta (1978) in a recent publication has evaluated the impact of industrialization on a tribe. The factory town of Jhinkpani is the field of study. He is of the opinion that the tribals in general will be marginally placed in any industrial organization if they cannot acquire the requisite education and skill which are beyond their means. They do not lack in motivation, but they do not possess the resources and social arrangements for acquiring the requisites for a transition to an industrial culture.

The Two Cities

I have dealt here with the different types of researches on urbanization and industrialization in Chotanagpur. Now we will see these studies in the light of our new sub-discipline of urban and industrial anthropology. The development of urbanization in this part of the country is mostly related with the industrialization. In the case of the development of the two premier cities it can be said that they have followed Warren Weaver's three stages of development in the history of scientific thought (Jacob, Jane: 1965). These are, to quote, "dealing with problems of simplicity, with problems of disorganized complexity and problems of organized complexity as life sciences". These two cities developed from rural to urban areas [Ranchi in 1872 and Jamshedpur (Sakchi) in 1911 Census]. For a considerable period of time these were mere urban centres, in the heart of the tribal villages. At a later stage the installation of large-scale industries in and around these centres facilitated their development into cities. The development of various industries resulted in disorganized complexity and they have now reached the stage of organized complexity. The organized complexity can be analysed into many problems or segments which are related with one another. Though the variables are many they are interrelated with one another. The approaches in studying both these cities by the anthropologists reflect their culture purpose of investing whole cultures. As students of culture we anthropologists should endeavour to study the urban and industrial societies through the inter-relation between culture, behaviour and social institutions. But we should avoid the error of equating macrocosm with microcosm.

The anthropologists with their knowledge of the tribal and peasant cultures can understand better the situation in which these tribals and peasants are overtaken by the process of urbanization and industrialization.

Centrality of Man

Though we are faced with various problems in the study of the larger perspective of the urban and industrial centres, e.g. problem of scale as against complexity in the social fields, the problem of holism and the interrelation of parts to the whole, the conceptual problem of studying culture in this field, we could overcome these problems and develop the new discipline into a higher standard if we do not neglect the basic fact of the centrality of man in the discipline as well as the methodological priority of man over all his creation,

So far as the new sub-discipline of urban and industrial anthropology is concerned we have just started to scratch the surface of a very complex problem. In Chotanagpur though, there are several gaps in our knowledge we have conducted considerable researches on this new field. Our researches range from the study of the impact of industrialization and urbanization on a particular tribe to the study of industrial and urban units as a whole through the intermediate stages of industrialized/urbanized villages, the impact on family organization, initial effect of uprooting of families in the industrial context, etc. Though most of our data are of a descriptive nature, in some of our researches we have conceptualized the way of life and the development of new type of regional sub-culture.

FIFTEEN

Makhan Jha

INDUSTRIALIZATION IN BIHAR
A Methodological Approach

AMONG the four dimensions of Indian civilization,* researches on urban dimension (Vidyarthi: 1978) based on sound methodologies and theoretical orientation, have been accelerated only during the analytical phase[1] of Indian anthropology.** When the urban centres or cities are to be considered for a suitable typology according to the urban morphology of the city, there may be nearly 11 types of cities in India, as

*For details refer to Dr. M. Jha's book, *Dimensions of Indian Civilization*, Classical Publishers, New Delhi, 1978, where the author has dealt with the four dimensions, viz., Tribal, Rural, Urban and Textual, as an integrated four cultural pillars of Indian civilization. This four dimensional approach is being applied by the study of South Asian Civilization.

**Recently, Dr. A. K. Ghosh has challenged the use and relevance of the term 'Indian Anthropology'. While writing on 'Indian Anthropology: an examination of concept', he says "to me it appears that it is a colloquial use in the form of an abbreviation" (in *Abstracts of the Sixty-sixth Session of the Indian Science Congress*, pp. 9-10, January, 3-7, 1979, Hyderabad). In the same pages while writing on the same theme, Dr. A. K. Danda has expressed his disagreement with Dr. Ghosh over the use of the term 'Indian Anthropology', and he further adds that "in spite of my awareness about the high proportion of subjective elements in Indian Anthropology, I do not see adequate reasons for its search for any new identity" (ibid).

classified* and discussed by Vidyarthi (1971: p.7). However, we may precisely categorize them into two broad groups according to the types of researches actually done on them, viz. firstly, the researches on the urban centres and cities[2] of the *pauranic* or the great traditional and historical types, and, secondly, the methodological researches done on the industrial centres specially with a view to assessing the nature and extent of impact of industrialization and social change in and around the industrial centre, in particular, and the country as a whole, in general. In this direction, the study of the emerging Hatia (HEC) industrial complex, carried out by Vidyarthi (1970), provided an excellent case study for throwing light on the form and processes of culture change caused with the emergence of factories in an underdeveloped area. The longitudinal, analysis of the various phases of industrialization taking place in the simpler tribal belt of Chotanagpur, as attempted by Vidyarthi (ibid), has been widely considered as a fundamental, theoretical and methodological contribution for developing "Industrial Anthropology".

Following this methodological model for studying an industrial complex, a band of alumni of the Department of Anthropology, Ranchi University, carried out researches on different industrial centres of this region, and recently some of them have taken up re-study of those industrial centres, viz. HEC, Bokaro, Patratu, etc., which were studied about a decade ago, which, I hope, would make significant contribution to the productive and elaborative phase of the full-fledged

*Dr. L. P. Vidyarthi, in his paper on 'Urbanisation, Industrialisation and Social Change in Tribal Bihar' (in the *Research Journal of Ranchi University*, Vol. VI & VII, 1971), has identified the following types of urban centres in India:

(i) Religious urban centres or Sacred Cities,
(ii) Administrative urban centres,
(iii) Urban centres of health resort,
(iv) Educational urban centres,
(v) Military urban centres,
(vi) Refugee urban centres,
(vii) Commercial urban centres,
(viii) Industrial urban centres,
(ix) Mineral towns,
(x) Port towns,
(xi) Railway towns, etc.

development of industrial means of production, industrial style of life and living and finally industrial society.

What is Industrialization

Industrialization is believed to be an important phase in socio-economic development "seeking to increase, improve and diversify productive capacities and to raise levels and standard of living" (Vidyarthi: 1970, p. 2). It is an effective and radical process of culture change. It is also considered to be the change of an economy, a frequently fundamental alteration of existing skills and placing of new techniques in the organization of productive work. "If industrialization is understood as that state of affairs under which a sizable part of a given population derives its living mainly and directly from employment in the manufacturing industry, industrialization means transformation of non-industrial people into industrial workers" (ibid, quoted).

However, industrialization with its concomitants like urbanization, advancement in technology, and immigration of a plurality of communities exerts not only a tremendous pressure upon the tribal and folk society, but also sets in motion a new process of acculturation, which has been termed in social sciences as "disorganization of culture". The study of this "cultural disorganization" of a community or territory leading to the multi-dimensional developments has been of the greatest importance to the social anthropologists (Vidyarthi: 1969, 70, 71, Choudhury: 1978).

Study of HEC Industrial Complex

Though the first effect of industrialization was felt in Chotanagpur around 1856, when the coal mining industries in Jharia, Bokaro, Karnapura, etc., were founded, it was geared up in 1907 with the installation of Tata Iron and Steel Factory at Jamshedpur. Thus, the twin industries of coal and iron marked the beginning of the large-scale exploration of minerals and other industrial resources of Chotangpur, which further led to the growth and development of several industrial urban centres and in this way this area has been exposed to urbanization for a long time which has been called as "industry-based urban explosion" (Vidyarthi: ibid).

With this history of industrial development in Chotanagpur the foundation of the HEC industrial complex at Hatia near Ranchi attracted the attention of Vidyarthi, who attempted to make a longitudinal analysis (1958-68) of the different phases of industrialization. He has categorized the phases of industrialization into three, viz., firstly, the formulatory phase which included the uprooting of the tribal villages, its problems of rehabilitation and reaction; secondly, the constructive phase which saw the installation of the factory, the township, communication network, etc.; and, thirdly, the productive and elaborative phase of the full-fledged development of industrial means of production and industrial style of life.

Among these three phases of industrialization of the HEC, Vidyarthi mainly concentrated on the first two phases of the industrial era. He examined the setting up of the pre-industrial stage, gradual implications of the dislocation and disorganization of an established order and society, formation of a new society, re-adjustment of the people in the new environment, new economy and new behaviour, growth of a new type of social and political leadership like trade unions and business organisation, etc. Thus, special emphasis was placed on understanding the re-orientation of the people in the industrial society and on the formation of a chain of relationship between the industrial, urban and rural societies in terms of economy, social behaviour, customs, fashions and inter-personal relationship.

However, as the factory had not reached full production and the HEC industrial complex was still in the process of expansion, the details of the third phase of industrialization were not attempted by the author. But the time has now come to undertake the study of this third phase of industrialization and the research projects are being finalized on a large scale to take up the study not only of the HEC industrial complex, but also of the basic industrial zone* of Central India.

*A big research project on the "Study of Basic Industrial Zone of Central India" is being taken up by the Department of Anthropology, Ranchi University, Ranchi.

The Basic Industrial Zone of Central India

When we survey the basic industrial zone of Central India, comprising the adjoining regions of Chotanagpur, viz., some districts of West Bengal, Orissa, Madhya Pradesh, etc., which a large number of tribes like the Munda, Oraon, Santhal, Kharia, Gadba, Baiga, Gond, etc., are inhabiting in an overwhelming majority, we find that there has been a rapid growth of industrialization within two decades. However, within this basic industrial zone, Chotanagpur has been in the grip of an industrial revolution, and consequent to a rapid urbanization, comparatively in a short span of time, it has led this region to an industry-based urban explosion. Some of the recent researches reveal that in a few cases industrialization has led to over-urbanization, which gets reflected in congestion and overcrowding, formation of slums, particularly in the industrial and mining towns, lack of civic amenities like drinking water, electricity, under or unemployment, etc. However, in all these researches (Vidyarthi: 1970, 71; Choudhury: 1978) on the impact of industrialization reflected through the studies of the HEC industrial complex (Vidyarthi: 1970), the Patratu industrial complex (Singh: 1966), the Bokaro industrial complex (Sarkar: 1970), the Jamshedpur industrial complex (Martin Oran: 1958; Mishra: 1959; Sharma: 1960), the Rourkela industrial complex (Roy Burman & Rao: 1966; Reufel: 1977), etc., one thing stands out very prominently, that is, the extent of impact of industrialization varies from the core industrial zones to the fringe and marginal industrial zones. With a view to illustrate this point I will cite here a few examples based on re-study[3] (Choudhury: 1978) of three tribal villages, located at the core, fringe and marginal zones near the HEC industrial complex. These three villages are Hesag (core zone), Jia-Rappa (fringe) and Senegutu (marginal).

In all these villages there has been an increase in the number of non-tribals because of immigration, which is a very common phenomena linked with industrialization. In 1963 when village Hesag, located near the core industrial zone of the HEC, was studied for the first time, by Vidyarthi, there was a 40.2 per cent tribal population and 59.8 per cent non-tribal, but when, after a lapse of 15 years, this village was re-studied in 1977-78, the tribal population was found to be only

35.9 per cent and the non-tribal 64.1 per cent. However, in spite of some changes in the demographic features of the tribal population, industrialization has definitely brought a multi-dimensional development to the tribals, especially in the field of economic development, psychological and political awareness, educational, hygienic and sanitational conditions etc.

In the early sixties, when the construction of the HEC was in progress, the tribals had mixed feelings regarding this growing industrialization; they were not certain about the advantages and disadvantages from it. However, a definite shape is indicated by the latest re-study. For instance, in 1963 only 47 per cent inhabitants of village Hesag expected advantages from the HEC, which increased, in 1977, to 75 per cent. Similarly, in village Jia-Rappa (a fringe village) 54.5 per cent people had expected advantages from the HEC in 1963, but, in 1977, 68.6 per cent people clearly pointed out the advantages, as reported by Choudhury (1978). He further pointed out that, at the level of marginal village, Sonegutu, 60.8 per cent people, expected a great advantage as early as in 1963, which has gone up to 80.9 per cent in 1977. Thus, these figures show that changes have been brought about by the impact of the forces radiating from the industrial complex of the HEC, though the extent of their influence on the core, fringe and marginal levels varies. For instance, at the level of physical expansion, the villages located at the core and fringe levels of an industrial complex tend to undergo a great physical transformation and after a lapse of time, become a part of the urban complex. "Slums" and "Jhuggis" are considered undesirable, but necessary by-products of industrialization and urbanization. These phenomena invariably occur in an urban complex. However, since the HEC complex has been located on the doorsteps of the tribal villages, there has been no congestion, as the rural areas offer enough space for horizontal expansion.

Schemes for providing education, health services, sanitation, communications, etc., were initiated after independence, but the tempo of their implementation has accelerated only after the advent of industrialization.

Under the influence of industrialization and urbanization,

people have also accepted urban modes of dress, diet, transport, recreation, etc. Modern means of mass recreation are replacing the traditional village-level recreation and such changes are more pronounced in the core and fringe villages.

The tribals of the fringe village, as the re-study reveals (Choudhury: 1978), show a dual loyalty to modern industry and traditional agriculture. However, modern life, specially a core village of the industrial complex, shows that industrialization has brought tribals and non-tribals together, although this has not succeeded much in synthesizing the two groups of people, because the forces of separatism are still actively operating among them.

The researches on industrialization have shown that under its impact, leadership has been trade union-oriented instead of the traditional village panchayats, where powers were concentrated in the hands of the village elders. The attitude pattern of the tribals vis-a-vis the coming of industrialization has been, in recent years, by and large, that of acceptance and appreciation of the Government for bringing advantages to the tribal community. The tribals, who were initially rather indifferent towards industrialization specially during its formative and constructive phases because they fearing that mechanization would throw them out, are now responding positively. This augurs well for the healthy growth of industrialization in other tribal areas also.

The study of the HEC industrial complex as well as the re-study of three tribal villages near it, as referred to earlier, reveal that though the tribals have retained some of their indigenous old customs, specially regarding birth, death, etc., the characteristics of industrial urbanization seem to be in direct conflict with the rural style of life. Because of this conflicts and tensions have been noticed in several areas in the industrial complexes. As the situation exists today, a policy for the co-existence of the tribal-rural and urban-industrial societies has to be drawn up.

Works So Far

Following Vidyarthi's work on the HEC industrial complex, which is the first of its kind in Indian anthropology, as far as its microcosmic and longitudinal study of various aspects of the different phases of industrialization is concerned, two alumni of Ranchi, viz., R. Singh and J. Sarkar, studied the two emerging industrial complexes of Patratu Thermal Power (1966) and Bokaro Steel Plant (1970).

By 1966 the Patratu complex had entered its first phase; and Singh's study analyses its impact on the traditional culture, the problems of rehabilitation of the uprooted 200-odd families and the emerging industrial society. Even from the study of the first phase, it was revealed that there was great discrimination in the payment of compensation for the land acquired by the Government. The most affected were the families which lost their main source of livelihood, i.e. agriculture, and had adopted other sources of livelihood. Before the establishment of the industrial complex, the villages around Patratu were isolated and a barter system prevailed there. However, according to the study of the preliminary phase the people and other inhabitants around this industrial complex became money-minded. The workers coming from far-off villages still believed in, and maintained, kinship relationship with their co-villagers, while the workers of core villages near the factory site had developed "individualism", although the religious institutions and practices of all castes and tribes reflect minimum transformation.

These were the salient features of the study done about 14 years ago, when the Patratu industrial complex had not fully entered into the second and third phases of industrialization. But now the situation is entirely different. The Patratu Thermal Power Station is now a full-fledged industrial complex and in the fourteen years many qualitative and quantitative changes have taken place in and around the industrial complex as well as in the villages located near the factory site. It was therefore felt necessary to make a re-study[4] of the impact of the Patratu industrial complex and this re-study is in progress.

The establishment of the Bokaro Steel Plant, which was studied by Jayant Sarkar for its industrial impact when it was still in its formative stages (1967-69) resulted in a total acquisition of 32,390 acres of land for various purposes like plant, township, dam, railway yards, etc. The acquisition land displaced almost 6,066 families. As agriculture was the primary occupation of about 94 per cent, of the total displaced persons, they were compelled to abandon their traditional occupation after their displacement.

Traditional village life in which the jajmani system, the cycle of festivals and rituals all had their place, was breaking down, and this was reflected in the sense of hopelessness that seemed like a pall over the lives of the uprooted villagers.

Besides the uprooted villages, the neighbouring villages, located near the Chas, Jodhadih, Chandakeyari, etc., have also been affected to a great extent. It has been further reported that many so-called upper castes of these villages have opened shops and other businesses near the factory site or have got themselves employment in the factory to ensure a permanent and stable income.

Again, as this study was made about a decade ago, when the third phase of industrialization had not started, it was also decided to make a re-study[5] of the Bokaro industrial complex and the re-study is now in progress.

Another new steel township of Rourkela, located in the midst of the tribal belt of middle India, was begun in 1956 in the original village Rourkela and little more than two decades it has become a big steel city with a population of nearly two lakhs covering an area of 30 sq. miles. The steel city of Rourkela has been responsible for uprooting 30 villages with 2,500 households constituting a total population of more than 15,000 of different tribes and castes.

Roy Burman made a preliminary study of the first two phases of the industrialization. Rao's paper (1969) also threw some light on the impact of industrialization of the Rourkela industrial complex. Besides these two preliminary works on Rourkela; Reufel, a Research Scholar of the University of Bonn (West Germany) attached to the Department of Anthropology, Ranchi University, Ranchi, also made a brief study (1977-78), at doctoral level of impact of industrialization. However, as Rourkela also falls in the basic industrial zone of middle India, we plan to make a re-study of the Rourkela industrial complex also.

Though some reports of the studies of the effects of the later phase of the Jamshedpur industrial complex are available

Martin Oran: 1958; Mishra: 1959; Sharma: 1960) the earlier reports are completely silent on the fate of the people of 18 villages with an area of more than 16,810 acres of land which were occupied by the Tata Iron and Steel Company as early as in 1907. However, through the first report surveying the life and living of Jamshedpur, undertaken in 1918 by Principal Harold of Poona, we know that there were many tribes and castes like Bhumij (249), Santhal (66), Ho (14), Brahmin, Kamar, Gaur, Tanti, Napit, Kumhar, Dhoba, Rajput, etc., who were uprooted from their villages. Agriculture was their main source of livelihood and the area was surrounded by thick forest and remained completely isolated from the outside world because of its geographical location between the two rivers, the Swarnarekha and the Kharkai. The earlier reports are silent about any rehabilitation programme for the welfare of those uprooted villagers, although the uprooted families were given preference in employment in the factory to do unskilled work. However, owing to the unfamiliarity with the job as well as a fear complex, very few could continue and this has been confirmed by the later studies (Mishra: 1959) in which, out of 5 per cent sample (a total 421 families), taken from 16 such old villages, only 13 per cent claimed to be of local origin, while 87 per cent migrated from other parts of the tribal areas to take up jobs in the industrial city of Jamshedpur.

As the later researches, carried out by Martin Oran (1958), Mishra (1959), Sharma (1960), etc., have been done during the productive and elaborative phase of industrialization of the Jamshedpur industrial complex, many significant facts regarding immigrants, growth and development of township, network of communications, transformation of traditional institutions, etc., have emerged therefrom. But, as these works were also done nearly two decades ago, and as many developments have taken place since then, specially the installation of small subsidiary plants, offices, business and marketing centres, residential colonies, etc., it needs to be re-studied afresh, and, therefore, in our study of the basic industrial zone research project, we have also included the re-study of the Jamshedpur industrial complex.

As Chotanagpur and its neighbouring areas are rich in mineral deposits, it has also caused the growth and development of various mining towns, where mining labourers have been migrating for more than a century. Anthropologists have been attracted to the study of these mining towns and the problems of the mining labourers; recently two anthropological studies on this theme have been completed at doctoral[6] levels and many more are in progress.

Finally, it may be concluded that researches on the industrial complexes of Central India, in general, and Chotanagpur in particular, have been in progress in which the teachers and alumni of the Department of Anthropology, Ranchi University, Ranchi, as well as a few researchers from outside, have made significant contributions for the development of industrial anthropology, which is comparatively a new branch of our discipline.

The form and content of industrial anthropology, like of any other anthropological researches, are growing and developing at a rapid speed. Industrial anthropology throws light on the complex institutions of the industrial societies, which were not within the purview of classical anthropology, although the study of culture change was initiated in Indian anthropology nearly four decades ago.

As mentioned earlier, the urban and industrial centres are developing at a rapid speed and hence transformation is taking place in the societies, irrespective of castes and tribes, inhabiting around these industrial complexes. The processes and elements of culture change taking place among the so-called industrial societies are certainly different from those operating in the peasant and rural societies near the countryside or specially beyond the marginal villages. The researches on the industrial complexes have also brought out that urbanization in Central India with special reference to the Chotanagpur Plateau during the last four decades has been positively correlated with industrialisation; the industrial-urbanization has led to a tremendous growth of the means of communication and transport, investment of foreign capital, technical know-how and accessibility to world-wide markets; owing to explosive industrial-urbanization, there have been considerable migration from the rural areas to urban-industrial centres; industrial-urbanization in middle India, specially, in Chotanagpur, has greatly affected the folk and primitive tribal population, who earlier had led a homogeneous, distinctive and folk style of life. The large-scale industrialization has also geared up the general economic development without making much effort to benefit the uprooted villagers, the local and regional inhabitants. Some of these problems and the impact of industrialization of the HEC industrial complex, as a case study have been dealt with by Vidyarthi (1970, 71) and the research methodologists followed by him in that study are being applied for the study and re-study of different industrial complexes of middle India, with a view to arriving at a concrete and broader conclusions concerning the form, nature and concepts of industrial anthropology, on the one hand, and throwing light on the universality and acceptability of the major findings of the earlier researches, as envisaged above, on the other.

REFERENCES

1. For details see Dr. L. P. Vidyarthi's book, *Rise of Anthropology in India* (two volumes), Concept Publishing Co., New Delhi, 1978.
2. For details refer to the researches on the "Sacred Complexes" done by Dr. L. P. Vidyarthi, Dr. M. Jha, Dr. B. N. Saraswati and others on the traditional cities of India and Nepal. Also refer to Dr. Jha's book *Rising India: An Urban Anthropological Approach to Puri*, 1978.
3. For details see Dr. G. N. Choudhuri's Ph.D. thesis on the 'Impact of Industrialisation: A re-study of three tribal villages near H.E.C.', unpublished, 1978.
4. For details see the Ph.D. outline of Shri C. M. Jha, Lecturer in Anthropology, Mander College, Mander, Ranchi, who is working on the "Impact of Industrialisation of Patratu Thermal Power Station: A re-study" under the guidance of Dr. M. Jha.
5. For details see the Ph.D. outline of Abinash Chandra Mishra, UGC Junior Research Fellow, Department of Anthropology, Ranchi University, Ranchi. He is working on the "Impact of Industrialisation of Bokaro: A re-study", under the guidance of Dr. Vidyarthi.
6. For details refer to the doctoral theses of M.F. Srivastava and A.K. Haldar, who have studied the coal miners of Chotanagpur. Also refer to the Ph.D. outline of S. S. Lahiri, who is studying the "Socio-Economic Problems of Coal Miners of Chotanagpur—a case study of Barkakhana Coal Mine" under the guidance of Dr. M. Jha.

SIXTEEN

Ajit Kumar Singh

ANTHROPOLOGY OF TRIBAL DEVELOPMENT IN BIHAR

ANTHROPOLOGISTS sometimes are also called social doctors for prescribing both curative and preventive measures for removing permanently social weaknesses. To me, the application of anthropological knowledge to the welfare and development of the oppressed and poor gave rise to a discipline which has come to be known as "Applied Anthropology". Along with other developments in the theoretical and methodological fields of anthropology, problem-based investigations for the effective formulation and implementation of development programmes also took a turning point in the fifties. The emphasis on "fact collection" turned to the problem-oriented analysis. The planners and administrators who were concerned with tribal rural and urban development themselves began to realize that they needed the assistance of anthropologists in their work in several important ways. The anthropologists offered solutions to the human problems confronting the planners and administrators. They pointed out several socio-cultural factors which had to be taken into account if development was to really succeed among the rural people whose lives are still largely governed by tradition. With their knowledge of the problems of the poor, anthropologists can surely help in drawing up more concrete developmental plans and implementing them, and also assist the planners and administrators in their effort to see that the benefits of economic growth do indeed reach the needy.

MAJOR PUBLICATIONS ON DEVELOPMENTAL STUDIES

Applied Anthropological Researches in India date back to 1949. Except Elwin's problem-based monographic publications, more or less systematic and analytical publications about tribal problems were attempted in the tribal number of *Eastern Anthrcpologist* (1949), to which a number of foreign and Indian anthropologists as well as social workers contributed papers on different aspects of the problems of the tribes of India.

Then onwards other anthropological journals like *Man in India*, *Journal of Social Research* and *Indian Anthropologist* have, also, from time to time, deal with various problems of the tribals and offered solutions. The special issues of the *Journal of Social Research* (Vols. II & III, No. 2) deserve special mention. They are on applied and action anthropology and have been brilliantly edited and published in the form of a book entitled *Applied Anthropology in India* (1965) by Dr. Vidyarthi. The book, in its four sections, covers a wide field of applied and action anthropology. It deals with general concepts, principles, problems and postulates of applied anthropology and with various problems of tribal welfare. It also deals with concrete case studies, and applied physical anthropology. The book also reveals the various problems of Bihar.

Pragmatism in Development (1969) by Dr. B. N. Sahay evaluates the approaches to the application of anthropology to welfare development and socio-cultural factors in the modernization process with special reference to Bihar. The book is divided into three broad sections—Section One introduces the development and welfare programme with special reference to tribals; Section Two presents the main body of the book linking every aspect of social anthropology with that of development and welfare; Section Three is a resume of the socio-cultural factors which act as a barrier to development and welfare and attempts to evolve 12 basic principles of approach to tribal development.

Prof. Sachchidananda, in his paper 'Planning, Development and Applied Anthropology in India' (1973), commented on the roles of administrators, and observes: "They do not want to be told what to do and how to proceed in the tribal areas . . . .

They dislike the brakes which the anthropologists might want to apply in the light of their researches . . . If any anthropologist raised any objection and cautioned them against the hazards involved in a particular field they were just brushed aside."

In 1974, Prof. Vidyarthi published a paper 'Tribal Development in Independent India and its Future' which gives an account of the various measures taken by the Government for tribal development since independence. It provides a complete inventory of the various official committees set up by the Government to inquire into the problems of the tribals and also provides relevant information on the tribal situation in the field of employment, education, health and other related matters. He suggested that tribal development programmes during the Fifth Five Year Plan should be organized in terms of micro, meso and macro areas and regions, and special emphasis should be laid on the extremely backward groups in the macro regions.

Anthropology in Development Process (1977) edited by H.M. Mathur attempts to introduce the planners and administrators to a core of anthropological writings relevant to their development work, and help promote a more systematic study of the anthropological contribution to development problems.

Prof. Vidyarthi's *Rise of Anthropology in India* (1978) is the most monumental, scientific and exhaustive work in this line. In two volumes the book records the researches conducted in different Indian societies and presents an exhaustive view of all aspects of anthropology. The second volume devotes a full section to 'Applied Anthropology' reviewing extensively all the applied and action researches conducted in the various regions of the country by various agencies.

There have been some developmental studies made especially in Bihar and the following are their various aspects:

Development Blocks

Two reports deserve special mention, namely, Elwin Committee report of 1960 on the Special Multipurpose Tribal Blocks and Dhebar Committee report of 1961 which evaluated tribal development schemes gave recommendations for the Scheduled

Areas and Scheduled Tribes. This is reflected throughout both the reports while discussing the problems of development of agriculture, shifting cultivation, forest, animal husbandry, health, cottage industry, rural housing, co-operation, communication, education and the problem of the staff and their training. Both reports lay adequate emphasis on the training of personnel in the tribal life and culture which includes a systematic knowledge of social anthropology.

The Bihar Tribal Welfare Institute carried out specific surveys in some tribal development blocks in different districts like Karra (Ranchi district), and Boriazor (Santhal Parganas district) comprising different tribal communities like the Munda, Santhal, Paharia, Ho, Oraon, Kherwar and Korwa. The survey reports were submitted to the Department of Community Development, Government of Bihar. These surveys were intended to find out the difficulties of the area, the needs of the people and to allot priorities. Currently the Institute is undertaking evaluation of the Chakradharpur Tribal Development Agency.

Dr. L. R. N. Srivastava also worked in Dumri Block of Ranchi district and brought into light the exploitations, educational problems, political consciousness and economic conditions of the Block.

In the field of applied anthropology, Shri Ajit Kumar Singh wrote a paper "Community Development Programmes in two Tribal Villages of Bihar" (1977) in which he has pointed out the causes of the failure of the Community Development Programme. Later, he submitted a Ph.D. thesis (1978) entitled *Approaches to Tribal Development in India* which is based upon micro-level study of Bishunpur Block (Bihar). In his thesis, Shri Singh evaluated the various measures taken up by the Government for tribal development and gave 52-point recommendations for tribal development.

Education

Prof. Vidyarthi, in his two papers (1955, 1957), discussed at some length the educational problems in the tribes of Bihar and suggested some ways to bring literacy among the illiterates. Again, Dr. N. K. Ambasta (1966) wrote a doctoral thesis which highlighted the problems of education of the tribal communities of Bihar. Dr. L. R. N. Srivastava deserves special mention in the field of education. He wrote a paper on "Education for the Tribes" (1967) in which he discussed the types of education, methods of education, content of education, medium of instruction, organization of school, selection of the teacher, wastage and stagnation in tribal schools and the need for a uniform policy. In his Ph.D. thesis (1968), Dr. Srivastava dealt with the problem of education and modernization among the Munda and Oraon of Ranchi and came to the conclusion that the educated people are more emphatic, more rational, have a high level of participation and achievement motivation. They are more exposed to mass media and are more mobile.

Dr. N. K. Dasgupta (1969) also studied tribal education in the Santhal area and brought out details about the tribal economy with reference to education. Sachchidananda also wrote a paper (1974) on the educational problems of the tribes of India in general and of Bihar in particular. Sita Toppa (1974) wrote a doctoral dissertation on tribal education and highlighted several aspects of education among the Oraon of Ranchi district. Recently V. Kumar (1978) was awarded the Ph.D. degree for his thesis "Higher Education among the Scheduled Tribes of Bihar".

Health

Prof. Vidyarthi's attempt in the field of health and culture deserves special mention here. The anthropologists of Ranchi University with the assistance of the local doctors have initiated an Action Research Programme on socio-economic as well as on health survey in village Kamre. The programmes are aimed at finding out the relationship between cultural and other factors and problems of health of the villagers. This helping-and-learning process aims at providing an insight into the Action Research Programme. In the Journal of Social Research, Dr. P. D. Sharma (1972) has also written on the health survey of Kamre village.

Recently a project report was submitted to the Ministry of Social Welfare by Prof. Vidyarthi and Dr. Upadhyay (1978) on the food habits of the people of Bihar. In their study they included all the four culture linguistic zones of Bihar, namely,

Bhojpuri, Naghi, Maithil and Tribal. Their study gauged the actual calory intake by the people of different zones.

Rehabilitation

Prof. Vidyarthi has examined the working of the Rehabilitation Scheme among the Sauria-Pahariya of Santhal Parganas (1963). A very comprehensive project on rehabilitation schemes among the tribes of Chotanagpur was taken up by Dr. V. S. Upadhyay (1965). With reference to the Parahiya, Birhor, Hill Kharia community of Chotanagpur he has shown how these communities have been changing in various spheres of life. In the context of rehabilitation schemes among the tribals, the works of Mr. Hari Mohan (1973) and Dr. D. P. Sinha (1959) may also be noted. The two have noted, in general, economic and social changes among the Sauria-Pahariya and Birhor respectively.

Forest

Dr. B. K. Rai in his Ph.D. thesis, "Man and Forest in Chotanagpur" (1967), has examined the forest policy and management of forests in Bihar and the role of forest in the life of agricultural tribes, shifting cultivators, hunting and food-gathering tribal communities. He fully illustrates the role of forest in their economic and socio-cultural life. The place of the forest villages, established by the Forest Department, has also been studied. The tension and conflict between the tribals and the Forest Department have also been considered.

Student Unrest

Student unrest is the burning problem in the present situation. Prof. Vidyarthi has written two papers (1967, 1972), one abstract (1973) and a book (1975). During his study he identified four distinct groups associated with campus unrest. These are: (a) students, (b) teachers, (c) university executives and (d) visible and invisible outsiders. He further opines that so long as the interdependence of these four elements is properly maintained the campus shall function as a harmonious system and its equilibrium maintained. Unrest or disequilibrium results when stress is caused by any one of the four.

Conflict and Tension

Dr. A. B. Saran (1961) studied the nature and extent of murder and suicide among the Munda and Oraon tribes of Ranchi district. A book, *Conflict, Tension and Cultural Trends in India* (1969), edited by Prof. Vidyarthi presents various themes of conflict and tension as well as social and economic changes in the tribal and rural societies. Dr. S. P. Sinha (1969), in his paper on tribal unrest, highlights the problems of tribal administrations in Chotanagpur and Santhal Parganas. He opines that the tribals are fast losing their traditional autonomous system of tribal administration, and it is not being replaced by a more effective system. He further emphasizes the need for devising machinery to end exploitation and backwardness in the tribal areas.

Leadership

In the form of several papers and a book, Prof. Vidyarthi has made a valuable contribution to the leadership studies (1967) in terms of substantive reporting from the tribal and rural villages. The book also provides certain theoretical and methodological leads relevant to leadership studies. Again, Dr. B. N. Sahay has written a Ph.D. dissertation (1967) on the changes in the leadership pattern among the Malei and Santhal of the Santhal Parganas. Prof. Vidyarthi and Dr. K. N. Sahay have studied some aspects of tribal leadership in Bihar and given their findings in a book entitled *The Dynamics of Tribal Leadership in Bihar* (1976). The A. N. Sinha Institute of Social Studies is also conducting a study on tribal participation in Panchayati Raj with special reference to Ranchi district.

Land Alienation

Dr. Kumar Suresh Singh, in his paper, "Agrarian Issues in Chotanagpur" (1972) examines at length the causes, incidence and extent of land alienation in Chotanagpur. He emphasises the need for a new orientation of land policy in the industrial areas located in the tribal belt which is facing new challenges and responsibility.

Dr. S. S. Sinha (1968) has also dealt with the problem of land alienation of the tribals in and around Ranchi and taken some cases of Tana Bhagat.

Indebtedness and Exploitation

Dr. N. Mishra has written a paper in the *Research Journal of Ranchi University* on tribal indebtedness and indigenous banking system in a tribal village (1973).

Recently, the Bihar Tribal Welfare Research Institute made a study of bonded labour in Palamau district and made several recommendations to the Government of Bihar.

Scheduled Caste Problem

Dr. Vidyarthi and Dr Mishra (1975) have published a paper dealing with some economic problems of the Scheduled Castes of Bihar.

Dr. Sachchidananda, in his book, *Harijan Elite* (1976), has studied five major Scheduled Caste communities, viz., Dusadh, Chamar, Dhobi, Pasi and Musahar. His study has produced winds of change among the Harijans, and brought out the differences between the elite and the masses, and the differential impact of development among the five castes.

Child Welfare

The A. N. Sinha Institute of Social Studies, Patna, is currently engaged in studying the problems of tribal children in the Oraon area of Ranchi district. In the study an attempt has been made to find out the role of the Dhumkuria in the socialization process of Oraon children.

Summing Up

As the problem-oriented researches started very late, we have no adequate data on the various problems of the different societies. As is clear from the review, up till now the anthropologists were mainly concerned with the study of tribal problems. But there are also some other castes or some Scheduled Castes who have for centuries faced crisis after crisis, whether it is food, or clothes or a roof over their heads. And unfortunately these oppressed people have not yet been able to catch the attention of anthropologists. Therefore, credit must go to Prof. Vidyarthi who initiated the applied researches (specially in Bihar) and wrote regularly on the different aspects of tribal problems.

There is wide scope for applied anthropological researches

specially when entire societies are in the process of change. And as we come across the studies on different aspects of the problems it becomes obvious that a number of problematic studies, viz., on agriculture, family planning, economic problems of all the poor people, crime, exploitation, current tribal unrest in Chotanagpur, etc., are still untouched, and need urgent research attention.

It is very unfortunate that the role of social anthropologists has not been well defined in the bureaucratic machinery either by the State or the Central Government. Of course, there are a number of research institutions to assist the administrative machinery in their action programmes but there is still a much wider field to be covered, and in this social anthropologists have much wider role to play. Anthropologists must also organize themselves to bridge the existing gulf between them and the bureaucrats.

SUGGESTED READINGS

Ambasta, N. K., Tribal Education in Bihar, a Doctoral dissertation submitted to Ranchi University, 1966.

Das Gupta, N. K., *Problems of Tribal Education and the Santhals*, Bharatiya Adimjati Sevak Sangh, New Delhi, 1969.

Dhebar, U. N., "Report of the Scheduled Area and Scheduled Tribes Commission", New Delhi, 1961.

Elwin, Verrier, "Report of the Committee on Special Multi-purpose Tribal Blocks", Ministry of Home Affairs, New Delhi, 1960.

Kumar, V., *Higher Education among the Scheduled Tribes—An Evaluative Study*, Ph. D. thesis, Ranchi University, 1978

Mathur, H. M., *Anthropology in the Development Process*, Vikas Publishing House Pvt. Ltd., Delhi, 1977.

Mishra, N., "Tribal Indebtedness and indigenous Banking System in a Tribal Village," *Ranchi University Research Journal*, Vol. IX, 1973.

Mohan, Hari, *The Chero : A Study in Acculturation*, Bihar Tribal Research Institute, Ranchi, 1973.

Rai, B. K., *Nature and Man : A Study of Interaction between Man and Forest in Bihar*, Ph. D. Thesis, Ranchi University, 1967.

Sachchidananda, "Planning Development and Applied Anthropology in India", *Indian Anthropologist*, Vol. 3, 1973.

Sachchidananda, "Tribal Education in India", *Vanyajati*, Vol. XII, No. 1, 1974.

Sachchidananda, *Harijan Elite*, Thomson Press, New Delhi, 1976.

Sahay, B.N., *Changing Leadership Pattern among the Maler and the Santhal Parganas* (Bihar), Ph. D. thesis, Ranchi University, 1967.

Sahay, B. N., *Pragmatism in Development*, Book Hive, New Delhi, 1969.

Saran, A. B., *Nature and Extent of Murder and Suicide among the Munda and Oraon tribes, Ranchi*, Ph. D. thesis, Ranchi University, 1961.

Sharma, P. Das, "A Health Survey of Kamre Village, Ranchi", *Journal of Social Research*, 16 : 82-st, 1972.

Singh, K. S., Agrarian Issues in Chotanagpur in his edited book *Tribal Situation in India*, Indian Institute of Advanced Study, Simla, 1972.

Singh, A. K., "Community Development Programme in two Tribal Villages of Bihar", *Journal of Social Research*, Vol. XX, No. II, Sept. 1977.

Singh, A. K., *Approaches to Tribal Development in India : A Case Study of Bishinpur Tribal Development Block in Chotanagpur*, Ph.D. thesis, Ranchi University, Ranchi, 1978.

Sinha, D. P., "Research and Development : A Case Study of Bihar Resettlement", *Journal of Social Research*, Vol. II, No. 1, 1959.

Sinha, S. P., *The Problem af Land Alienation of Tribals in and Around Ranchi* (1955-56), Bihar Tribal Welfare Research Institute, Ranchi, 1968.

Sinha, S. P., "Tribal Unrest : An Urgent Research Problem", *Bulletins of Cultural Research Institute*, Vol. VIII, No. 1 & 2, 1969.

Srivastava, L. R. N., "Education for the Tribes in Applied Anthropology in India", 1967.

Srivastava, L. R. N., Education and Modernisation among the Munda and Oraon, unpublished Ph. D. dissertation, Patna University, 1968.

Toppo, S., *Education Then and Now Among the Oraon*, Ph.D. Thesis, Ranchi University, 1974.

Upadhyay, V. S., *Tribal Rehabilitation Scheme : A Study of Directed Social Change in Chotanagpur*, Ph.D. thesis, Ranchi University, 1965.

Vidyarthi, L. P., "Education in Tribal Bihar", *Man in India*, Vol. 35, No. 1, 1955.

Vidyarthi, L. P., Anthropology, Authority and Tribal Welfare in India", *Eastern Anthropologist*, Vol. XI, No. 1, 1957.

Vidyarthi, L. P., *The Maler : A Study in Nature-Man-Spirit Complex*, Book Land, Calcutta, 1963.

Vidyarthi, L. P., *Applied Anthropology in India* (*Principles and Caste Studies*), Kitab Mahal, Allahabad, 1967.

Vidyarthi, L. P., *Leadership in India*, Asia Publishing House, Bombay, 1967.

Vidyarthi, L. P , "A Socio-Psychological Study of University Students," *Journal of Ranchi University*, Vol. IV & V, 1967.

Vidyarthi, L. P., *Conflict, Tension and Cultural Trends in India*, Punthi Pustak, Calcutta, 1969.

Vidyarthi, L. P., "Causes and Remedies of Student Unrest", *Behaviormetrics*, Vol. II, No. 2, 1972.

Vidyarthi, L. P., "Student Unrest in Chotanagpur" (abstract) I. C. S. R.

Research Abstract Quarterly, Vol. II, No. 4, Orient Longman, New Delhi, 1973.

Vidyarthi, L. P., "Tribal Development in Independent India and its Future," *Man in India*, Vol. 54, No. 1, 1974.

Vidyarthi, L. P., *Student Unrest in Chotanagpur*, Book Land, Pvt. Ltd., Calcutta, 1975.

Vidyarthi, L. P., and Mishra, N., "Economic Problems of the Scheduled Castes of Bihar : Some Preliminary Observations", *Journal of Social Research*, Vol. XVIII, No. 2, 1975.

Vidyarthi, L. P. and Sahay, K. N., *The Dynamics of Tribal Leadership in Bihar*, Kitab Mahal, Allahabad, 1976.

Vidyarthi, L. P. and Upadhyay, V. S., Revival of the Indigenous Nutritive Dietary Habits and Recipes of the People of Bihar (Unpublished Project Report), 1978.

Vidyarthi, L. P., *Rise of Anthropology in India*, Vol. II, Concept, New Delhi, 1978.

SEVENTEEN

Sarat Borbora

AREA—APPROACH IN ANTHROPOLOGICAL RESEARCH IN BIHAR
A Case Study of the Asur

AN ANTHROPO-GEOGRAPHICAL research project covering the Netarhat group of plateaus (*pats*) has been organized by the Department of Anthropology, Ranchi University, under the supervision of Prof. L. P. Vidyarthi. Being supported by grants from the University Grants Commission, the research project attempts to make a comprehensive academic study of the *pat* region forming the north-western tip of Ranchi district and southern portion of Palamau district, Bihar. Besides contributing to our knowledge about the all-too-limited *pat* anthropology by portraying and projecting profiles of communities of the region that comprise a spectrum of ethnic groups, the area research opens up in its trail avenues for inter-disciplinary research in respect of these tiny plateaus.

Such area studies, or "region-oriented" studies which deal with people and cultures within certain geographical bounds have both positive and negative aspects (Roy Burman, 1978: iv, v). "On the positive side, these promote multi-disciplinary research so that the findings of one discipline can serve as reference material for studies in another discipline. But the area studies make it difficult to know exactly what priorities are being given to different aspects of the life of the people." Priorities are given in the present area study in terms of the needs of studying a number of selected communities, and considering, besides physical and nutritional aspect, etc., certain specific socio-economic, cultural and religious processes.

The project is to cover the ecological, demographic, ethnological and other aspects of the life and culture of the *pat* dwelling people, putting much emphasis, however, on the various ecological and socio-economic problems. The study will further examine in detail the adaptability of the population of the area to their habitat through their crude technology and interactions with various ethnic groups.

Attempts are being made to collect data on the basis of a universal frame which will facilitate cross-cultural and also cross-regional comparisons of the data. The study is also meant to help in identifying the economic and social processes involved in the gradual transformation of these *pat*-dwelling communities.

Regional studies were undertaken at different times covering different areas in India. Studies of the type done among the Nayars by Gough (1952), the survey of the actual great variety of regional kinship system by Karve (1953), Miller's village studies in North Kerala (1955), Mayer's studies on castes and kinship in Central India (1960), etc., deserve special mention.

Saksena's (1964) regional study covering the tribal economy of five M.P. tribes also deserves mention as his analysis seems to be a "valuable contribution to the study of the economy of a tribal region". A regional approach to the study of basic industrial zone of Durgapur-Ranchi-Rourkela-Bhilai is being undertaken by the Ranchi University (Vidyarthi, 1978:448).

The Anthropological Survey of India also has a project to study Arunachal Pradesh as a cultural area. Another project under the area study is taken up by Lal on ecology and demography of the same region. While the first project deals with the "interrelations among various dimensions of customs of the diverse groups of people" living in Arunachal, the other project "focuses mainly on the pattern of techno-economic and cultural adaptation" of the people of the region (Vidyarthi 1978, 1:122).

Over and above many such area studies by an individual or by a team of researchers, large-scale researches such as an inter-disciplinary research covering the varied aspects of the life and culture of the Andaman and Nicobar Islands by the Ranchi University Anthropology Department with the collaboration of the National Government Survey, the anthropo-ecological studies to be conducted in the Garhwal Himalayas by Garhwal University, etc., are in the preparatory stages.

A number of tribes and castes are concentrated round the Netarhat plateau proper and the group of plateaus contiguous to it. These flat or somewhat undulating table lands are the home of such tribes as the Oraon, Munda, Asur, Korwa, Birjia, Kisan, and such castes as the Ahir, Ghasi, Turi, Lohar, etc.

These isolated plateaus are believed to be composed of Deccan lava, now converted into laterite and bauxite as a result of weathering (Ahmed, 1965: 1,23). The *pat* region is about 3,600 ft. above sea level, that is, these plateaus rise a further 1,000 ft. to 1,200 ft. above the Ranchi plateau. The soil capping of these flat-topped plateaus is very thin, though in places it may be 20 ft. or more in thickness.

The annual rainfall of the *pat* region, which probably, at an early time, was "one continuous mass" forming a single plateau, is about 70 to 75 inches. The region escarpments intercept the rain-bearing winds from the south-east (Bay of Bengal) and monsoon clouds, and thus ensure a more dependable supply of moisture. The rain-water is absolutely necessary for agriculture. While without sufficient rain, agriculture is sure to suffer, the rain is also a dangerous force, swiftly eroding the exposed hill-sides, the soil cover being loose due to extensive and regular ploughing.

The climate of the *pat* region is pleasant throughout the year. It is much like that of the Ranchi plateau, the only difference being that in respect of certain climatic factors the *pat* climate has some marked accentuation. The *pat* region is rainier, cloudier, cooler in summer and colder in winter than the Ranchi plateau. Hoarfrost (*pala*) occurs at night and continues to remain on the grass till late in the morning during December/January. The *pala* causes much damage to the winter crops and the young trees. Because of this, people do not feel encouraged to practise double cropping. With about 75 to 80 inches normal annual rainfall *pats* are the rainiest tracts of Chotanagpur.

Tribal people flourish in the whole *pat* region to such an extent as to make the rural scene in these tiny plateaus wear a "distinctly tribal complexion". Among these *pat*-dwelling people the Asurs (total population 7,026) are an example by itself. Although one of the original settlers of the region this artisan group, once smelters and suppliers of iron to the neighbouring people, took to agriculture only recently. The techniques of agriculture and the rituals connected with its various stages were borrowed by them from their agricultural neighbours, the Oraons and Mundas.

Since the Asurs form bulk of the *pat* population and a lot of spade work has been done in the form of field-investigations by the author during 1977-79 covering several villages the Asur case study can conveniently be presented as representative of things that happen elsewhere in the area among other groups of people. It is observed that in these regions any Asur village is likely to be "representative of a larger class of relatively similar villages" which fact will help us analyze the *pat* ecology in the framework of an anthropo-ecological model. It is felt that the study of the Asur which has an orientation of the cultural ecological concept depicting the intimate "man-nature-spirit" interactions and inter-relationship during various phases of the life of the people can also be used as a guideline for a study of the other groups since the neighbouring groups also occupy almost identical eco-systems. Ecology in the *pat* region works as a levelling factor among the diverse ethnic groups so far as their cultural ethos and world view are concerned.

On analysis of the Asur case study, it is observed that nature, besides directly providing them with various raw materials, also provides them with lands for agriculture. Their adaptive strategies evolve measures for drawing at least a part of their sustenance from forests in the form of readymade eatables. Forests and *pat*-region people, as is the case with tribes elsewhere in India, are inseparable. The economy of the people is intricately linked up with forests, because the forests are the "basic matrix" in which the rural economy and culture of these forest-based communities are cast.

By making an ecological approach to the study of the Asurs' material culture and the socio-religious life, the role played by ecology and the people's adaptive strategies vis-a-vis their physical environment, are brought out.

The village houses throughout the region reflect the available materials such as earth and stone for making the walls and tiles and wood and bamboo for the framework. The construction of such rather strong and cosy houses is made possible by the availability of materials in the forested ecology and the people utilize to the maximum the abundance of these building materials. Big-sized houses are, however, rarely built now a days as it is becoming increasingly difficult to procure materials for house construction for existing ecological conditions determine the size of the house and also free labour from co-villagers.

The belongings of a house for necessary for subsistence activities and for processing the raw materials for consumption and other uses are likewise shaped and manufactured from the raw materials available in nature.

The forested ecology is still the direct source of supplementary food supply to the people, although it has inevitably lost its previous significance due to recurring exploitations. Although the forest belts have suffered much denudation, these serve the people as one of the important economic basis. In an analysis of the forests as a source of food materials, one thing becomes evident that for the *pat*-dwelling people, hunger for whom is rather perpetual, the forests are still a dependable source of food, and during the "hunger months" maximum utilization of these is made. People remain busy in collecting roots, fruits, tubers, leaves, honey and other eatables from the forests during this period. Poor as the technology is, the implements for collecting are restricted to some varieties of axes and hoes and the gleaning activities are always carried on individual family level. The appetite for hunting and fishing and craving for some protein food are satisfied by undertaking these activities in the nearby forest areas and pools of water.

Agriculture is the mainstay of the *pat*-dwelling people. The similarity in the eco-system of the arid, rocky region and the technological level of the people give a uniformity to the intricate agricultural processes. The sustenance is derived by the people from two varieties of lands lowland (*don*) and upland (*tanr*). The upland areas are covered with laterite soil which is almost unfit for cultivation being deficient in mineral constituents. Without liberal use of manure these rain-fed lands produce only meagre crop. The lowland irrigated soil is, however, rich and fertile deriving its richness from the washings from above. Because these areas lie at the bottom of the depression they suffer less from the effects of drought.

As there is a scarcity of water forms in the flat summits, irrigation of the upland cultivable areas does not seem to be economically feasible. During rains, the soil cannot arrest water and remain moist due to the inclination of the hill sides. Many upland areas are, however, totally unproductive, and strewn with huge quantities of rocks and stones are almost as good as abandoned. Reclamation measures undertaken in respect of these lands are very costly and even then the lands are likely to be of marginal productivity which is a pointer to the "areal limit to which agriculture can be pushed up" in this arid country.

Although the villages have limited quantities of lowland irrigated areas, the people make the maximum use of it by growing paddy and wheat in it—even though double cropping is not always possible due to scarcity of seeds and/or vagaries of nature.

Contiguous to the settlements sites or sometimes lying central to these, the fenced, well-protected, richly manured upland *bakhri* fields produce at least three or four crops a year—the maize crop heralding the end of months-long hunger period, and also two oil crops which are the only cash crops of the region.

In the whole region a particular style of plough agriculture, involving the age-old steps of ploughing, sowing, weeding, reaping and threshing form the dominant sector of economy.

The agricultural technology of the *pat* people as can be generalized from the Asur case study seems therefore to be well geared to make a successful adaptation of such assortment of crops as lowland paddy, dry-land paddy (*gora*), two varieties of millets which thrive in poor soil and without much water, maize, barley, wheat, two main varieties of oil crops and varieties of pulses into the ecological system. Although the yield of millet and other crops in rain-fed conditions is "variable and unpredictable", the selection of crops and the timing of sowing and reaping and the organization of the human elements in these intricate processes prove the ingenuity of the cultivators.

The similar qualities and characteristics of the soil, the same unpredictable monsoon rain, climate, the grains sown and produce harvested through the application of well-organized human effort and an identical technology from one of the basic parameters of the subsistence activities and material culture of the *pat*-dwelling people.

An analysis of the agricultural ecology reveals that the cultivators of the region have a set of technologies by the application of which they cope with their immediate physical environment or "successfully establish productive relationships" with the available lands. It becomes clear from a detailed study of the agricultural technology and agricultural ecology that ecology, at present, puts a limit to their resources and production. In order to maintain a harmonious relationship with their eco-system, the people in the economic sphere have to interact outside the periphery of the settlement. The application of agricultural technologies to an environment involve interaction even between people of different villages. When the cultivated lowland areas of two settlements lie close, equal distribution of water to the fields is ensured by cultivators owning these lands cooperating and cutting channels from the water source.

In the agricultural ecology of the *pat*-dwelling people, bullocks, cows, calves and buffaloes form the vital and indispensable element. The *bakhri* lands, the most productive upland tracts nearest to the settlement sites, are kept productive by the manure produced by these animals. These animals are also used for ploughing, harrowing and threshing operations. The ecological circumstances favour maintenance of a large population of these animals, as the villages have wide stretches of waste lands or uncultivated forest tracts which serve as grazing lands.

At the level of generalization, villages in the *pat* region seem to be the product of interaction of groups of people, their various technologies and immediate physical environments. Agricultural technologies initiate a lot of interaction between the people of neighbouring villages, transcending the boundaries of hamlets within a revenue village (*mauza*), as these facilitate exchange of goods from a surplus village to a deficient one, ideas for agricultural improvement, or the urge to experiment with an innovation and also technical know-how regarding irrigation, crop rotation, use of fertilizers, insecticides and such allied matters. The recruitment of surplus and redundant labour from different areas is also ecologically significant.

Scarcity in the *pat* areas is rampant and is accentuated by the very nature of the unproductive laterite soil. Moreover, as there is a discernible disparity between man-land ratio due to increase in population, the present economy is incapable of providing sustenance for the whole year, not to speak of generating a surplus. Most cultivating families are, therefore, on the lookout for avenues of earning a livelihood from one source or another. Here also ecological situations play a crucial role, by providing the bases for exploitation and creating a number of wage-earning facilities. They work in the bauxite quarries or forest copses or in building road for keeping the arteries of communication alive and bring different tribal and non-tribal people in contact with each other.

The identification of these changes in the sphere of economy concomitant to the introduction of these wage-earning facilities and also in response to the various welfare measures introduced by the Government under Community Development Projects would reveal the extent of economic and political transformation of the communities.

In an overall survey of the Asur villages and the fringe of other ethnic villages, it can safely be concluded that the fundamental ecological relationships taking place between the animals, food crops, human beings and the wild vegetation are alike in the villages. This symbiotic relationship—the cause of the successful adaptation of the communities to their physical environment—although vulnerable "in each of its four components", as Andress (1966:301-2) observed, has not yet caused any apprehension of a breakdown in the *pat* region.

The tribes and castes of the region live in double-ethnic or multi-ethnic *tolas* (hamlets), a number of which combine to form a village or revenue *mauza*. Each of these small *tolas* is, however, a totally independent socio-economic entity. These minimal units belonging to a village may be spread over a wide area.

The integrated nature of *pat* population is reflected when

people of a village at inter-*tola*, or even at inter-village, level are brought together during the observance of a sacred ritual or common secular festivals, frequently breaking the "rural isolation". The agricultural technology of the people is indirectly involved in it as its application involves interaction with the spirit beings as well. The set-up of the multi-ethnic revenue villages or *mauzas* is such that these have common places of worship located at a traditional venue where the people owing allegiance to the same set of religious functionaries and the same host of spirit beings gather during observance of the principal rituals. Because of identical ecological conditions there is similarity in the selection of crops and in the cycle of planting and harvesting, leading to similar observance of agricultural rituals at various pre-harvesting and post-harvesting stages.

The similarity in the religious and secular festal observances and the common identification of the deities are instances of syncretism prevalent in a *pat* region. This shared religious tradition—a product of sharing the same eco-systems—facilitates social interaction within the village and between villages lessening the chances of conflict and acrimony between neighbours.

The ecological and physiographical situations of a *pat tola* put a limit to the village cultivated areas. Such a *tola* contains 30-35 households on an average. Although settlements are located in flat terrains, the hill-top environment, the difficulty in obtaining water and the limitations of productive agricultural lands put a limit to the population of a settlement. As population of a small *tola* cannot produce enough even to support themselves throughout the year, and as the difficult terrain and lack of transport hinder easy movement, the people do most of the specialized work—from repairing and remodelling of wooden or metal parts of farm equipment to tile-making—themselves on self-help or co-operative basis. Even personal hygiene services such as hair-cutting or shaving of beard are also provided as a gesture of help and co-operation by one to another.

There is, however, a definite attitude of hierarchical arrangement of tribes and castes in terms of purity-pollution ranking. The Birjias, and such castes as the Turi, Ghasi,

Chamar, etc., are regarded as inferior in status to the Asur, Munda and Oraon, the numerically larger tribes who regard themselves to be on a par.

Different physiographic features in the same geographical region have produced different ecological riches. The settlements which are situated in flat lands for down the *pats* represent a totally different ecological situation. Here the flat well-irrigated lowland areas form the bulk of the cultivated areas and, as a result, the production is much more than that in the *pat* lands, and people are economically better off, although the agricultural technology is of the same level. As these are located at a much lower height, there is not much interaction between them and the *pat*-dwelling people.

Conclusion

To the study of the *pat*-dwelling tribes and castes the concept of "cultural ecology" can conveniently be applied. While studying the Asur, the same concept was used as a methodological tool of study to show the intimate connection between the three elements, namely, nature, man and spirit, for a successful adaptation, following Vidyarthi's (1963) depiction of the Maler (another forest-based high-hilly tribe) where too cultural ecology formed one of the orienting concepts. The ecologically oriented pattern of life of these *pat*-dwelling people is dependent upon the interaction and inter-relationship between lands, animals, forests and people forming the same social group. The sphere of the pre-existing inter-relationship between people of the same ethnic group is widened to include people from other areas, belonging to the same or other ethnic group, providing a "series of pathways between communities".

Due to close association for centuries among the Mundari-speaking Asurs, Mundas and Birjias and the Kurukh-speaking Oraons of the region and because of sharing identical eco-systems much acculturation has taken place. Sharing a common *tola* by different tribes/castes, although in unequal proportion, accentuates the acculturative processes. As a consequence, among the sequential processes, competition and conflict are almost totally absent in the villages. In multi-ethnic villages specially the interacting groups while maintaining separate ethnic identity take part in the socio-economic and religious functions of the *tola* and village thus making these associative or co-operative adjustment processes commodious for all.

It is hoped that the panorama unfolded by the area research of the Netarhat *pats* will generate interest of the academicians and people in general, and the basic data will be utilized by the planners to set in train speedily ameliorative measures in regard to the living conditions of the people in this region, since the data are likely to meet the requirements of the times for planning and development, and also for revamping some of the existing *pats*.

Since the area study concerns itself with the indepth study of representative villages of *pat* communities in respect of specific economic, socio-cultural and religious problems and also with the physical, nutritional aspects, etc., on the basis of a universal frame, being more or less synchronous, it would provide a cross-cultural perspective of the socio-economic and cultural profiles of the people in the region

SUGGESTED READINGS

Ahmed, E., *Bihar, a Physical, Economic and Regional Geography*, Ranchi University, 1965.

Andress, J. M. Quoted in Berremen, *Eastern Anthropologist*, Vol. 30, No. 2, 1977, 1966.

Gongh, E. Kathleen, "Social Structure of a Tanjore Village", *Economic Weekly*, Vol. 4, 1952.

Karve, Irawati, *Kinship Organisation in India*, Poona, Deccan College, (first edition), 1953.

Mayer, A. C., "Caste and Kinship in Central India", London, International Library of Sociology, 1960.

Miller, Eric J., "Village Structure in Northern Kerala", *In India's Village*, M. N. Srinivas, (ed) Bombay, Asia Publishing House, 1955.

Roy Burman, B. K., *Editorial in Indian Anthropologist*, IV-V Vol. 8, No. 2, 1978.

Saksena, R., *The Maler : A Study in Nature-Man-Spirit Complex of a Hill Tribe of Bihar*, Bookland Pvt. Ltd., Allahabad, 1963.

Saksena, R., *Rise of Anthropology in India*, Vol. I, Concept Publishing Company, Delhi, 1978.

EIGHTEEN

Amitava Das Gupta

STUDIES ON TRIBAL RELIGION IN BIHAR

THE CENSUS OF INDIA, 1971, revealed that the tribals in Bihar form 31 per cent of the total population of the State. This tribal population, constituted by 29 different tribes and some unclassified ones (See Appendix), is concentrated in the seven southern districts of Bihar collectively known as Chotanagpur and Santhal Parganas administrative divisions.

Due to this enormity of tribal diversity, it has not been possible yet for researchers, tribal welfare organizations or even the administration to make complete and detailed studies of all the physical and cultural characteristics of each of these tribes. It will, therefore, be realized that though the scope is large, pure studies on the religions of all these tribes are yet to be completed. These need much time and money to conduct.

Our present state of knowledge of the tribal religions of Bihar is mainly confined to those of the Oraon, Munda, Maler, Ho, Kharia and Asur, based on the monographic accounts on these tribes, various published papers, Government records in the shape of gazetteers and census publications, doctoral dissertations, etc. In fact, we can mention only one work, *Oraon Religion and Customs* by S. C. Roy to be the single complete study of a tribal religion in Bihar.

Such being the background of the studies on tribal religion in Bihar, it would be better to review them in their thematic sequence in the order of development. For such an assessment, Prof. Vidyarthi's model of the phases of the development of Indian Anthropological Research is found to be most suitable. On an all-India level, Prof. Vidyarthi has classified the development of social anthropological studies and research into three phases: *formative* (1774-1919), *Constructive* (1920-1949), and *Analytical* (1950-). This division, however, does not mean that one stage strictly follows after the completion of the previous stages; some element of over-lapping of the stages is also noticeable. Furthermore, Prof. Vidyarthi has pointed out that "there have been strikingly different rates of development in the different parts of India". Emphasizing this point, we find that in the context of the studies on tribal religions of Bihar, while maintaining the three stages, slight modification is necessary in the chronology.

Analyzing the phases of tribal religion studies in Bihar, we find that the *Formative Phase*—characterized by preliminary studies on tribal religion and some of its specific aspects through a simple descriptive approach—began in 1872 with the publication of *Descriptive Ethnology of Bengal* by E. T. Dalton. This phase continued till 1927. The *Constructive Phase*—characterized by sound theoretical orientation supplemented by field investigation and interpretative approach—began in 1928 with the publication of *Oraon Religion and Customs* by S. C. Roy. The phase came to an end in 1939. The latest on the *Analytical Phase* began with the publication of Dr. D. N. Majumdar's analytical paper on 'Bongaism', in 1940. This phase continues to date and is characterized by a systematic and analytical approach based on sound methodology.

Formative Phase (1872-1928)

With the establishment of the Asiatic Society of Bengal at Calcutta in 1774 by Sir William Jones, a trend began to study "nature and man" in India in keeping with the scope of the society. Enlightened administrators, missionaries and anthropologically oriented persons began to take notice of and study the customs, manners and religion of the tribal groups.

Following this trend, Dalton (1872), Risley (1891), O'Malley and other British scholarly administrators began studies of the tribal cultures and their religions in Bihar. Their reports though not based on modern anthropological methodologies and encyclopaedic in nature, however, contained basic data on the religions of the tribes they studied. Such data lacked depth and analytical context as these were meant for gazetteers and government handbooks. The approach to such studies was of a simple, descriptive nature.

At the beginning of this century, Bradley Birt (1903) and Bainbridge (1907) improved upon the earlier studies and published their works titled *Chotanagpur: A little known Province of the Empire and The Saoras of Rajmahal Hills* (in essay form) respectively. In his book Bradley Birt attempted the first holistic study of contemporary Chotanagpur and its tribes. His study, however, was mainly confined to the customs, festivals and village life of the Oraon, Munda, Birhor and Kharia. His approach was in the nature of a traveller's account based on his personal observations. In spite of this non-anthropological approach his book remains a source of our baseline data. Bainbridge, unlike Birt, confined himself exclusively to the study of the Saora tribe of Rajmahal Hills. Approaching the study in the traditional British style of giving references to specific villages and informants he gave profuse information on topics of religious importance. Among other details, he showed special interest in describing the rites of passage, festivals, rituals and the religion of the tribe.

It was at this time that Rai Bahadur Sarat Chandra Roy, designated as the Father of Indian Anthropology, appeared on the scene of tribal studies in Bihar. His first book, *The Mundas and their country* was published in 1912. The book, though a monumental achievement for the first Indian scholar in the field, unfortunately gave very little account of the Munda religion in its last chapter. However, such was the impact of the book that the contemporary European anthropologists like Frazer, Rivers and Marret highly acclaimed the work. The British administration awarded Roy the Kesar-i-Hind Silver Medal and made available funds for future research. Encouraged by his success, in 1915, Roy published his two-volume monograph *Oraons of Chotanagpur*. The second volume of the book solely dealt with Oraon religion. Showing a deep understanding for their religious beliefs and practices, Roy vividly described the rituals, festivals and the magical content of the Oraon religion. This book earned great appreciation from foreign scholars, including

Sir James Frazer and A. C. Haddon, and firmly placed tribal studies in Bihar on an international plane.

It was at this time that the Bihar and Orissa Research Society was founded at Patna in 1915, making available a suitable platform for further research and publication of material in its journal. Roy initiated the journal with a series of articles on the theme of 'Totemism among the Oraon' (1915), Birhor (1916) and Asur (1917). In the following years (1917-1919) while Roy confined his study to the theme of marriage and funeral customs among the Birhors and Bhuiyas, two other scholars, S. Haldar and G. N. Sarkar, for the first time, attempted to study the religious life of the Ho, publishing their findings in two papers titled 'Ho Auguaries' (1917) and 'Birth and Funeral Ceremonies of the Hos' (1921) respectively.

With the founding of *Man in India*, the first anthropological journal in India, by S. C. Roy, in 1921, further impetus was provided to the young ethnographers to publish their findings. Accordingly, we find D. N. Majumdar publishing a paper on the 'Traditional Origin of the Ho' (1924) in which he examined briefly the Ho concept of the supernatural world including a brief description of the chief deities. In the meantime, S. C. Roy turned his attention to the study of the new religious movement, among the Oraon, the Tana Bhagat movement, and published his findings in *Man in India* (1:4,1921). At the same time he carried out research on diverse themes and published papers on the Oraon Pantheon (1922), Exorcism (1923), Magical Practices, Omens and Dreams (1924), Totemism among the Birhor (1925), the Bull-roarer in tribal religion (1927), etc., but his most important contribution at the time was a paper on the Birhor tribe (1925) in which he examined the Birhor's religious beliefs and practices, 'Primitive religions in the Chotanagpur' (1928), etc. Besides Roy, Majumdar continued to publish a series of papers on the Ho, on the themes of birth rituals (1925), the supernatural world (1926), and death rituals (1927).

The Constructive Phase (1928-1939)

It was in 1928 that the Constructive Phase of tribal religion studies based on "interpretative approach" was initiated in Bihar by S. C. Roy with the publication of his book on *Oraon*

Religion and Customs. It was of pioneering significance, being the first instance of a monographic study on the religious aspect of a tribe. Based on the contemporary British trends of research on magic science and religion the book describes the various spirits, deities and supernatural powers of the Oraon. It gives a vivid picture of the initiation ceremonies and their ritualistic aspects, the role of the supernatural agencies in the life of the Oraon, and the rites of intensification. It also exhibits typological classifications of the different festivals of the Oraon and the nature and context of their magic and magical performers, and includes an assessment of the revivalistic trends in Oraon religion. Taking up the trend from S. C. Roy, D. N. Majumdar published his findings on the Korwas. He wrote two papers, 'The Cycle of Life among the Korwas' (1930), and 'The Korwas and their country' (1930). In the latter, he has given the first account of the Korwa religion through an interpretative approach. Majumdar's most remarkable work of the period was, however, the paper titled 'The Spirit of Bongaism' (1936).

After a gap of several years, S.C. Roy, in collaboration with his son R. C. Roy, and Majumdar, published two significant books in 1937. Roy's 'The Kharias' was a 600-page monograph in two volumes on the Kharia tribe, the second volume exhaustively dealing with the Kharia religion. In it Roy also dealt with the impact of Christianity on the Kharia religion and concluded:

> Under economic stress and strain the cheerful, nice and agreeable Kharias accepted Christianity on a large scale.

Majumdar's book, *A Tribe in Transition*, though mainly dealing with the process of change among the Ho, gave a consolidated account of their religious beliefs and practices for the first time. Majumdar's most significant work on tribal religion before the close of the Constructive Phase was a study of the impact of Christianity, published in a paper titled 'Tribal Population and Christianity' (1938) which examined closely the attitude of the tribals regarding conversion to Christianity and the various problems arising as a consequence of such conversions.

To sum up, we find that during the 11 years covered by the Constructive Phase of the tribal religion studies in Bihar, a number of specific trends developed:

Firstly, we find that at the beginning of the phase, the study of religion occupied a secondary position while more emphasis was given to the study of the total culture of the tribal groups.

Secondly, a coordinated plan for the study of tribal religion was absent among the scholars, resulting in diversification of topics and an unsystematic selection of tribes.

Thirdly, most authors gave primary importance to the study of rites-de-passage, totemism, magic, witchcraft, festivals, and the concepts of gods and spirits.

Lastly, these trends persisted for a time in the next or Analytical Phase.

The Analytical Phase 1940 Onwards

The joint session of the Indian Science Congress and its British counterpart (British Association) held in 1938 provided to Indian and foreign anthropologists a common forum for meeting, deliberating and reviewing the progress of anthropology in India. It also provided leads for future anthropological investigations in India on a more sophisticated level. Accordingly, Indian anthropologists began to contemplate a new trend in anthropological investigations, critical analysis of data on tribal culture and religion in place of descriptive ethnography.

Following this trend in respect of tribal Bihar, D.N. Majumdar, in 1940, published his first analytical paper on tribal religion. Titled 'Bongaism', it exhaustively dealt with a critical analysis of the concept of the "Bonga" or "the all-pervading impersonal super-natural power", a belief which is common to the Mundas and their cognate tribes in Bihar. With this paper, the credit goes to Majumdar for initiating the Analytical Phase in the study of tribal religion in Bihar. It was at this time (1942) that India lost its foremost ethnologist of the day, S.C. Roy who had published at least 91 papers, of which 25 were studies on tribal religion, and a number of monographs each including a study of the tribal religion of Bihar in its contents. In spite of this great setback the analytical studies continued in Bihar and, till his death in 1960, Roy's able disciple, Majumdar, published a number of papers in Hindi and Bengali. His noteworthy work was the publication of *The Affairs of a Tribe* on the tribal dynamic of the Ho in 1950. The book very critically studies the roots of Ho religion and his earlier views on Bongaism among the Ho.

During the post-Independence period Indian scholars came in closer contact with foreign anthropologists particularly American, as a result of mutual visits. Due to this increased contact there was rethinking and formulation of new trends of study and research in social anthropology including primitive religion. As a consequence of this contact, we find the publication of: *A Study of Munda Village life in India* by a Japanese scholar, K. Sugiyama, in 1954. While analyzing the religious beliefs, Sugiyama makes a critical study of the concept of the "rice mother" among the Mundas. In the same year, D. N. Majumdar's essay on Bongaism came under severe critical analysis in a paper titled 'Religious beliefs of the Ho' by G. S. Royetall. In the following years, we find the publication of a number of analytical papers on particular aspects of tribal religion in Bihar.

It was in 1960 that a new trend in the problematic study of tribal religion in Bihar was noticed in the form of a paper by R. O. Dhan titled 'The Problem of the Tana Bhagats'. It was a critical analysis of the reformist movement in Oraon religion, the trend of which was first pointed out by S. C. Roy in his paper 'A New Religious Movement among the Oraon' published in 1921. In 1961 with the publication of *Aspects of Religion in Indian Society* by Prof. L. P. Vidyarthi, new avenues were opened in the methods of scientific and critical examination of data on tribal religion. The publication of Vidyarthi's *The Maler* in 1963 added a new dimension to the study of tribal religion in Bihar. On the basis of the revolutionary concept of 'Nature-Man-Spirit Complex' formulated by him, Vidyarthi had studied the religion of the Maler tribe of the Santhal Parganas since 1953 and published his above book based on sound scientific methodology, giving a lead to the future scholars.

While such novel researches were being conducted by individual scholars, the Social Studies Division of the Census of India under the able guidance of Dr. B. K. Roy Burman undertook a systematic study of the fairs and festivals of India in preparation for the 1971 Census volume. In the volume on Bihar, edited by S. D. Prasad, we find adequate data on these in tribal areas of Bihar, thus opening a new avenue for further researches in this field. Such studies, though not analytical in nature, exhibit the carrying over of the trends of the constructive period into the analytical, as mentioned above.

In the latest trend of study on tribal religion in the State we find the remarkable work of Dr. K. N. Sahay. Based on his doctoral dissertation on the impact of Christianity among the Oraons, he developed the theme further and published his highly analytical book, *Under the Shadow of the Cross* in 1977. The most remarkable book of the following year, *The Rise of Anthropology in India*, by Vidyarthi, though historically oriented and analytical in nature, gives profuse information about the study of tribal religions in India.

Before concluding, mention must be made of the most recent and comprehensive analytical essay on the theme of the 'Bhagat movement in Bihar" by Sachchidananda. In his essay, 'The Bhagat Movement in Chotanagpur' in *Indian Movements*, Sachchidananda gives a critical analysis of the Movement, saying that it should be viewed in the context of a nativistic or revitalization movement taking place in tribal India.

In conclusion, we may add that at present we are in the middle of the Analytical Phase of tribal religion studies in Bihar, and there remains vast potentiality for further study which must be tapped, particularly in view of the various movements and conversion processes which will considerably disturb the originality of tribal religious beliefs and practices in future. Therefore, the need for fundamental research may be suggested to cover the basic religious beliefs and practices of each of the hitherto untouched tribes. At the same time, more sophisticated researches, like those on the study of the symbolic content of rituals and myths, should be undertaken along with the studies on festivals, witchcraft, etc., in respect of those tribes on whom we have the basic data. Such studies should follow an integrated approach combining an interpretative and analytical content.

APPENDIX

THE TRIBES OF BIHAR

The following are the Scheduled Tribes of Bihar according to the Constitution of India Order, 1950.

1. Asur
2. Baiga
3. Bathudi
4. Bedia
5. Bindhia
6. Birhor
7. Birja
8. Bhumij
9. Chero
10. Chik Baraik
11. Gond
12. Gorait
13. Ho
14. Karmali
15. Kharia
16. Kharwar
17. Khond
18. Kisan
19. Kora
20. Korwa
21. Lohra
22. Mahli
23. Mal Paharia
24. Munda
25. Oraon
26. Parahiya
27. Santhal
28. Sauria Paharia
29. Savar
30. Unclassified

SUGGESTED READINGS

Bainbridge, R. B., The Saoras of Rajmahal Hills, *Memoirs of the Asiatic Society of Bengal*, 1907.

Bradley Birt, F. B., *Chotanagpur* : *A Little Known Province of the Empire*, Smith Elder & Co., 1903.

Chattopadhaya, G., "The festival of Jatra or Harmagya of the Hos", *Journal of the Asiatic Society of Bengal*, Vol. 22 (s), 15-19, 1956.

Chattopadhaya, G. & Biswas, S., "An annual festival of the Hos", *Man in India*, Vol. 135 : 3, 185-191, 1955.

Dalton, E. T., *The Descriptive Ethnology of Bengal*, Calcutta, Council of the Asiatic Society of Bengal, 1872.

Dhan, R. O., "The problem of Tana Bhagats", *Bulletin of the Tribal Research Institute*, p. 110, 1960.

Diwakar, R. R., *Bihar Through the Ages*, Longman, Calcutta.

Elwin, V., *The Bongas*, Oxford University Press, London, 1939.

Elwin, V., *The Agaria*, with a Foreword by S. C. Roy, Oxford University Press, Calcutta, 1942.

Gupta, S. P., *Tribes of Chotanagpur Plateau*, Bihar Tribal Research nstitute, Ranchi, 1964.

Haldar, S., "Ho Auguaries", *Journal of the Bihar and Orissa Research Society*, 3, 279-281, 1917.

Leuva, K. K., *The Asur, a study on Primitive Iron Smelters*, Bharatiya Adim Jati Sevak Sangh, New Delhi, 1963.

Majumdar, D. N., "Traditional origin of the Ho : together with a brief description of the Chief Bongas (gods) of the Hos", *Journal and Proceedings of the Asiatic Society of Bengal*. Calcutta, Vol. 20, 193-198, 1924.

Majumdar, D. N., "Birth ceremonies of the Hos of Kolhan", *Man in India*, 190-198, 1925.

Majumdar, D. N., "Ho beliefs about natural phenomenon and rituals rainmaking", *Indian Science Congress*, 1926 Presentation, 1926.

Majumdar, D. N., "Death and connected ceremonies among the Hos of Kolhan", *Journal and Proceedings of the Asiatic Society of Bengal*, 23, 277-285, 1927.

Majumdar, D. N., "The cult of the dead among the Ho", *Proceedings of the Indian Science Congress*, 15, 318, 1929.

Majumdar, D. N., "The cycle of life among the Korwas", *Proceedings of the Indian Science Congress*, 17, 396, 1930.

Majumdar, D. N., "The Korwas and their country", *Proceedings of the Indian Science Congress*, 17, 395, 1930.

Majumdar, D. N., "Forms and functions of primitive religion", *Proceedings of the Indian Science Congress*, 18, 45, 1931.

Majumdar, D. N., "Disease, death and divination in certain primitive societies", *Man in India*, 13, 115-149, 1938.

Majumdar, D. N., "The spirit of Bongaism", *Proceedings of the Indian Science Congress*, 23, 397, 1936.

Majumdar, D. N , *A Tribe in Transition*, Longman Green & Co., Calcutta, 1937.

Majumdar, D. N., "The Tribal Population and Christianity", *Modern Review*, 1938.

Majumdar, D.N., "Bongaism", in *Essays in Anthropology Presented to Raibahadur Sarat Chandra Roy*, Maxwell & Co., Lucknow, 1942.

Majumdar. D. N., *The Affairs of a Tribe*, Universal Publishers Ltd., Lucknow, 1950.

Majumdar, D. N., "Religious life of the Ho", *Man in India*, Vol. 34, 1954.

Majumdar, D. N., *Chotanagpur Ki Kharia Jati* (Hindi), 2 Vols. 2.

O, Malley, L. S. S., *Bihar and Orissa Gazetteers*, Palamau, 1907.

O, Malley, L. S. S., *Bengal District Gazetteers*, Singhbhum, Saraikela, Kharswan, 1910.

O, Malley, L. S. S., *Bihar District Gazetteers Santhal Parganas*, Govt Press, Patna, 1938

Prasad, N., *Land and People of Tribal Bihar*, Bihar Tribal Research Institute, Ranchi, 1965.

Prasad, S D., "Fairs and festivals of Bihar", *Census of India*, Vol. IV, Part VII B, 1971.

Risley, H. H., *The Castes and Tribes of Bengal*, Calcutta, 1891.

Roy, G. S., "A magico-religious ceremony in connection with the death of a Ho boy", *Man in India*, 34 : 3, 1954.

Roy, G. S., "Religious beliefs of the Ho", *Man in India*, Vol. 40 : 3, 169, 1960.

Roy, S. C., *The Mundas and their Country*, City Book Society, Calcutta, 1912.

Roy, S. C., "Magic and Witchcraft on the Chotanagpur Plateau", *Journal of the Asiatic Society of Bengal*, New series; 10 (presented at the 1st Indian Science Congress, 1914.)

Roy, S. C., *The Oraons of Chotanagpur : Their History, Economic Life and Social Organisation*, Bar Library, Ranchi, 1915.

Roy, S. C., "The corn spirit and the tree spirit in Chotanagpur", *Journal of the Bihar and Orissa Research Society*, 1 : 1, 1915.

Roy, S.C., "Orientation of grave stones and houses in Chotanagpur", *Journal of the Bihar and Orissa Research Society*, 1:2, 277-80, 1915.

Roy, S. C., "Probable traces of totem worship among the Oraon", *Journal of the Bihar and Orissa Research Society*, 1 : 1, 53-56, 1915.

Roy, S. C., "Birth and childhood ceremonies among the Oraons". *Journal of Bihar and Orissa Research Society*, 1 : 1, 31-46, 1915.

Roy, S. C., "Divine myths of the Mundas", *Journal of the Bihar and Orissa Research Society*, 2 : 2, 201-214, 1916.

Roy S. C., "Totemism among the Birhors". *Journal of the Bihar and Orissa Research Society*, 22, 250 254, 1916.

Roy, S. C., "A general account of the Birhors", *Journal of the Bihar and Orissa Research Society*, 2 : 4, 457-467, 1916.

Roy, S. C., "A note on totemism among the Asur," *Journal of the Bihar and Orissa Research Society*, 3 : 4, 567-571, 1917.

Roy, S. C., "Marriage customs of the Birhors", *Journal of the Bihar and Orissa Research Society*, 4 : 1, 62-90, 1918.

Roy, S. C., "Birth, childhood and puberty ceremonies of the Birhors", *Journal of the Bihar and Orissa Research Society*, 4 : 2, 214-231, 1918.

Roy, S. C., "Death and funeral customs of the Birhors", *Journal of the Bihar and Orissa Research Society*, 4 : 3, 307-321, 1918.

Roy, S. C., "Religion of the Birhors", *Journal of the Bihar and Orissa Research Society*, 4 : 4, 455-482, 1918.

Roy, S. C., "Birth, childhood and puberty and death customs of the Pabri Bhuiyas", *Journal of the Bihar and Orissa Research Society*, 5 : 4, 618-619, 1919.

Roy, S. C, "Ethnographic notes and querries (on primitive economics, sociology. religion and magic)", *Man in India*, 1 : 1, 66-72, 1921.

Roy, S. C., "Ethnographic notes and querries (on primitive economics, arts and crafts, sociology, religion, magic and notes on castes and tribes)", *Man in India*, 1 : 2, 164-65, 1921.

Roy, S. C., "A new religious movement among the Oraons", *Man in India*, 1 : 4, 266-321, 1921.

Roy, S. C., "Notes and querries (on beliefs, customs, myths of the Birhor tribe)", *Man in India*, 2 : 1 & 2, 111-112, 1922.

Roy, S. C., "Gods of the Oraons", *Man in India*, 137-157, 1922.

Roy, S. C., "Exorcism in Chotanagpur", *Journal of the Bihar and Orissa Research Society*, 9 : 1, 118-139, 1923.

Roy, S. C., "Magical practices, omens and dreams among the Birhors", *Journal of the Bihar and Orissa Research Society*, 10 : 3, 209-220, 1924.

Roy, S. C., "Totemism and Religion", *Journal of the Bihar and Orissa Research Society*, 11 : 2, 162-176, 1925.

Roy, S. C., "The Birhors : A little known jungle tribe of Chotanagpur", *Man in India*, VI, VII, Ranchi, 1925.

Roy, S. C., "The Oraon feast of Sal flower", *Journal of the Bihar and Orissa Research Society*, 12 : 3 (216-242) (1926).

Roy, S. C., "Exorcism among the Oraon of Palamau district", *Journal of the Bihar and Orissa Research Society*, 12 : 4, 477-497, 1926.

Roy, S. C., "The bull-roarer in India", *Journal of the Bihar and Orissa Research Society*, 13, 54-61, 1927.

Roy, S. C., *Oraon Religion and Customs*, 1928, Editions, Indian, Calcutta.

Roy, S. C., "Primitive Religion in Chotanagpur", *Journal of the Bihar and Orissa Research Society*, 14, 65-74, 1928.

Roy, S. C., "Studies in Indian Anthropology", *Presidential address 6th All India Oriental Congress*, Patna, 1930, 320, Calcutta, 1930.

Roy, S.C., The Kharias, 2 Vols, *Man in India*, I : VI, XIV (306); II : IV (307-530), Ranchi, 1937.

Roy Banerjee, Chattopadaya, Religious beliefs of the Ho", *Man in India*, Vol. 34 : 4, 288-299, 1954.

Sachchidananda, "The Bhagat movement in Chotanagpur", *Indian Movements*, Ed. S. C. Malik, Indian Institute of Advanced Studies, Simla, 1978.

Sahay, K. N., "Tree cult in tribal India". *Tree Worship in India*, Ed. Sankar Sen Gupta, Calcutta, 1964.

Sahay, K. N., *Under the Shadow of the Cross*, Institute of Social Science and Applied Anthropology, Calcutta, 1976.

Sahay, V., "Bihar Ki Ho Janajati" (Hindi), *Vanyajati*, 12 : 2, 1964.

Sarkar, G. N., "Birth and funeral ceremonies among the Hos", *Journal of the Bihar and Orissa Research Society*, 5, 1918.

Sugiyama, K., *A Study of Munda Village life in India*, Takai University Press, Tokyo, Japan, 1954.

Vidyarthi, L. P., *Aspects of Religion in Indian Society*, Kedarnath Ramnath, Meerut, 1961.

Vidyarthi, L.P., (Ed.), "Aspects of religion in Indian Society", Vol. IV No. 1-12, *Journal of Social Research, Prof. Majumdar Memorial Volume*, 1961..

Vidyarthi, L. P., *The Maler, a study in Nature-Man-Spirit Complex*, Bookland Pvt. Ltd, Calcutta, 1963.

Vidyarthi, L. P., *Rise of Anthropology in India*, Vol. 2 Concept Publishing Company Delhi, 1978.

NINETEEN

Abnindra Narayan Sandhwar

STUDIES ON NATURE-MAN-SPIRIT COMPLEX
A Case Study of Tribal Bihar

RANCHI has carved a significant position in the anthropological world for which credit goes to late Rai Bahadur Sarat Chandra Roy—the Father of Indian Anthropology—and later to Prof. L. P. Vidyarthi. Teaching and research in anthropology in India in general and in Bihar in particular cannot be understood without proper reference to the contributions of Prof. Vidyarthi and his students. It is because of his untiring efforts and tremendous zeal that the Department of Anthropology, Ranchi University, has found a place in the national and international map of the anthropological world. Within 26 years of his association (founder-member of the faculty established in 1953) with this Department, Prof. Vidyarthi, along with his colleagues, students and research scholars has produced a vast, valuable material on different aspects of Man. He has developed a number of valuable concepts which need mention here, viz., Sacred Complex, Nature-Man-Spirit Complex, Campus Unrest, Cluster Development, etc.

The concept of Nature-Man-Spirit Complex, which is the topic of my discussion, was evolved by Prof. Vidyarthi in 1963 in his book, *The Maler*. It is a highly commendable work because not only does it give detailed ethnographic aspects of the Maler but also provides a methodological framework for studying different primitive and simple communities like the Maler, Birhor, etc. This framework helps in understanding the community in more realistic ways its eco-system, its various activities and supernatural world. Prof. Vidyarthi holds that Nature (forest economy, Khallu cultivation), Man (social organization, family life and lineage) and Spirit (Gossaiyan) together form a complex. It is significant to mention that the life of the Maler revolves around the forest and spirit world. It was definitely a shift from plain monograph writing to a particular conceptual framework. Ecology has a dominant role in shaping our socio-economic-religious life specially among such communities. And this can be best understood through this conceptual framework.

In view of its significance a few scholars have tried to test the Nature-Man-Spirit Complex concept and some have shown the relevance of the concept. R. K. Prasad[1] (1967) in his doctoral dissertation examines how the Parahiya living in three different ecological conditions (hill, valley and plain) with different social conditions shows inter-action between Nature-Man-Spirit.

Again, A. N. Sandhwar[2] while studying the Korwa tribe for his doctoral dissertation examined this concept. The Korwa, from ecological and economical points of views, may be divided into two broad groups, viz., Hill Korwa (Pahari Korwa) who primarily depend upon food collection from forest and basketry (previously they practised shifting cultivation) and Plain Korwa (Diha Korwa) who live in plains and primarily depend upon agriculture. Related to this, in a separate article entitled 'Occupational Rituals of the Korwa and the Nature-Man-Spirit Complex'[3] Sandhwar shows that there are clear-cut differences between the plains and Hill Korwa. Two sections of the same tribe living under two types of ecology have two types of econom y and other distinguishing cultural differences. Those who are associated with agriculture worship for the welfare and good yield of agricultural crops, whereas those who are associated with forest worship for the better yield of forest products. Their social organization is also framed accordingly. It shows relationship between Nature-Man-Spirit. The whole study indicates that different rituals associated with the occupational patterns vary in different villages which show that every village has its own Nature-Man-Spirit Complex.

A. N. Sandhwar along with Ajit Sahay and Rita Soni made another study in 1976 among the Birhor tribe of

Hazaribagh and Giridih districts—the Birhor is a nomadic, hunting and food-gathering tribe. The study gives a clear account of Nature-Man-Spirit Complex. The Birhors' whole life revolves round the forest. Their economy, social organization and spirit world are inter-related. Right from morning till late in the evening, males, females and children (above the age of eight years) roam in the forest in quest of food and other materials. Their process of socialization, rituals, practices and pantheon are related to the ecology and the mode of their economic life.

Another significant work has been done by Sarat Borhora on this concept. His study of the Asur of the Netarhat group of Plateau (*pat*) for which he did his field work during 1977-79 is ecologically oriented. He, however, presents his data on the Asur's life and culture in such a way as to bring out the mutual interactions and intimate inter-relations maintained by these people with the three elements, namely, Nature-Man-Spirit. To deal with each of these, the Asur have evolved suitable adaptative strategies. The conclusion of Borbora's thesis is that only through intimate interactions among these three elements the Asur have so far been able to successfully adapt themselves to this inhospitable mountainous *pat* country.

Besides these, there are a number of research scholars of the Department of Anthropology, Ranchi University, who are examining this concept. Mention may be made of S. P. Sinha, Chaturbhuj Sahu, N. C. Samaiyar, A. Das Gupta, etc. S. P. Sinha's main focus in the study is to examine Nature-Man-Spirit inter-relation among the minor tribes of Chotanagpur, while N. C. Samaiyar is examining it among the Birjia tribe, Chaturbhuj Sahu is working on the developmental aspect of the Birhor tribe considering the significance of the phenomenon of Nature-Man-Spirit Complex. A. Das Gupta, in his study of the 'Ho Rituals and Symbolism' has also marginally applied the concept of Nature-Man-Spirit in the context of his explanation of the supernatural world of the Ho. This he demonstrates through the dependence of the Ho on Nature on the one hand and the Spirit on the other for his very survival, for it seems that without this Nature-Man-Spirit Complex the culture of the Ho would not have attained the state of development it has now achieved.

It would not be out of place here to mention two doctoral researches conducted by Prof. Vidyarthi's students outside Bihar. These have been done exclusively in the framework propounded by Prof. Vidyarthi. Ranjit Kumar Sinha[4] has done work on the Pando tribe of Madhya Pradesh while Vijoy Shankar Sahay[5] has worked on the Nicobarese. Both works show the relevance of the concept of Nature-Man-Spirit Complex.

Numerically the number of researches on this line is small. Nevertheless they show the relevance of the concept. The model as a methodological framework provides a big asset for anthropological researches of this type. Life and culture of communities in the holistic way can be best understood through this concept, though it has ample scope of further remodelling of the framework. The Nature-Man-Spirit Complex may vary from community to community and village to village. But there is need to undertake many more such studies for its wide application.

REFERENCES

1. R. K. Prasad, *Parahiya : A Study in Cultural Ecology*, a doctoral dissertation submitted to Ranchi University in 1967 and later published from Ectu-Ethologica Institute, Vienna, in 1978.
2. A. N. Sandhwar, *The Korwa of Palamau : A Study of their Society and Economy*, a Ph.D. dissertation submitted to Ranchi University in 1972 and later published by Eata-Ethnologica Institute, Vienna, in 1978.
3. A. N. Sandhwar, 'Occupational Rituals of the Korwa and the Nature-Man-Spirit Complex', *Research Journal of Ranchi University*, Vol. X-XI, 1974-75, p. 147.
4. Ranjit Kumar Sinha, Ph.D. Dissertation on "A Study of the Nature-Man-Spirit Complex of Chattis Garha" (a doctoral dissertation submitted to Ranchi University in 1977).
5. V. S. Sahay, "The Nicobarese : A Study in Nature-Man-Spirit Complex" (a doctoral dissertation submitted to Ranchi University in 1978).

PART IV

TRAINING AND INFLUENCE OF RESEARCH

TWENTY

M. R. Chakravarthi

TEACHING OF PHYSICAL ANTHROPOLOGY IN BIHAR

PROFESSIONALLY I am engaged in that branch of anthropology which is concerned with the study of innate differences and shall, therefore, restrict my observations mainly to the point of view of Biology and its relation to Anthropology. Physical and Cultural Anthropology developed as two separate disciplines. A specialist in one of these disciplines, in most cases, could not unfairly be described as one who agreed not to know what was going on in the other. In such circumstances, it was not surprising that the two seldom met. Historically, physical anthropology grew out of the medical and zoological sciences. For many years, its principal representatives were medical men working within the medical or zoological forum. Cultural anthropology, on the other hand, developed largely from the side of the humanities, so that when it became a university subject it was usually pursued in a department which was far removed from that in which the physical evolution of man was being studied. Even when the physical and cultural anthropologists were brought together under the same roof and were subsequently joined by the archaeologists it took years before some evidences of cross-fertilization were to be observed.

During the first ICAES held in London in 1934 the meeting discussed the teaching of anthropology and ethnology in universities. The main recommendation of the first two ICAES, was, however, to establish a section of biometry and biotypology essentially for a department of anthropology. While the

British anthropologists had always made a point of combining the physical and cultural sides of the subject, seeking to bring ethnology and cultural anthropology together in their common relation to environment and appealing to the whole complex of conditions in order to solve the ethnological problems, the west European anthropologists, however, identified anthropology as biological anthropology. The American anthropologists followed an intermediate path.

The physical anthropologist can most efficiently assist the cultural anthropologist in two different and distinct ways: he can help him in interpreting his data, and can ask him questions, that is to say, point out the need for fresh data. A human society may be said to consist of men, animals, plants, inanimate objects, natural and manufactured, and traditions. The physical anthropologist is concerned with the first three.

In Bihar, the usefulness of teaching physical anthropology and ethnology was aptly realized as early as 1920 by late S. C. Roy. His readership lectures on the subject concerned are still informative. Another piece of information related to the somatic affinity of the Brahmins of Bihar by Chatterjee (1934) reminds us of the Huxley memorial lecture delivered by Haldane at London in 1956. "I am speaking to the anthropologists. And the smattering of anthropology which I have acquired leads me to the conclusion that anthropologists are mainly interested in the differences between human groups, less so in the differences within groups and rather little in the characters which are common to all groups and to almost all members of these groups."

Obviously, teaching physical anthropology in Bihar has to be considered in the context of six traditional querries:

1. Why teach physical anthropology?
2. Who should learn physical anthropology?
3. Who would teach physical anthropology?
4. When to teach physical anthropology?
5. What to teach in physical anthropology?
6. How to teach physical anthropology?

Admittedly, the existing syllabus of physical anthropology in Ranchi University has to be redrafted and reframed with reference to these six basic questions. Meaningful teaching can only thus be obtained.

The present-day concept of physical anthropology touches upon vast areas in bio-medical sciences. It should create a public awareness, create an atmosphere to think for a better life and a better generation. The students of humanities, natural and biological sciences are all eligible to learn the subject. Essentially the biologists with adequate training in biometry and with a sound background of cultural anthropology would be eligible to teach the course. The subject must be taught through a graded course especially because of its diversified field areas. The courses should be delivered through lectures and practical demonstrations. Thus, a meaningful and well-based syllabus has to be developed. In this connection, a reference may be made to the course content of the Human Genetics and Physical Anthropology so carefully drafted in consultation with experts by the author while instituting the department in 1972 at Andhra University.

The distinction between structural and functional studies in physical anthropology, of course, is blurred. Typically, knowledge of a population structure is critical to understanding questions of function. Indeed such knowledge can be vital in devising the most penetrating design for a functional study. Contrariwise, one can see the structure of a population as the historical product of the ways in which it has functioned in the past, and both types of study are ultimately concerned with explaining the nature and form of human variety. But once the focus shifts from concern with genetic structure and population affinities to the way individuals and populations adapt or fail to adapt to their environments, priorities for attention change. Interest in adaptive processes has provided a new impetus to classical anthropometric and other quantitative traits, because, whatever their determination, many of them clearly affect or reflect the capacity to survive and reproduce i.e., fitness. There are many components to adaptation: individual adaptability in development, physiology and behaviour, genetic adaptations produced by classic Darwinian natural selection and group adaptations which may be biological, cultural or bio-cultural and which in man are especially important. Analysis of these components and the way they interact to determine fitness may be one of the major themes of interdisciplinary research programme in this part of the country under the auspices of the Department of Anthropology, Ranchi University.

I have stated earlier that traditionally, physical anthropologists were concerned with describing and interpreting the patterns of geographical variety which are found to be so striking in the human species. The characteristics first examined were, naturally enough, the visually obvious ones, and for their detailed study a variety of increasingly refined anthropometric and anthroposcopic techniques were devised. Many of these characters show rather striking geographical patterns, with populations differentiated on a broad continental basis. This permitted, and indeed encouraged, the drawing up of racial taxonomies, an activity which received a great deal of attention. The activity, however, was not merely one of classification, for on the Darwinian premise that similarity indicates phylogenetic affinity, it was taken that the taxonomies attempted to express the evolutionary history of the species. Ascertaining this, history has always been and remains one of the main goals of teaching physical anthropology. It was well recognized that for this purpose the characters first available for examination had a number of disadvantages. Most of them, for instance, are influenced in their expression by the immediate environment in which the individual develops. Similarities and differences, therefore, are to some extent determined by non-genetic factors which are not relevant to establishing evolutionary affinities. At least as important is the fact that such genetic basis as there is to anthropometric variation, both within and between populations, is typically complex. Within any one population and in groups that are hybrids between two or more, generally normal or Gaussion form is displayed, without the appearance of discrete classes. Such variation has so far remained intractable to precise genetic analysis and, in particular, although caused by particular inheritance has not in any case been reduced to the level of identification and localization of responsible genes. This means not only that individuals of similar or identical phenotype may be genetically very different but also that even if each phenotype is genetically unique, there may be no linear relationship on the particular scale of measurement between the magnitude of phenotypic difference and the magnitude of genotypic difference.

The situation is changed radically with the discovery of an ever increasing number of characters which show discrete variation within and between populations. The development of these characters is not affected by immediate environmental factors and because the mode of inheritance has been precisely established it is possible to identify and, to some extent, locate responsible genes. Many of these characters have been identified in blood, mainly because this tissue is easy to collect and handle, and the variants often reach polymorphic proportions within populations. They include the various blood groups systems, haemoglobins, serum proteins and a rapidly increasing number of enzymes. For them, populations can be characterized for gene frequencies and in population comparisons of these frequencies, it is found, typically, that what varies is the level at which the polymorphism is set. On the whole, the pattern of geographical distribution is less distinct than for many of the quantitative traits and change in gene frequency with distance tend to be clinical. Also there is rarely close concordance in the distribution of different characters. Having said that, it is nevertheless true that broad continental patterns emerge and taxonomies of man based on polymorphic system are broadly in harmony with those based on anthropometric traits. A fairly large body of information had gradually accumulated on the distribution of polymorphic systems in this region of the country. Although, mainly through survey work, the broad patterns of genetic variation in man in Bihar have become known, the causes remain obscure and controversial. Essentially, the issue of debate is whether genetic differentiation of populations is dominated by the stochastic processes which are bound to occur in small populations, and Mendelian populations have been small throughout most of human evolution, or whether it is dominated by natural selection, which can be seen primarily as a set of deterministic processes.

The position is, thus, in a state of considerable flux, but the point of importance here is that concern with the question of what are the causes of genetic variety has led physical anthropologists and especially human population geneticists to concentrate increasingly on unravelling the detailed genetic structure that exists within populations and population systems, since the diversity which exists between populations is the consequence of forces which operate within them. This has necessitated the development of refined and sophisticated techniques and procedures for field studies and the modern human biologist has to spend many months or years working with a comparatively small group of people, whereas his predecessor could quite quickly and easily sample the physical variety which existed in a population.

The modern approach and the types of problems, both logistic and academic, have to be overcome. An important development in human population genetics which has followed the increasing concern with within-population phenomena is the incorporation of demographic studies with the genetic ones. It has long been recognized that forces determining the genetic structure are or are manifest in demographic conditions. Population size and changes in it affect the magnitude of stochastic processes and the probabilities of inbreeding.

Another area which has attracted the concern of population geneticists is the social structure of populations. This not only influences demography but also genetic structure directly through the prescribed mating systems. Although genes are often distributed as though mating were at random, such mating is in fact rare, especially in any extended population and the form and nature of deviations need to be known. Associative marriage is particularly a function of social systems. These systems also frequently determine the actual definition of population. What may, at the first sight, appear to be a single Mendelian unit is often a set of multiple units separated by social breeding barriers. Then understanding of the social structure of a population can be vital in recognizing biological kin as compared with social kin.

Traditionally, human population biologists have worked with societies which have simple economies and are exposed to the rigours of natural environments, and, as has already been argued, there is a good case for this, since these are the environments under which most of human evolution occurred. But ever increasingly people are living in essentially man-made environments, particularly urban ones, and the effects of these conditions which form the evolutionary point of view, are very new, and are in great need of investigation in this region. This need is as much practical as academic.

There is, therefore, an urgent need to initiate studies of urban biology especially to know as much about the structure and function about the urban populations as possible.

I have tried to offer my views in the foregoing observations as to what should be a meaningful course content of the present-day physical anthropology in Indian universities. The Anthropology Department of Ranchi University has studied the cultural aspects of many population groups in this region and has earned international laurels but unfortunately has shown very poor performance so far as the physical aspect of the discipline is concerned. May be, if we redraw our present syllabus and include a few modern important courses, we would be able to be with the times in this discipline also.

TWENTY ONE

Jyotirmoyee Sarma

SPREAD OF EUROPEAN CULTURE THROUGH CHRISTIANITY

THIS SHORT paper consists of thoughts and reflections rather than intensive research. It is based on the opportunity offered to me by the Provincial Sister of the Ursuline Order of India of the Roman Catholic Church, which has its headquarters in Belgium, to accompany her on her official inspection of several convents. This unusual invitation came on account of her friendship with some persons known to me in Ranchi. She understood that I wanted to visit some tribal villages, and did make it possible for me to visit five villages near the convents. The villages visited are : Tongo and Katting near the mission of Tongo in Bihar, Nayatuli near Kunkurhi, Patrapura near Dharamjaigarh, and Kattar near the mission of Jhingo, the last three being in Madhya Pradesh.

I stayed in the convents for a fortnight in May, 1979. I was offered the rare hospitality of staying on the very premises occupied by the nuns. I silently observed whatever I could see. But everyone knew that I wanted to see the nearby villages for academic reasons.

To the villages I was accompanied by a Sister, or a lay girl of the convent staff, as guide and interpreter, and also to restrict my questioning. So I did not ask many questions in the villages, and turned my attention more to the nuns themselves.

Most of the nuns I met were of Oraon ancestry. I could not fail to be impressed by the life of devotion and service accepted by these women, and at so early an age. A nun becomes ordained at the age of 18 or 20 years. The cult of virginity and the state of sisterhood as practised by the Roman Catholic Church is completely alien to the original Oraon culture, as it is to the rest of the Indian society. Among the Hindus occasionally some women may become *sannyasinis* and among them some may have married at one time, or some may have become widowed. But it is compulsory for the Catholic nuns never to have married. The Roman Catholic Church, with its emphasis on the discipline and dignity of womanhood, has raised the position of women in society in general. That it has opened this path of dignity to so many women whose ancestors were Adivasis is no small matter indeed. So with deep appreciation, I present my observations.

Throughout the world the empire building of the European powers has been associated with the spread of Christianity, and India is no exception. Regardless of the humble teachings of Christ, Christianity has been the professed religion of the European people, and, therefore, a symbol of the dominant nations. Although various indigenous cultural traits have been interwoven into it in various parts of the world, Christianity is distinctive of the European civilization, and persons who call themselves Christians are expected to bear some rudiments of European cultural traits.

Christianity first came to India with the advent of St. Thomas. Myths prevail that he was an apostle of Christ and he landed on the Malabar Coast in A.D. 52[1]. The Malabar Church is related to the East Syrian Church of the near East. The East Syrian Church also regarded St. Thomas as its founder.[2] Christianity gained fresh impetus in India with the coming of the Portuguese traders. Their colonies were at first established in western India also, as Vasco da Gama came to Calicut in A.D. 1498 for the first time, and for the second time to Cochin in A.D. 1502. Missionaries came wherever their colonies were formed.

In Eastern India Christian missionaries and the Christian churches of various denominations came with the advent of the Portuguese, the French, and the British. The Bandel Church in Hooghly district of West Bengal claims Portuguese origin in the 16th century. In spite of the efforts to make converts among all levels of people, however, Christianity did not gain firm roots in eastern India. The fact that the teachings of Christ were not antithetical to Hindu ethics was hardly appreciated by the people. The conspicuous traits which created social distance were that the professed Christians ate forbidden meats and drank wine, their women were not secluded, and married men of their choice at mature ages; even after marriage the women mingled with men in social gatherings, and in most respects did not abide by the rituals practised by the Indian people.

The social histories of the 18th and 19th centuries in India indicate that there were two kinds of reactions of Christian proselytizing influences. One, some persons with outstanding family backgrounds became Christians in order to become totally identified with the Europeans. The classic example of this was poet Madhusudan Dutt. At the time of his conversion he had proclaimed European culture to be superior to that of India. Many others, of literary eminence, had similarly accepted Christianity, like the family of Aru and Toru Dutt. The other was movements to resist the growth of Christianity as supplementary to the growth of Indian Nationalism. Among the intellectuals, deeper concentration on the Vedas and the Upanishads led to the development of the Brahmo Samaj which eliminated many of the Hindu rituals, and made people conscious of current social problems. At about the same time grew the devotional cult of Sri Ramakrishna which brought to its fold not just the intellectuals, but people from all walks of life, with the simple assertions that all religions are the same, and all paths lead to the worship of the eternal divinity. These revivals in the Hindu religion helped keep the conversion of Hindus to Christianity to a low level in eastern India. The Muslims also fended for themselves. Being persons of strong religious faith, they kept away from Christianity. Just as European rulers and European merchandise were to be forsaken, there was no place for European religion in Indian life.

However, although conversion to Christianity was resisted by the Hindus and Muslims, many of the secular amenities introduced by the Christian missionaries were retained and considered desirable. These were mostly in the realms of education and social service. Schools and colleges founded by the missionaries were considered to be the best in any locality. There boys and girls learnt the English language, and through contacts with some European teachers and students learnt the European food habits, how to wear European clothes correctly, and the European ways of spending leisure. In other words, boys and girls who attended Christian schools were considered to be more modern, better educated and more disciplined than those who attended non-Christian schools. This is so even today. Thus there is the paradox : institutions founded and managed by various religious orders and under the influence of self-sacrificing nuns and priests have become the status symbols in modern Indian society where the students resist the religious thoughts of Christianity but eagerly learn the European ways of life.

Hinduism believes that all religions are the same, whereas one of the basic tenets of Christianity is that it is the only true religion. Christians are expected to preach and spread the Gospel, and bring all the non-believers within its fold. The churches in Europe and America collect vast sums of money and distribute them to their foreign missions. The missionaries dedicate their lives to the service of humanity and especially the underprivileged. It is not compulsory that they should convert all the persons to whom they offer their services, but some conversions do take place and add greatly to the dignity of the order, and reflect the merits of the religious personnel through whom the conversions are made. The missionaries are, therefore, always looking for new fields for their activities. In India the Adivasis captured their attention. Not only were they the people whom the missionaries could help in many ways, they were also the persons who did not have the intellectual background, nor a systematic philosophy with which defend their indigenous religions as did the Hindus and Muslims.

K.N. Sahay, in an article,[3] tells us of the economic hardships the Oraon suffered in the early 19th century, and now a leading missionary, Father Lievens, with the object of helping them "set to studying the agrarian troubles and tenant laws of the native people".[4] He helped the Oraons successfully fight legal battles against the oppressive landlords, and thereby was able to convert many whose confidence he had won. He had made it known that he would help only the Christian converts. Most likely there were more men like him who set themselves to rectify many of the grievances of the tribal people in the Chotanagpur area as well as in the rest of India.

Christianity has been accepted in Chotanagpur for more than a century. The history of the original missionary activities in the Ranchi area is found in the writings of S. C. Roy. The first Christian Mission was established in Ranchi in 1845 by the German Evangelical Lutheran Mission. Four Oraons were the first Christian converts made by this Mission in 1850. In a few years the number of Adivasi converts increased with the expectation that the European missionaries would help them in their land disputes with the landlords. In 1869 there was a split in the German mission. One section of it joined the S. P. G. (Anglican) Mission in Ranchi. These two missions continued to make Christian converts in Ranchi District until 1883 when a Catholic Mission was started near Ranchi.[5]

The Catholic Mission was most successful in making Christian converts.

> Soon after the Catholic Mission began to work in the District, there were phenomenal mass conversions to Christianity. The Catholic Fathers wisely permitted their converts to retain as much of their tribal customs, feasts and festivals as did not militate against the Christian creed, and they took a keen and zealous interest in the material welfare of their converts. And this was the secret of their phenomenal success.[6]

Roy pointed out that many of the Adivasi Christians tend to group together, and converts of one denomination tend to stay separately from converts of other denominations.[7] This seems to be the situation even today. But I also observed that some persons find their tribal ancestry to be more of a bond of unity than the division between the Christian and non-Christian. Thus, sometimes marriages take place between Christians and non-Christians of the same tribe provided that the boy and girl belong to inter-marrying clans. The difference in religious ideologies does not seem to be an important issue in some families. In many villages Christian and non-Christian Oraons live in close proximity without apparent conflict. Many of the Adivasis do not suffer from the Hindu "pollution" complex, and this probably leads to harmonious relations between the two groups. As all the Adivasi Christian children go to Mission schools, many of the non-Christian Adivasis who live near Christian Mission schools and hospitals also send their children to these schools, and also go to these hospitals without any inhibitions. The religious authorities these days do not compel people for conversion, but keep their doors open to everybody. The Mission establishments in Jhingo, M. P., have existed for only six years. In a nearby village of the Korwa tribe, consisting of seven households, six of the families claimed not to have anything to do with the Christians. The Korwa families are extremely poor. Men spend little time in gainful work. They cultivate barley and rice of poor quality, but hardly enough for their needs. Rice is dehusked with a stick by hand. When these people fall ill, in six houses the women asserted that they perform rituals in which the diseases are driven away with a *kula*. In the seventh house, however, the mother took her two ill children to the convent hospital where they got well. She does not perform any Korwa rituals at home, but at the time of the *naya dhan* ceremony she takes her offering to the convent bungalow and asks the sisters for their blessings. She does not go to the Church. Apparently she is not a person who evaluates ideologies, but is more interested in the results.

The State of Bihar provides free education to all persons of Adivasi origin. As a result many non-Christian Adivasis also are now highly educated. This has led to the development of nationalistic feelings and the desire to identify themselves separately from their Christian counterparts. In an article,[8] Kartik Oraon clearly asserts that Christians are not tribals. His argument is that by becoming Christian, people become part of the large society of Christians throughout the world. So they should no longer identify themselves with their ancestral tribes. Jyoti Sen, in an article,[9] further describes the development of self-conscious or national feelings amongst the tribes. In this context I would like to quote an instance. In May, 1979, there was an armed robbery in the convent of Tongo (near Chainpur). The priests were forced to part with money and valuables. Although this incidence was recorded by the police as an ordinary armed robbery, shoutings of "Ham loke ka country se nikal jao" (get-out of our country) and "Jai Hind", made me wonder if the robbery was not politically motivated. Since none of the culprits were caught, nothing further may be known of this particular event. I learnt subsequently that robberies in the missions were not infrequent. I think this should receive careful consideration from all aspects.

In another village near the convent of Dharamjaigarh, M. P., an educated gentleman of the Cherwa tribe distinctly displayed feelings of tribal nationalism. He was a school master, and all his sons and daughters went to school and college. He lived in a large clay house with a big compound, which had been built by his grandfather. He proudly showed me around his house. The rooms were comfortably furnished and he indicated that he was quite adjusted to the modern world. He had nothing to do with the Church or Christianity. He mentioned that the Tribal Research Institute helped the Adivasis a great deal. He had learnt that Sarna was only one of the many names of Mahadeva. The image of Sarna is a stone, and so is the form in which Mahadeva is worshipped.

Regardless of the adoption of many indigenous ways of life by good Christians, such as the singing of hymns with tribal tunes, reception of visitors with dances and washing their feet, sitting on the church floors where chairs are lacking, many European culture traits are retained among Christians. The Christian names sharply differentiate the Christians from non-Christians. In Oraon villages where all are Christians I found myself in a completely different world. All have names of Biblical or European origin. Surely people with such names could not help having different conceptions of themselves from others very like themselves but whose names were different. Lately, churches have started christening children with Hindi names, but I did not find any such name in the Christian villages I visited.

The sisters are trained in the model of their European counterparts, and the Missions are organized on the pattern of those in Europe. Various European items of food are cooked by the nuns, and learnt by the students. Very fine embroidery work, in Belgian tradition, is taught in work centres and is looked after by a trained staff of local women. Some of the embroideries are sent to Europe, where they are in demand. Management of home and village is taught at school. The students are taught interior decoration, and systems of hygiene much in the European tradition.

Although most of the villagers tend to arrange marriages according to the traditions of clan exogamy, Christians may marry other Christians regardless of ethnic differences. Marriages between persons of different tribes, as long as they belong to the same church, are not uncommon. The emphasis on education enables Christian Adivasis to get higher ratings for competitive occupations. Some even go to Europe, with the help of the missionaries, and from there reach even a higher stage of professional aspiration. In other words, the Christian Adivasis have their range of communication extended to very wide limits. Thus the missionaries offer the same kind of social mobility to the Adivasis as they do in the urban areas with the distribution of European cultural traits.

In conclusion I would like to suggest certain research problems for future studies. In the three Oraon villages I visited, the families of Lohar, weaver, potter and Ahir were not Christians. The Christians called these families Hindus, but each of the families I visited denied performing any Hindu rituals. They lived surrounded by the Christians and sent their children to the Mission schools. But they do not go to church. Marriage partners are sought from other families of their own caste who live in similar tribal villages. Roy had mentioned the presence of these functional castes in Oraon villages.[10] I do not understand why these people do not identify themselves as Christians, and wonder if there is any kind of status differentiation between Hindus and Christians in the village society. Do these people command higher status by calling themselves Hindus than they would by calling themselves Christians?

REFERENCES

1. Brown, L. W., *The Indian Christiansomas of St. Thomas Account of the Ancient Syrian Church of Malabar*, University Press, Cambridge, 1956, p. 43.
2. Ibid., p. 66.
3. Sahay, K. N., 'Impact of Christianity on the Uraon of the Chainpur

Belt in Chotanagpur : An Analysis of Its Cultural Processes,' *American Anthropologist*, Vol. 70, No. 5, 1968, pp. 923-942.

4. Ibid., p. 925.
5. Roy, S. C., 'The Effects on the Aborigines of Chōtā-Nāgpur of their Contact with Western Civilization,' *Journal of the Bihar and Orissa Research Society*, Vol. XVII, Pt. IV, 1931, pp. 378-380.
6. Ibid., p. 380.
7. Ibid., pp, 390-391.
8. Kartik Oraon, 'Tribes and Tribalism of India,' *Journal of Social Research*, Vol. VII, No. 1-2, 1964, pp. 36-52.
9. Jyoti Sen, 'Problems in Tribal Transformation,' *Man in India*, Vol. 46, No. 4, Dec. 1966, pp. 319-330.
10. Roy, S.C., *The Oraon of Chotanagpur*, The Brahmo Mission Press, Calcutta, 1915, pp. 170-180.

TWENTY TWO

Rajiv Ranjan Prasad

DE-ISLANDING ANTHROPOLOGICAL RESEARCH MATERIALS

IT WAS Aristotle who, for the first time, said that "Anthropologists are those who talk about themselves". He was right. We, the anthropologists, are primarily concerned with the study of mankind. We study mankind at different levels of civilization, e.g., tribal society, rural society, urban society, etc. But we fail to communicate our findings to the general mass of people. We write about our findings and research materials in the anthropological journals which are largely read by those scholars whom we call anthropologists and who are already, more or less, acquainted with such type of findings. Thus, we make our knowledge "islanded"; an island of anthropologists.

Hence, it was realized that de-islanding of the anthropological research material was the urgent necessity for the survival and progress of the discipline.

According to my understanding, the main factor responsible for the poor and deplorable status of anthropology is the lack of communication of our data to the general mass. We have also not been able to keep pace with the allied disciplines like Sociology, Economics, Political Science, Social Work, etc. It is quite unfortunate on our part that being the pioneers in the tribal studies, we have failed to project the tribal style of life in the mainstream of the Indian society. We study the tribals, their leadership dynamics, peculiar customs of the natives, etc., but the general mass learns about the different customs of tribals, tribal movements like Jharkhand movement,

Backward Class Movement, etc., not through our writings but through the writings of journalists. This, in fact, should have been our legacy. But we merely keep talking about the social structure, social organization, culture contact and change, acculturation, etc., using anthropological jargon which hardly conveys anything to the general masses and to the administrators and planners who are interested in such material. Therefore, it is high time that we thought in terms of making the "Science of Man" known to him. And I think it is quite relevant because we always keep talking about national integration as our broad aim. And we are not going to succeed in this noble objective unless the human diversities are bridged or diminished by exposing them to different societies. This we cannot do until we start communicating the peculiar cultural practices of one particular society to the other and so on. This will help the Indian masses in understanding each other's culture, values, norms and thus in developing a sense of brotherhood. For the achievement of this noble idea, let us ensure that the anthropological findings do not travel straight to the archives and become islanded knowledge.

Also it is quite imperative that the aim of anthropology should be not only the scholarly interest, it should also concern itself with the understanding of the socio-economic problems which confront the human society and the nation. In fact, we do not lack in knowledge but we lack in its manifestation. We cannot prove the worth of our knowledge unless it is exposed to the planners, administrators, scholars of allied disciplines, and above all to the lay man. We should not remain under the impression that we would submit our findings, suggestions, etc., to the Government, planners, administrators, etc. only when asked to do so. But I wonder if there is any other way of doing it except that we ourselves show them through our writings that we too have something to contribute to the development-oriented plans, social welfare projects, etc.

It is, therefore, quite necessary that the subject matter of anthropology be generalized and simplified for the general mass. However, this does not mean that fundamental research, and scientific studies of the society be given up. In fact, they should be divided into two parts:

1. Scientific studies to build up second theories, healthy models, methodologies for the proper understanding of society, and
2. De-islanding the findings of anthropological researches in an all-pervading environment of knowledge.

While we have already made substantial progress in the scientific studies of man and society, little or no attempt has been made in the direction of making anthropology a popular subject. I strongly feel that there is a vast scope for the teaching of journalism in the curriculum of anthropology. This can be done by introducing a new sub-discipline in anthropology which can be termed as ethno-journalism. By introducing the teaching of journalism in anthropology, our students and research scholars will find themselves in a better position to convey their findings not only to the scholars, but also to the planners, administrators and even lay men. This will also help in popularizing the subject matter of anthropology. Our writings in the popular magazines will give us recognition, identity, and raise our status in the realm of social sciences.

The State of Bihar provides a vast spectrum of cultural types. We can certainly hope that with the introduction of teaching of journalism in the curriculum of anthropology, the cultural types which exist in Bihar shall be amply projected in the mainstream of Indian society.

TWENTY THREE

Sita Toppo

BIHAR AND THE TEACHING OF ANTHROPOLOGY

IN BIHAR the Department of Anthropology was established in 1953. Since then the department has been busy popularizing Anthropology, the science of man. But it could not become as popular a subject as history and political science. The reason is that anthropology is a field science, and as such its study involves much expense. All colleges whether constituent or affiliated, even the Universities, dare not establish departments of anthropology. Even in the case of Ranchi University, anthropology is being taught only in 10 of its 62 colleges.

Anthropology is a fascinating subject, no doubt. But as it is quite unknown to the past generation, the teachers find it difficult to motivate students to offer anthropology as an optional subject. However, the teachers make their best efforts to fascinate students who offer Anthropology, a new subject, at the intermediate level. But at this level teaching of anthropology is totally theoretical.

Two types of courses in anthropology are taught at the Bachelor of Arts stage—general anthropology and practical physical anthropology for the Pass Course students and anthropology with depth for the Honours students. The Honours students are being taught with specialization in certain special branches of anthropology. To get a glimpse of the varied human life, the Honours students have to do field investigation for three weeks and have to submit a field report. Besides, they do physical anthropology practical and keep record. But it is felt that the general students get afraid of doing the practical. Anthropology is better equipped now than at any other time to contribute both in theoretical perspective and in field detail. Now it is not merely the study of culture as a whole, but it has developed a close relation with psychology. The students are being taught sociology, social psychology, prehistoric archaeology, applied anthropology and ethnography, and learn the applicability of anthropological knowledge among the groups of ethnic minority of India in general and Bihar in particular.

At the post-graduate stage the field investigation is conducted for six weeks under the guidance of professors who try to help them make analogies and inquiries. They try their best to give proper training in research design. And it is realised that after the Masters degree in Anthropology, a research student needs no spoon-feeding for his Ph.D. research work, at least for collecting data and approaching the field. The students are being taught both the synchronic and diachronic methods of approach for field investigation. I may say that the Department in a short period of 25 years has produced a good number of Ph.Ds.

Sociology, Pass Course, was only a subject of examination, i.e. those who wanted to appear in sociology sat for the examination privately. But this year sociology is being introduced at B.A. level in which anthropology is being taught.

At post-graduate level students are being taught about the emergence and development of man from physical, cultural and social points of view. This way they study the origin and history of man's cultures, his evolution and development and the structure and functioning of human culture in every place and time. In prehistoric archaeology, they try to reconstruct human history and determine the types of historical phenomena in its different sequences. They realise how, in the past, man struggled for his existence and invented amenities of life on the basis of his experiences.

A study of History of Anthropology is made to obtain some knowledge about the various schools of anthropology and their contributions. For specialization in social anthropology which usually involves mapping out the nature and type of social relationship in a community and arrangements of social structure, the students select special papers like Dimension of

Civilization to know culture, and civilization and thinking about Indian civilization. In Human Relations principles of sociology and social psychological relations are being taught.

The third type of specialization is in Tribal and Rural Welfare in which Applied and Action Anthropology with field experience is being given. For specialization in physical anthropology Human Genetics is being taught with special physical anthropology practical work.

Method of teaching is just giving lectures, doing practical work of physical anthropology and prehistoric archaeology and conducting field work for research design. Dissertations are also offered by some of the students on specific topics.

The medium of instruction is generally Hindi at the undergraduate level while at post-graduate stage it is English. This makes anthropology a complex subject. It is suggested here that English must compulsorily be a side subject at the undergraduate level.

Another problem which the department has to face is that some students come to this department without any anthropological background and the department somehow manages to give the general base in Anthropology to bring them on the level of those who come with their Honours degree in this subject. This way the Department of Anthropology becomes feeding department.

There is some scarcity of anthropology books in Hindi; but if available, these become more popular. Anthropological thought is considered a tough subject and not many books are available to all students when actually needed.

In various universities like Mithila, Patna and Bhagalpur, Anthropology is being taught as a special paper in M.A. (Sociology). In B.A. (Sociology) too one paper is of social anthropology.

In the BPSC Competitive Examination, Anthropology is included in Sociology. It is unfortunate that Anthropology is not treated as an independent subject. In the Union Public Service Commission, Anthropology was only among higher or additional papers meant for critical knowledge of Physical Anthropology, Social (Cultural) Anthropology and from tribal India sides. But now anthropology has no important role in the selection for the Indian Public Services.

Some administrative officers, and men of responsibility, not understanding the tribal system of land tenure, introduced uniform methods of revenue collection, and had unintentionally alienated tribal land to the members of advanced population. This is the reason why anthropology-based education is being imparted in administrative training institutions. This helps much to lessen the exploitation and oppression of the rural and tribal people by the elite. For this reason, anthropology-based training is being imparted by Community Development and Panchayati Raj Training Institutes to the Block Development Officers and Village Level Workers and by the Administrative Training Institute to the future administrators.

For Diploma in Mental and Social Psychiatry (DMSP) and Diploma in Psychiatric Social Work (DPSW) at the Institute of Psychiatry, Kanke, Cultural Anthropology-based training is being imparted.

In B.Ed. course Social Anthropology is being taught as compulsory but extra paper. The National Council for Educational Research and Training occasionally makes the provision of Summer Institutes and arranges lectures on anthropology to broaden the outlook of elementary school teachers in rural areas who generally have caste bias.

In the Post-Graduate Department of Psychology, Social Anthropology is taught to facilitate understanding of human behaviour in a particular time and space.

Anthropology is a field science and it helps the process of mental growth. It unfolds what is within and prepares an anthropologist for the responsibilities of adult social life. It disciplines the mind.

It seems there is no scope for an anthropologist in the matter of job selection in India as in the U.S.A. in Government agencies like "Smithsonian Institute, National Park Services, Trust Territory of the Pacific Island, Department of State, Department of Defence, Library of Congress, Government of American Saoa, National Science Foundation, Veterans Administration, Extension Service of the Department of Agriculture, Bureau of Indian Affairs" (Sturtevant, William C. : 1970).

"Other organisations that have hired a few anthropologists include some independent research organisations, a few philanthropic foundations, some hospitals, particularly, mental hospitals, state and local health and advertising companies, a few business houses with interests abroad, and law firms working on Indian claim cases. These are not numerous. Television, radio, documentary movies and related concerns are sources of part-time employment for a few trained anthropologists"

(Sturtevant, William C. : 1970).

But it is true that an anthropologist usually obtains his first job through the University department in which he receives his advanced degree. Subsequent jobs are offered to the professionals on the basis of their reputation in their respective fields which mainly depends on his publications.

But it is clear that no one could take up the study of anthropology in expectation of large economic rewards, though rewards of another nature are there. Job security is relatively great, and the researcher gets his major satisfaction from earning his living by doing what he enjoys most.

Teaching of anthropology helps in a natural, harmonious and progressive development of man's innate powers. Teaching in anthropology is a part of total culture. It varies according to time, space, society and individual. Anthropologists, specialised in a particular model, teach the same subject vigorously. They pass on anthropological knowledge gained by them to another generation and show ways and means for improving upon the existing knowledge. But in various institutions, colleges and universities methods of imparting anthropological knowledge differ.

Anthropology forms a special environment that has been designed by society with a view to imparting training and influencing the mental and moral disposition of its members. Every individual is born at a particular time, space and environment and is put in the midst of certain fixed social environmental arrangements. The anthropologist knows that the unconscious influence of the environment is subtle and pervasive which affects the whole personality of the emerging anthropologists.

For Physical Anthropology courses in general zoology,

genetics, comparative anatomy, physiology, ecology, palaeontology, and biological statistics should be included if possible. For Archaeology, courses in such fields as geology, history, the art of elementary surveying, and climatology will be useful. For Ethnology courses in sociology, linguistics, psychology, economics, history, statistics, geography, art and musicology are advantageous. For Linguistics, as many languages as possible, psychology, history may be included. A course or two in English composition will not be wasted, regardless of the future specialization.

Attending summer schools for specialized training and participation in excavations under expert supervision is very useful. There is often considerable duplication between under-graduate and post-graduate anthropology courses and because of that the students lose their interest in anthropology. To avoid this and to increase their interest, the interdisciplinary studies also make such collateral training profitable. Anthropology is liberal enough to give a few applied anthropology jobs for pursuing anthropological research in a spare-time activity in later years. It is almost always advisable to change to another University after completing undergraduate work. Next, the basic groundwork for formal anthropological training can be laid in the post-graduate, preparatory course at college or honours level.

Students of anthropology must get a knowledge of the social problems, like social disorganization, crime, punishment and cure, fashion, unemployment, poverty, student unrest about casteism and communalism, problems of stratification of caste and class and the alarming growth of population. Some important traditional social institutions and associations of Indian culture like family, marriage, position of women, purushartha, ashrams, unity and extension must be known to all. An anthropologist having a Master's degree in Anthropology must have the clear conception of various concepts and aspects of Indian society and groups. Some topics are quite rotten which must be replaced. There are some specific topics and papers which are pretty hard for the teacher and the taught, to teach and to learn, e.g. Prehistoric Archaeology, a subject which is not meant for all.

The teacher should try to make students experience the

knowledge, to make it pleasant and delightful. To arouse students' curiosities, audio-visual aid is much useful because experiences are the only reality. Tutorials on a topic or the semester system of education will be more utilitarian. Particular topic will be fixed for a particular period of time. Lessons must be planned. Only then the teacher can know about the problems and grasping capacity of his students. Problems are the foundations of thinking and can reconstruct our experiences.

To my mind the college curriculum should be an embodiment of the wonders of discovery, the pride of self-cultivation and the brimming joy of the flux of life. The college students lack the proper guidance of their teachers as generally teachers behave like paid social workers. The tribal students by nature are shy and submissive and, therefore, dare not consult their college teachers and are always in a disadvantageous position resulting in poor examination results. Therefore tutorials in each topic are essential.

Again I cannot understand why some junior teachers, who can teach better than some of the senior teachers, cannot become the examiners and question setters for the University examinations of their own students? Why invite two external examiners for their students whose interest and attitudes and weaknesses in a specific topic are unknown to them?

I think that in the quest for excellence, particularly in the field of education, our hearts should be broad for all, free from all "isms" and complexes.

TWENTY FOUR

B. M. Mukherjee

TEACHING IN ANTHROPOLOGY IN BIHAR
Retrospect and Prospect

THIS STUDY is based on the personal acquaintance of the author with the varied types of anthropological literature and his long association with the educational institutions in Bihar which impart anthropological training either as regular courses or certain time-bound programmes. As is known to me, anthropology could possibly be called the mirror from which our faces get reflected in order that we know the self (man). There is hardly any need to go into its detailed subject-matter and scope. The science of man appeared in India at a comparatively later stage than in the West. The lead was of course given by the Britishers although some of the early writings of Indian scholars and humanists have shown much interest in this line. But these were not recognized by the then anthropologists of Western origin. Calcutta University started a Department of Anthropology for the first time in this country in 1921. But before that Rai Bahadur S. C. Roy had already started conducting anthropological researches in his individual capacity. Primarily, he, a lawyer, developed a keen interest for the entire land of Chotanagpur (then included some parts of Bengal and Orissa). His first book in the form of a tribal monograph entitled "Mundas and their country" was published in 1912. He was the first Indian who delivered the readership lectures in Patna University on the various branches of Anthropology in 1915. In the same year another book was published on the Oraons of Chotanagpur. He continued anthropological research from 1910 till his death in 1942. Roy was bestowed the honour of being called the father of Indian ethnology. Again, he received the Kaiser-i-Hind silver medal in 1913 and the title of Rai Bahadur in 1939 besides many other awards. He was elected honorary member of the Folklore Society of London in 1920 and in the same year held the President's position of the Anthropology and Archaeology Section of the Indian Science Congress Association. The great scholar was also elected President of many national and international Seminars on Anthropology and Archaeology. He was the founder-editor of the first anthropological journal, "Man in India", started in 1921. Again, it was Roy's indefatigable endeavour to inspire Sir Ashutosh that resulted in the teaching of anthropology at Calcutta University. He acted as visiting lecturer at Calcutta University for several years after its inception. He also imparted his knowledge to some of the famous Indian anthropologists like D. N. Majumdar, N. K. Bose, L. P. Vidyarthi and others. The preceding paragraph suggests that the seed-bed of anthropological teaching and research was prepared only in Ranchi.

The British administrators like Dalton, Hutton, Campbell, Anderson, Bodding, O'Malley and others wrote many anthropological papers on the tribes and castes of Bihar which appeared primarily in two journals—*Journal of Bihar and Orissa Research Society*, Patna, and *Man in India*, Ranchi. Articles on Bihar were also published in all-India journals like *Anthropological Society of Bombay*, *Asiatic Society of Bengal* and others. These writings presented a comprehensive methodology and ethnology on the basis of which Professor Vidyarthi categorized this stage as Constructive Period preceded by Formative Period in the development of Indian anthropology.

It was during the analytical period of Indian anthropology that the Post-Graduate Department of Anthropology was started in the Ranchi College under Bihar University. The following year witnessed establishment of the Bihar Tribal Research Institute at Ranchi. These two institutions went on exploring the life and culture of Chotanagpur and Santhal Parganas under the supervision of trained anthropologists like Sachchidananda, Vidyarthi, Saran, Mrinal Roy, B. K. Srivastava and others.

The Anthropology Department of Ranchi University in India was started only after Calcutta, Delhi and Lucknow and till now is the only University in Bihar which offers a course in anthropology both at Honours and Master's level. At present anthropology is taught in nine Colleges of Ranchi University and offers the Honours course in Ranchi College only. At the intermediate level a course in anthropology provides some basic and primary topics concerning customary laws and social institutions. In B. A./B. Sc. Pass Course anthropology provides three times more detailed study than intermediate with physical anthropology practical and field work in the syllabus of this University. Depth study is only imparted in the Honours Course. Now I shall turn to the courses of study in which a complete paper on social anthropology expects the students to understand family, marriage, kinship, social organization, totem, taboo, religion and primitive economy. These topics are taught for the basic concepts and to show the unity and diversity in human society. The above mentioned topics also furnish some theoretical base line for the beginners. Another paper has been prescribed for the methods and techniques for anthropological field work with the exclusion of various approaches. This course is more practical and subtle. It has another paper on physical anthropology and prehistoric archaeology. The next paper is on Ethnography and Applied Anthropology consisting of varied topics like life-styles of Indian tribes, caste studies (only theoretical concepts), problems of culture change and culture contact, loss of ethnicity, retribalization and tribalism, resettlement programmes, problems of exploitation, indebtedness, seasonal migration, loss of habitation and economic displacement, different approaches to their welfare programmes, constitutional safeguards and the Government's welfare measures and its evaluation, and also the study of Christian missionaries approaches in the tribal development. But the paper does not give attention to the studies of later Indian applied anthropologists like J. K. Bose, P. K. Bhowmick and others. What may be suggested here is that the syllabus of honours course requires slight modifications and alterations with a view to feeding the students current situational consequences in our own society On the other hand, if we take up the issue of distribution of marks in various branches of

Anthropology in B. A./B. Sc. honours course, we will not find it uniform. There should have been more emphasis on the pattern of paper distribution. Instead of six papers in the Honours Course there should be eight papers of which two, carrying 200 marks, be with practicals both in Social Anthropology and Physical Anthropology and Prehistory. The remaining six theoretical papers could be distributed as under:

Ist paper : Tribal Ethnography of Chotanagpur and some non-Indian tribes
2nd paper : Physical Anthropology
3rd paper : Prehistoric Archaeology
4th paper : Social and Cultural Anthropology (to include studies of regional material culture)
5th paper : Research Methodology
6th paper : Special Paper (Sociology or Social Psychology) or Human Geography as selected by the student.

Each theoretical paper should be of 100 marks making a total of 600 plus 200 marks for the practicals of the 200 marks for practicals 100 should be fixed for Social Anthropology providing 50 marks each for Field-work and Technology Practical. The other 100 may be equally divided between Physical Anthropology Practical and Prehistory Practical.

Turning to the Post-graduate teaching in anthropology in Ranchi University, I am thinking aloud about the existing courses of M.A./M. Sc. After Dr. Sachchidananda, Dr. Vidyarthi took over as Head of the Department of Anthropology, his pioneering efforts gave new stimulus to it and consequently it flourished more rapidly than any other faculty of this University. Dr. Vidyarthi has also restructured the Department both academically and administratively. I would now like to discuss the syllabus which consists of eight papers, each of 100 marks. The first paper offers theoretical training, concepts and terminologies of social anthropology. Some of the concepts of sociology are also included. Contents of the paper are kinship, detailed study of marriage, concepts of society and culture, theories of religion, magic, totem and taboo, topics related to economic anthropology and political anthropology. But what lacks is the modernization of the contents.

For example, the kinship study does not explain the advanced theories such as componential and formal analysis. The course is unconcerned about the structural and linguistic analysis of kinship. Also, it would have been better to include some of the cultural anthropological chapters in this paper to give the student a clear conception of two distinct traditions—cultural and social. Alongside, a chapter on culture change (theoretical framework) furnishing the various anthropological approaches to the study is also needed to better equip the student. The second paper is on research methodology, comprising the logic in anthropology, different strategies and techniques for field work, methods of psychological anthropology, statistics, different steps in scientific investigations and formulations of research projects. It also covers different approaches like historical, monographical, ethnographical, evolutionary, functional-structural analysis, ecological and culture area approaches. Then is required a thorough study of two anthropological books for evaluation and review purposes. Besides, the student has to work in the field from time to time for at least ten days in order to apply field techniques learnt in the class. Here I take the opportunity to appreciate this paper because of its self-contained nature and full coverage.

The third paper has two parts, physical anthropology and archaeological anthropology, each carrying 50 marks, and are categorized as A and B. The first part (physical anthropology) includes details of the theories of organic evaluation, human origin, possible phylogenetic explanations. Relevant fossil forms, race and racism, principles of genetics also come under this part. So far as the general physical anthropology is concerned, it is sufficient for the social anthropological students. But a few additions would be helpful. There appears to be a need to cover some aspects of bio-social studies. From the point of population group and their food intake, human growth could be a better comparison. At the same time one more topic should be incorporated as warranted by the changing situations. Impact of family planning, people's attitude to sterilization, the incentive behind it, the unchanged attitude of the Muslims towards family planning demand special attention, and need to be included in the

M.A./M.Sc. course in anthropology. The second part consists of geomorphology, geochronology, prehistoric ecology, economy, tools and tool-making techniques, dating of artifacts, palaeolithic, mesolithic, neolithic cultures of India and Europe, ancient civilizations, and palaeolithic art. This part of the paper is quite lengthy and particularly prehistoric cultures of India and Europe overburden the students. For this reason prehistory is little learnt by the average student. So, it is suggested to curtail this chapter and prescribe either the European or the Indian stone age culture.

The fourth paper has two groups of practical courses. Group 'A' is concerned with general physical anthropology practical containing osteology, dating and sexing of bones with special reference to stature, dossires, ossification, centre and epiphyseal union. Then craniometry, sonatometry and their tabulation and analysis are also done. In Group 'B' detailed study measurements, sketching of the prehistoric tools, selected technological implements, primitive implements for agriculture, fishing, hunting, basketry pattern and some other museum specimens are to be done in the laboratory. But the Department has impecunious laboratory and museum for prehistoric teaching. The syllabus does not either prescribe field work in prehistoric archaeology.

The fifth paper really demands special attention. It deals with purely theoretical formulations. Various schools of anthropological thought, eminent American anthropologists, French and German sociologists, social thinkers and some Indian anthropologists have been included. Different thoughts and concepts to the study of Indian civilization enrich the subject matter which are shown from various dimensions. Lastly, it examines the contribution of Indian anthropologists in the formulations of theories related to Indian situations and indigenization. The sixth paper imparts field training under the supervision of a teacher for a period of six weeks. This demands scientific preparation beforehand. A series of discussions on the synopsis of individual students in open symposia take place. After returning from the field every student is required to present his paper and findings on the individual topic in a series of seminars. Thereafter each of the student is required to submit his/her field dissertation for the final examination when it is evaluated.

Lastly, there are a number of specialised groups constituting the remaining two papers of 100 marks each. This part is selective where the student's choice and interest is taken into account. He is required to take an examination for offering the special papers. Special groups are on social anthropology, advance physical anthropology, linguistic anthropology, dimension of Indian civilization, human relations, tribal and rural welfare and also on dissertation. The last category of the special paper (dissertation) carrying 200 marks has been envisaged for a very special kind of advance research work on a specified problem. But this group is offered only to a student of exceptional merit who has to work under a senior teacher. It combines very useful training and research and may be said to be of the level of M. Phil. course. The dissertation enables the students to develop new ideas and independently handle situations for their work for Ph.D.

The discussion in the present paper gives the impression that the various courses in anthropology have not been related to the Indian situation to the fuller extent wherever necessary. The entire programme seems to reflect the perspective of the American School of anthropology to a great extent. What, however, is striking is that it seems to shut itself off from the regional tribal population. Even the course on teaching of tribes does not include the local tribes for acquainting the fresh students who directly jump into anthropology post-graduate courses. Further, it is evident that at some stage the course provides studies on Indian village and caste stratification. I agree that there is much conceptualization of research methodology paper but, at the same time, I disagree that there are any systematic practicals on technology, material equipment and pre-history. Then there is a great disparity between the under-graduate and post-graduate class lectures. Here, language is the problem. The students who are accustomed to Hindi lectures in the under-graduate courses suddenly face the problems of lectures in English at the post-graduate level. This has proved to be a big handicap for at least 50 per cent of the students.

Besides the Anthropology Department of Ranchi University there are other universities in Bihar where one paper on anthropology has been included in the sociology curriculum, for example, Patna and Bhagalpur. Magadh University provides one paper on anthropology as selective in the post-graduate Psychology Department. In the B. Ed. course social anthropology is taught as an extra paper throughout the state of Bihar Again in Geography post-graduate courses a paper on human geography is opted by the students. Some of the universities in Bihar offer one paper on social anthropology in the B.A. Sociology Honours Course.

An institute of the Government of India like the Development Officers' Training Centre presently known as Community Development and Panchayati Raj Training Institute, Ranchi, from time to time organizes orientation courses in applied anthropology for the officers engaged in tribal and rural development programmes.

The discussion so far and critical appraisal of teaching in anthropology in Bihar gives an impression that anthropologists' procedure should be of associative nature rather than of eliminative. Again the author believes that an anthropologist's professional responsibility is only to reveal the truth, and all other responsibilities are extra-professional. It is not guaranteed that some fruitful results would come. Therefore, the action anthropological teaching does not impress the author. For, the present-day need is not only syllabus-bound teaching programme but also reinterpretation which brings out many things. Firstly, efficacy in ethnography is acquired. Secondly, mistakes committed by early ethnographers are detected. These help achieve a degree of refinement.

The teachers and students must realize while doing anthropological field work in India that they are not making some other culture study but only self-study.

TWENTY FIVE

Arbind K. Sinha

ANTHROPOLOGY
A Question of Relevance

> Man has sought to gain knowledge about his environment and myriad phenomena that surround him in natural elements and other inanimate objects and in plant and in animal life. But man himself has also been an object of study: man has tried to understand his human behaviour in relation to others. Emerging from this attempt are the social sciences, which study man and his works from various standpoints.
>
> (*Chitamber* : 1973 : 6)

THE STUDY of man and his environment is not a new phenomena in India. We always keep our eyes and ears open to it. History says that the ancient travellers to India like Fahiyan and Huensiang kept a good account of India, Indians and the Indian culture. But, were they social scientists? Also the claim of Bradley-Birt's work (Bradley-Birt : 1903) as an anthropological document is still not out of controversy. We also know that the report of a social scientist is the outcome of systematic and scientific research. And the field of social science is vast. Any sensitive social scientist, conscious of happenings in his surroundings and then in a place at a distance, frames a problem and starts searching for a solution. In this search he comes across a new question. This is a continuous process. It is termed as "Social Research" (Sinha : 1978 : 169). As far as the question of anthropology as a subject is concerned, it is the youngest of the social sciences and focuses on the study of human culture in its entirety.

Anthropology, initially confined to the study of aboriginals, started in India as a hobby of British administrators who tried to understand the tribes and tribal culture in order to run the administration more effectively. The eighty-year-old history of Indian anthropology has much to say about its conception, birth, growth and maturity. The present paper limits the discussion to the geographical boundary of Bihar with special emphasis on cultural anthropology which is closely associated with the father of Indian anthropology—late Rai Bahadur Sarat Chandra Roy.

Right from the early writing of Bradley-Birt in 1903 or the memoir written by Bainbridge in 1907 to the present seminar papers, the anthropology has covered a wide range starting from tribal ethnography to impact of industrialization, tribal religion to the sacred complex of Deoghar, shifting cultivation to the dimension of recent agricultural development, and primitive technology of Munda to satellite communication and community. The trend in world anthropology has left its impression. The British school of anthropology shaped the anthropology of Bihar in unidimensional researches whereas the American influence, as appears from researches done in post-independent India, lead it to multidimensional approach. We can understand the present functional structure in anthropology through the following Fig. 25.1 :

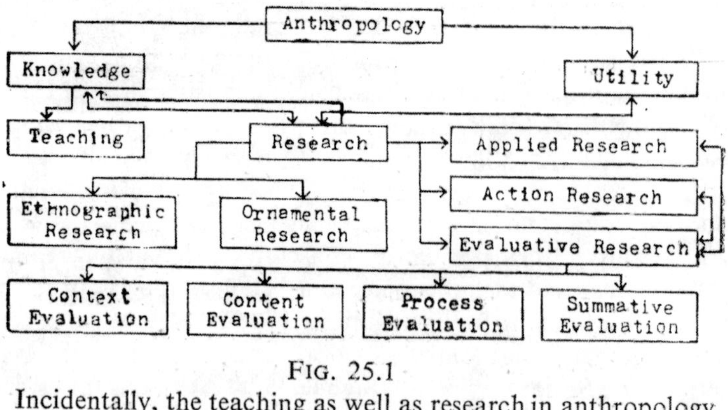

FIG. 25.1

Incidentally, the teaching as well as research in anthropology in Bihar is mainly confined to Ranchi. Ranchi University (formerly Bihar University) opened a Department of Anthropology in 1953 and a Tribal Research Institute was established in 1954. Both have more than 25 years of experience.

A Serious Question

The responsibility of this unit is to build a body of knowledge but has no deep concern for its practical use. The learned teachers of the Department, the only university department in Bihar, have done their best and, in the 25 years of its existence, produced many trained anthropologists who could be absorbed in the different wings of research, the field of teaching has saturated. Nobody will disagree with me that in the field of teaching there is almost zero scope. Intake capacity of this Department is 32 students and output between 20 and 25 anthropologists per year. One gold medallist is produced almost every year. And in the last 25 years only nine colleges could offer anthropology as a subject. And even if Bhagalpur University starts teaching anthropology, as is suggested by some, the chain problem of production of anthropologists and demand for more places of teaching is expected. This raises a serious question; if this problem is not solved what is the relevance of this subject of anthropology?

There is a moral dilemma amongst the social scientists about their role in the profession as well as society. Blalock says:

> The scientist as scientist is not directly concerned with applications to which his findings of theories are relevant, although as a citizen he may be very much interested in these applications. When playing the role of scientist he must inevitably take a stand, if only to 'stand aside' while others apply his knowledge. This dual role is never easy to play. If the scientist becomes an extreme partisan he may find that he loses his objectivity and his ability to analyse data impartially. But if he becomes completely unconcerned as to how knowledge is applied, and if he takes an extreme "science for science's own sake" position, he may become willing to sell his services to the highest bidder. (Blalock : 1970 : 11)

Paddington writes:

> Anthropologists are sharply divided among themselves as to what role they should play in human affairs . . .

> (1) They should retire to an ivory tower and divorce themselves from practical which they cannot effectively influence ... (2) The anthropologist should concern himself with practical problems, but only as a fact-finder, but he should play no part in the formation or criticism of policy itself, and... (3) The anthropologist is the person most intimately aware of human problems, both general and particular, which are involved. He should therefore shamelessly make pronouncements on administrative policies and should provide facts relevant to the carrying out of policies which he approves.
>
> (Paddington : 1970 : 129).

Vidyarthi wants the anthropologist to be a social doctor and says :

> As a social doctor, an action social scientist combines in himself the responsibility for diagnosing the disease, prescribing the medicines, following up the treatment, changing the prescription and finally bringing about health and happiness in the society.
>
> (Vidyarthi : 1968: 177).

The aforesaid offers enough room for discussion, so we can switch over to the other aspect of the subject which covers research.

Among the researches in the field of anthropology, it is not surprising to find some of ornamental value. In a developing country like India in general and a backward state like Bihar in particular, where anthropology faces a great challenge and has an opportunity to make an effective contribution to it, we cannot afford ornamental researches for the sake of research.

We have been doing ethnographic studies for such a long time that now the time has come when there should be a comma, if not a full stop. So much has been done that we do not know what to do with it. It seems that we have built up a library, but nobody is coming to use it or we do not know how to read. There does not seem any logic in gathering data in the hope that someone may one day use it. No thought seems to be given to the fact that by the time that someone comes, the validity of the data will decrease. When you begin to doubt the data of Malinowski, or regard the findings of Radcliffe Brown outdated, when you examine the concept of Vidyarthi in the time dimension, how can you expect that people will accept your findings as they are?

One can disagree with my views and justify one's own piece of work as most useful one since no single piece of research can be classed as being entirely applied or unapplied. This I leave to the value judgement of the anthropologist community.

Anthropology, being the science of man, feels it a moral responsibility not only to take something from the responding unit (subject) but also to contribute to its well-being. Keeping this view in mind and seeing the pressing need of development of mankind the trend in Indian anthropology took a curve in post-independent period. Problem-oriented studies with same suggestive measures for a solution or study which can be used for any proposed programme led towards a new branch of anthropology—"Applied Anthropology". The Department of Anthropology, Ranchi University, teaches applied anthropology as one of the major papers. The Department of Anthropology, the Tribal Research Institute, Ranchi, and the A.N. Sinha Institute of Social Studies, Patna, have shown keen interest and carried out many applied researches. Researches on the impact of industrialisation (Datta : 1962 and Vidyarthi: 1970), Agro-social research (Sachchidananda: 1972), Socio-economic study of tribal market (Sinha : 1966), Unrest study among the universities (Vidyarthi: 1976), Satellite communication system and rural development (Agrawal and Sinha : 1977 and Sachchidananda and Jha :1977) and a few others are examples of the progress we have made in this direction.

Deaf Government

Anthropology in Bihar can claim to have done a good amount of work in the applied field. Some of these researches are indeed of high standard. But what has happened to them? Did they get justice? Is the purpose of applied research solved with mere publication of these reports? It is unfortunate to have to point out that the planners, the administrators and the government hardly care for it. Some pressure from a well-wisher in the government or the interest of a few top officials, may see a few anthropologists on some committees, but the proceedings of the meetings and functioning of the committees clearly indicate that the suggestions and recommendations made by the anthropologists fell on deaf ears. This is not the case in Bihar only. Barnett says : "No matter how tactfully it is phrased, the truth is that anthropologists and administrators do not, on the whole, get along well together." (Barnett : 1956 : 49). In such circumstances we feel uncomfortable and unsecure. As a result, our efficiency decreases day by day. Is it a healthy environment for survival of anthropology?

Another meaningful involvement of the anthropologist is in the field of "Action Research". As appears from its name, Action Research invites full involvement of the anthropologist, and its job is, as Vidyarthi says, "bringing about health and happiness in the society". Thus his involvement is from conception to the efficient execution of the programme, and he is supposed to see that it becomes a success. For this he will have to do all types of evaluations (see Fig. 25.2).

Unfortunately, very little has been done in this field. Vidyarthi, inheriting the quality of his Guru, Sol Tax, has been trying hard to take up such challenging tasks but has failed in his mission due to many problems—economic, academic, operational and administrative. "Kamre Action Research Project" could not go far because of untrained anthropologist like me and dearth of another man to follow up "Operation Self Help" was reduced to only applied research for lack of finance and co-operation from fellow "Rotarians" and "Birhor" project flopped due to bureaucracy. Nevertheless, this Centre for Agrarian Research Training and Education (CARTE) has recently initiated an action programme under the able guidance of Sachchidananda of the A. N. Sinha Institute of Social Studies. It has the privilege of having a trained anthropologist with it. Let us hope it will have a good future.

We have been advocating for a fuller participation of anthropologist in developmental programmes and often we say that they should not function merely as a camera but rather as a potter to give the desired shape to the object, before, a social doctor to bring betterment to the community as he has a better understanding of the community. But the review of the circumstances in which the above-mentioned action projects could not go ahead indicates the problem of getting a dedicated worker, proper allocation of finance and bureaucratic interference. Action programme is basically developmental programme which needs dedication and, as I have mentioned elsewhere (Sinha : 1968 : 173), we are not doing any research in the true sense. Anyway, the anthropologist should come forward to take up this challenging task. The government and policy-makers have also to make up their minds and the administration should not treat us as second-grade citizens. At the same time the researcher should also be honest on his part. It is a general tendency to submit reports after a long span of time which the planners cannot afford and the user agency wants a quick feedback. After all reports are not monuments that people will come to see after a decade.

Conclusion

In brief, we have discussed the status of anthropology in Bihar. The picture is more or less similar elsewhere in the country. It does not satisfy any of the expectations. The teaching field is saturated and there is almost no scope. Students of anthropology get enrolled for doctoral degrees, try to get some fellowship and pass their time. But what after that? Research is not research in the true sense. The circumstances under which a researcher operates are not congenial and we are not honest to ourselves as well as to our profession. The factors responsible for this may be many—anthropologists themselves, our guardians in the academic field, the administration, the policy-makers or the government. We are blamed as a defender of the weak and oppressed so much so that applied and action anthropology has come to be a bad name in many administrative circles. In this state of affairs there seems to be only two possibilities: (a) Either we do not prove ourselves of any use, or (b) The administration or government is not giving us recognition.

In either case what is the use of producing so many anthropologists every year? Without comparing the position of other disciplines we should think of ourselves because if our skill is fully utilized, there is ample job opportunity in several developmental programmes which along with work will give job satisfaction.

The important question before us however is whether we should allow this situation or improve the conditions or wind up this subject as a whole. This is most urgent as it is urgent to all who are concerned with anthropology and the question of its relevance is the most urgent to be discussed.

SUGGESTED READINGS

Agrawal, B. C. and Arbind K. Sinha, Ismailpur through Holistic Study : A Study of SITE, Space Applications Centre, Ahmedabad (unpublished), 1977.

Bainbridge, R. B., The Saorias of the Rajmahal Hills, *Memoirs of the Asiatic Society of Bengal*, 1907.

Barnett, C., *Anthropology in Administration*, Row, Peterson and Company, Evanston, 1956.

Blalock, H. M. Jr., *An Introduction to Social Research*, Prentice Hall, Inc., Englewood Cliffs, New Jersey, 1970.

Bradley-Birt, F. B., *Chotanagpur : A Little Known Province of the Empire*, Smith Elder & Co., London, 1903.

Chitamber, J. B., *Introductory Rural Sociology*, Wiley Eastern Private Limited, New Delhi, 1975.

Dutta, A. K., The Neighbourhood Unit Plan and its Impact on Jamshedpur City, *Journal of Social Research*, Vol. V. I, Bihar Council of Social and Cultural Research, Ranchi, 1962.

Piddington, Ralph, "Action Anthropology", in *Applied Anthropology Readings in the uses of the Science of Man*, Clifton (ed), Houghton Mifflin Company, Boston, New York, 1970.

Sachchidananda, *Social Dimension of Agricultural Development*, Delhi, National Publishing House, Delhi, 1972.

Sachchidananda and M. N. Jha, Communication in a Bihar Village: Barahsher, Space Applications Centre Ahmedabad (unpublished), 1977.

Sinha, Arbind K., Samajik Anusandhan : Pariyojana: Anusandhan Karta, (in Hindi) *Manav*, Vol. 6:3, Lucknow, Ethnographic and Folk Culture Society, Lucknow, 1978.

Sinha, D. P., *Cultural Change in an Inter-tribal Market*, Asia Publishing House, Bombay, 1968.

Vidyarthi, L. P., *Socio-cultural Implications of Industrialisation in India: A Case Study of Tribal Bihar*. R.P.C. Planning Commission, New Delhi, 1970.

Vidyarthi, L.P., *The Students Unrest in Chotanagpur*, Calcutta, Punthi Pustak, Calcutta, 1976.

Vidyarthi, L.P., *Rise of Anthropology in India*, Vol. II, Delhi, Concept ublishing Company, New Delhi, 1978.

TWENTY SIX

Vijoy S. Sahay

IN SEARCH OF RANCHI SCHOOL OF ANTHROPOLOGY

THE IDEA of a school of anthropology first entered my mind when I read what Kroeber said about Franz Boas—father, hero and Guru of American Anthropology—that "there is no 'Boas School' and never has been". (Haris, Marvin : 1968:262). Margaret Mead also, on one occasion, said, "there are no methods named after Boas, just as there is no Boas School".

I wondered then how was it possible that Franz Boas, who had trained perhaps the maximum numbe1 of internationally acclaimed scholars in the field of anthropology, and whose outstanding accomplishments as a teacher, administrator, researcher, founder and president of many societies, lecturer, editor and traveller were exhausting to behold, failed to establish "his" school.

The answer was in the underlying meaning of school itself. A school in anthropology meant "the body of pupils, or followers of a master, a system, a method or a doctrine".

The above is not meant to diminish the importance of Boas' contribution to the development of anthropology or of anthropological theories; nor should it affect his image of an unparalleled professional scientist. It, nevertheless, appears that compared to the two architects of British Social Anthropology, Brown and Malinowski, Boas made less conceptual frameworks in his anthropological investigations. He was an unparalleled field worker. He urged that theory should result from field work conducted as far as possible without theoretical pre-conception. Perhaps because of this dichotomy his students admitted only that Boas had trained them to pursue their own varied interests, mindful of the data, free of prejudice and distrustful of all schemes. Thus, they explicitly denied that Boas was the centre of a "school".

My idea of the Ranchi School of Anthropology showed the first signs of shaping itself in Port Blair in 1974 when I was there in connection with my doctoral work on the Nicobarese culture. The personnel of the Anthropological Survey of India, the largest anthropological organization of the world, called me a "man from Professor Vidyarthi's Department". My stay for field work in the island of Chwra was considered by them as a rigorous one. Also, my research problem was to test the hypothesis and concept of Nature-Man-Spirit Complex on the Nicobarese, which was, initially, propounded by Professor Vidyarthi in his study of the Maler (1963).

It was, however, just before the commencement of the Xth International Congress of Anthropological and Ethnological Sciences in New Delhi in December, 1978, that I felt that in a definite conceptual framework, lead by Dr. Vidyarthi, the pupils of the Ranchi School of Anthropology were heading towards a definite destination. Thus was established my idea of the Ranchi School of Anthropology.

This paper is not meant to enumerate the exhaustive account of anthropological works done by the Department of Anthropology, Ranchi University. Instead, it is an effort to explore the various aspects of conceptual frameworks initiated and applied by the researchers and teachers of this Department.

It should also be noted that Ranchi has been bestowed with several anthropological potentialities. It has been the home as well as centre of intellectual life of the "Father of Indian Ethnography", the late Rai Bahadur Sarat Chandra Roy. The first anthropological journal edited by any Indian, *Man in India*, is being published from here ever since 1921. Ranchi is not only inhabited and surrounded by various tribal folks, but there are several research institutions engaged in social and cultural researches and imparting training to the scholars here. Mention can be made of the Bihar Tribal Research Institute and the Community Development and Panchayati Raj Research Institute.

This paper may lead to the conclusion that the Ranchi School of Anthropology is not in the making but has already been firmly established. It has to go a long way, especially as far as the ancient Indian scriptures and thoughts and works of the great social thinkers of this subcontinent are concerned.

II

Ranchi has twice led the anthropological researches in India. It has been the home of two "veteran anthropologists of international repute", namely, S. C. Roy and L. P. Vidyarthi. With a band of disciples, they have brought to light many of the unexplored fields of Indian life and culture. Their conceptual frameworks and methodologies have given light to many young researchers of their respective times. They, however, represent two different "eras" of anthropological development in the country.

While Roy focused his attention on the tribes of Chotanagpur only, though his anthropological inquiry led him to conduct field work in the adjoining States of Orissa, Madhya Pradesh and Bengal, Vidyarthi's interest went throughout the length and breadth of the country : from Rameshwaram in the South to the Tharus living it the foothills of the great Himalayas in the north; and from the State of Meghalaya in the east to the sacred city of Dwarka in the west. His manifold anthropological interest went as far as the island culture of Andaman and Nicobar archipelago, which were once dreaded as the "island of the condemned" or the "land of the cannibals". Even to this day, there the wild tribes like the Jarawas and the Sentinalese live in complete geographical and socio-cultural isolation.

If Roy brought international repute to India by his selection as a member of the Council de Honour of the International Congress of Anthropological and Ethnological Sciences, Vidyarthi's election as the President of the Xth ICAES and IUAES (1973-78) marked the advent of a "New Era" in Indian anthropology.

The basic differences between these two geniuses of Indian anthropology lie in their intellectual background and general anthropological outlook. Roy's research in anthropology reflect complete British influence, whereas Vidyarthi's emphasis has been on "Indianness" in social sciences in general and anthropology in particular as early as 1964. Having been trained initially under the leadership of Dr. D. N. Majumdar in India, and later in America, Vidyarthi, in our opinion, entered as a professional anthropologist with slight American influence. However, very soon he realized that the methodologies developed in the study of the accidental culture were not accurately suited to the studies of the complexed oriental cultures. Hence, he began to advocate "Indianness" in anthropology.

In his presidential address at the Xth ICAES (1978) he said "India's ancient scriptures like the Vedas, the Upanishads, the Smritis, the Puranas and the (other) great epics provide a sensitive insight into the social realities. Therefore, the Indianness in social science has to emerge with a proper appraisal of these ancient texts, whose influences on the behavioural pattern of our countrymen cannot be neglected".

He also categorically lashed out against the comments of some of the Western scholars like Gunnar Myrdal (1968), who said that there was dominance of religion only on the thinking and practice of Indian folks. He also attacked the Western scholars who held that the Third World countries were not capable of pursuing research works. Thus, we find that in recent times Vidyarthi has, quite often, hit the traditional trends of anthropological inquiries to discover some stimulating and new trends of researches for the coming generations in this discipline. It is hoped that his incessant effort to bring Indianness in sociological and anthropological inquiries would certainly bring fruitful results.

III

From 1898 till his death in 1942, S. C. Roy lived in Ranchi. By profession he was associated with the Bar, yet he was a self-styled anthropologist. In the course of his ethnographic works he came in contact with British social anthropologists like James Frazer, W. H. R. Rivers, A. C. Haddon, Marriot and many others. The greatest contribution that Roy made to Indian anthropology was his persistently stimulating and persuading Sri Asutosh Mukherjee to initiate anthropological studies at the university level in Calcutta in 1921. It was certainly a landmark in the history of social sciences in India. Today, Roy is remembered as a meticulous monographer, author of several papers, editor of an epoch-making anthropological journal. *Man in India*, as also a teacher and supervisor of anthropological researches. It was Roy, who initiated several professional anthropologists including late D. N. Majumdar into ethnographic studies of several tribes of Bihar and Orissa. After Roy's death the rich traditions established by him were, to some extent, maintained by D. N. Majumdar.

Thus, Roy dominated the Indian anthropological scene for over three and a half decades. We find, however, that his works were purely of monographic nature and in the line of Imperial anthropology. He did not initiate any conceptual framework in his anthropological investigation. It was perhaps so because he lived at a time when anthropology in India was still in its infancy. The diversification and proliferation of this discipline had not taken place in India. Yet, Roy, though living in such a small town like Ranchi, laid the very solid foundations of anthropological researches in the country.

IV

Till Roy's exit from the scene of anthropology, Indiananthropology was virgin, so far as American influence was concerned. But after World War II the American influence in anthropology started at a global level. India also could not remain unaffected.

Soon after his return from America in 1958, Dr, Vidyarthi joined the Department of Anthropology in Ranchi, then under Bihar University. The curriculum of this Department, ever since its inception in 1953 has been comprehensive. The Department's progress under Dr. Vidyarthi's guidance has been excellent, and it has acquired sufficient potentialities to justify the establishment of the Ranchi School of Anthropology.

Dr Vidyarthi developed the "Concept of Sacred Complex" in his study of Hindu Gaya. This is by all means one of the finest structural approaches to the study of the complex and heterogeneous dimensions of Indian civilization. It has provided a good anthropological tool for the study of the important pilgrim centres and sacred cities of this vast subcontinent. Dr. B. N. Saraswati's work on the sacred city of Kashi, Dr. Sahchindra Narain's work on Deoghar and Dr. M. Jha's works on Janakpur and Puri and his recent effort to study the sacred centres of Hardwar, Rishikesh and Joshimath are the brilliant off-shoots of Dr. Vidyarthi's pioneering work in this direction. The Department has also conducted intensive field work in the sacred cities of Puri, Dwarka, Ayodhya, Janakpur, Rameshwaram and Deoghar.

Dr. Vidyarthi's study of Hindu Gaya was followed by an ecological-functional study of the Nature-Man-Spirit Complex of the Maler (1963). This study inspired many scholars including me to continue on the same lines. My work on the Nature-Man-Spirit Complex of the Nicobarese is based upon Dr. Vidyarthi's study of the Maler. I have tested the hypothesis and concept of Nature-Man-Spirit Complex, and discovered that it exactly fits and properly suits the interpretation of the Nicobarese culture. Similarly, a number of other scholars have tested this hypothesis in their works and found useful.

After these two theoretical concepts, Dr. Vidyarthi's interests turned to the conceptual framework of studying the impact of industrialisation and urbanisation in India. A study of Ranchi (1969) and Hatia (1970) is the result of his interest. Inspired by his study on the industrial city of Ranchi, a number of scholars are now working on the cities like Bokaro, Jamshedpur, Bhilai and so on.

Thus, besides the study of the Sacred Complex and the Nature-Man-Spirit Complex, Dr. Vidyarthi has done pioneering work on industrialisation/and urbanization, dynamics of tribal leadership, student unrest and on various aspects of applied and action anthropology. Dr. K. N. Sahay's (1976) study on the impact of Christianity in India and his concept of "spiritual anthropology" are the results of the Ranchi School of Anthropology, and constitute guidelines for future researches. Similarly, Dr. N. Mishra's (1977) studies on the scheduled castes, Dr. V. S. Upadhyay's inquiry into the tribal resettlement scheme, Dr. M. Jha's specialization on the Sacred complex and civilizational studies and Dr. V. S. Sahay's study on the Nature-Man-Spirit Complex of the

Nicobarese are the other achievements of the Ranchi School of Anthropology (for details, see the *Journal of Social Research*, Vol. XXI:11). In the field of applied and action anthropology also the Department of Anthropology has made commendable contributions. It is a matter of pride for this Department that the first and only Birhor was taught to read and write by the efforts of Dr. Vidyarthi. Besides, chiefly because of his efforts a number of projects have been completed in this direction.

V

To sum up, within the aforesaid limitations of this venture, we come to the conclusion that the Ranchi School of Anthropology, though it primarily received stimuli from the Redfieldian approach in its efforts to formulate hypotheses in the study of Indian civilisation, very soon made a departure and established its own existence. The sole credit for such a departure, no doubt, goes to Dr. Vidyarthi's penetrating anthropological insight.

His empirical studies convinced Dr. Vidyarthi that it required a pin-pointed conceptual tool to study the interwoven and heterogeneous nature of Indian civilisation. The concept of "Sacred complex" incorporation to the "Sacred centre", "Sacred specialist"and "Sacred performance" reflected a level of continuity, compromise and combination between great and little traditions. He also provided such terms as "Sacred cluster", "Sacred segment" and "Sacred zone" to describe the "Sacred geography" of a "local", "regional", or "universal", aspect of the great Indian civilization. Henceforth it becomes easier to regregate the ritualistic and festival aspects of the study of different dimensions of India's civilization.

We deem it necessary here to mention the interest of this Department to discover the socio-cultural elements in the ancient scriptures of India. In the recent past there have been extraordinary symposia and seminars organised in this Department to discover the same fact.

It is true that the modern anthropological thoughts are very much dominated by the Euro-American methods and concepts which are not very suitable for the study of the oriental culture. It is true that almost all the anthropological ideas of the western world have their base in the civilization of the ancient Greeks. But it is also true that equally fertile and more prosperous civilizations have existed on the earth prior to the Greek, viz. the civilizations of Egypt, Mesopotamia, China, and India. The western scholars now think that if the written records of these ancient civilizations are properly assessed, we may discover new facts about the anthropological ideas. It is held that the anthropological thought began whenever men first began to think about society and culture of their own or of their neighbours in the "naturalistic forms" devoid of any interpretation of gods, goddesses or mythologies. According to this standard we find that anthropological elements in the ancient scriptures of India remain very vague and shrouded. And it is a challenging task before the Ranchi School of Anthropology to give a shape and clarity to these elements.

To quote Dr. Vidyarthi (1978), "these ancient scriptures reflect the wisdom and provide guidelines for shaping the socio-cultural life in India". The patterns of nature-man relationship, man-to-man relationship and man-to-spirit relationship are explained in great depth. The basic elements of Indians' life-style lie in their traditional practice of the four Ashramas, four Purusharthas, 16 Sanskaras, etc., which still continue to influence the ethos, world view and the life of an average Indian". Dharma (wrongly translated as religion) is the first of the four fundamental principles of social ethics of man in the form of Purushartha. The word literally means "the meaning of man" or the "aim of being human". The other three principles are: Artha (wealth), Kama (desire) and Moksha (salvation). It is man's duty to fulfil the first three in order of priority and live with purity to achieve the last (Presidential Address of Xth ICAES, 1978).

In our opinion while it is true that a proper assessment of the ancient Indian scriptures would bring fruitful results in terms of anthropological thought it is also hoped that it will emancipate the Third World anthropology from the Euro-American concepts and methodologies. I wish to admonish the pupils of the Ranchi School of Anthropology or, for that matter, all those who are working in this direction that unless they discover the historical and geographical elements in the ancient texts propely, it is possible that their efforts to discover the socio-cultural elements would prove futile. Because any society or culture exists in a time and a space, and we are certainly not sure of the elements of time and space in connection with the ancient Indian texts.

Nevertheless, we hope that the pupils or the followers of the Ranchi School of Anthropology under the dynamic leadership of Dr. Vidyarthi would one day be able to discover the necessary and desired anthropological elements in the ancient Indian texts. To conclude we can very safely assume that according to our initial definition of a school we find that the Ranchi School of Anthropology has been fully established with a developed set of systems, methods and various conceptual frameworks under their lone master, Dr. Vidyarthi.

INDEX